LUCY KIRKWC

Lucy Kirkwood's pla_   _nildren (Royal Court);
Chimerica (Almeida/W   *SFW* (Royal Court); *small hours*
(co-written with Ed Hime_   _npstead); *Hansel and Gretel*, *Beauty
and the Beast* (with Katie Mitchell; National Theatre); *Bloody
Wimmin*, as part of *Women, Power and Politics* (Tricycle); *it felt
empty when the heart went at first but it is alright now* (Clean
Break/Arcola); *Hedda* (Gate, London); *Tinderbox* (Bush). *it felt
empty when the heart went at first but it is alright now* won the
2012 John Whiting Award, and was nominated for the Evening
Standard Most Promising Playwright Award, and the Susan Smith
Blackburn Award. *Chimerica* won the 2014 Olivier Award for Best
New Play, the 2013 Evening Standard Best Play Award, the 2014
Critics' Circle Best New Play Award, and the Susan Smith
Blackburn Award.

LUCY KIRKWOOD

Plays: One

Tinderbox

it felt empty when the heart went at first
but it is alright now

small hours

NSFW

Chimerica

with an Introduction by the author

NICK HERN BOOKS
London
www.nickhernbooks.co.uk

A Nick Hern Book

Lucy Kirkwood Plays: One first published in Great Britain as a paperback original in 2016 by Nick Hern Books Limited, The Glasshouse, 49a Goldhawk Road, London W12 8QP

Cover image: *Chimerica*, designed and photographed by Es Devlin

Designed and typeset by Nick Hern Books, London
Printed in Great Britain by Mimeo (UK) Ltd

ISBN   978 1 84842 619 1

Contents

Introduction	vi
Tinderbox	1
it felt empty when the heart went at first but it is alright now	99
small hours	151
NSFW	167
Chimerica	241

Introduction

I grew up on the border of Essex and London, and my maternal ancestors came from the Isle of Thanet, and I started thinking about *Tinderbox* at the end of four years of university in Edinburgh, as I prepared to go home. In 2006 it seemed to me like everything that had felt new and young and revolutionary for a while had revealed itself to be as old and reactionary as what came before it. So it was about change seeming impossible. A series of white men running the show. But it was also about how difficult change is for those at the sharp end of it. A country is a delicate organism and some parts are more exposed than others to the arrival of foreign bodies. I wanted to be honest but generous about this. Saul is a racist, but he is also a man who has been culturally and economically displaced by forces beyond his control. Modernity. Multiculturism. Weather. He's a crook and a murderer and – worse – very sentimental. But he is grieving, and while his grief is sometimes presented comically, I don't find it entirely funny.

I was lucky when Mike Bradwell commissioned me to write the play and when, after he left the Bush, Josie Rourke programmed and directed it. I remember her being very kind and calling me 'baggage' a lot. Lucy Osborne designed a stifling butcher's shop behind a red velvet curtain and ignited my passion for model boxes. We opened in May at the old Bush Theatre, then a tiny space above a pub, during a heatwave when the air conditioning was broken. Dystopian farce is a genre with a niche fan club anyway: it's fair to say it divided people. I think the play is better on the dystopia than the farce, but writing this introduction in the months after the Brexit vote it feels like its prevailing concerns are alive and kicking violently.

it felt empty… was developed closely with Lucy Morrison as a commission for Clean Break during my residency with the company. We had seen the Helen Bamber Foundation's installation about human trafficking in Trafalgar Square, and both of us were struggling with the idea of victims of crime being incarcerated as criminals. We worked with the Poppy Project (whose funding was diverted in 2015 in the name of Austerity to, oddly, the Salvation Army). The women we talked with had been victims of the most

inhumane crimes, not only by their traffickers but by the British
Government. They were angry, articulate and bitterly aware that their
suffering had begun with an ambition to improve their lives. Many of
them had a coal-black sense of humour. All of this went into Dijana.

I had the idea for the first two acts, and writing them made it clear
what the third one should be. I was roughly Dijana's age at the
time, and it felt important to show more how she was like me than
how she wasn't. It was supposed to go on in a disused shop unit in
the old Shepherd's Bush shopping centre. When this fell through
the Arcola gave us a vast warehouse space at fairly short notice.
Lucy gave me a beautiful and unflinching production, and Chloe
Lamford created a dazzling, grubby, Lynchian rabbit warren for the
audience to follow Dijana through. In the final act, the audience sat
on white goods still in their packaging.

small hours was entirely inspired by a request from Katie Mitchell
to write a one-woman show for downstairs at the Hampstead
Theatre, with Franz Xaver Kroetz's *Request Programme* as a
reference. Ed Hime and I wrote it in Brussels, taking it in turns to
type. In the stage directions we had specified that she would stop
and rewind the song at least five times, and in performance it was
never less than nine, which was unbearable and why Katie is a
great director. The audience sat in Maggie's living room, which had
very thick cream carpet. I remember how discomfited the small act
of having to take your shoes off made them. I am glad to see it in
print because so many people at the time seemed bewildered by the
idea of playwrights writing stage directions, not just dialogue. Here
is the proof.

NSFW was the first play where the structure presented itself quite
quickly. The spark was seeing my sister's CV, which was five or six
pages long and entirely filled with unpaid internships. It was never
intended to be specifically about the magazine industry or even the
media in general, but about how the industrialised workplace and
Capitalism itself compromises us, by substituting over time its
economic morality for our emotional one. No one in the play is
inherently corrupt, and most of the corruption we do see is self-
harming. Sam loses the woman he loves (and his love of women).
Mr Bradshaw and Aidan lose their souls. And as a woman of fifty,
Miranda's been wired to find herself disgusting by a culture she
herself has helped to enshrine. There's a line in Martin Crimp's
brilliant play *The Treatment* about corruption having three stations:

'The first is the loss of innocence. The second is the desire to inflict that loss on others. The third is the need to instil in others that same desire.'

Which I think is a good way of describing the 'Fall' of the play.

Simon Godwin cast it beautifully and Janie Dee was resplendent in an obscene leather dress. I remember lots of trouble being taken at the Royal Court to make sure the topless photograph of Carrie was ethically sourced. I think it's more about class than gender and it's a play that gets progressively less funny as it goes along.

Chimerica started as a commission at the National Theatre Studio, an incredible gift, as it gave me licence to think on a larger scale than young playwrights are usually advised to do. The problem was that when it was released after a period of development, there weren't that many other theatres with the capacity for an epic play with a cast of twelve. So it then went on a long journey before Michael Attenborough programmed it at the Almeida. The most important thing that happened in that time was that Headlong came along on a white horse and rescued it from the doldrums. Ben Power and I worked on it together for some time, pacing around Covent Garden, talking it out. The Occupy movement hadn't emerged when I first started writing, and Barack Obama was also a couple of years away. Later there were many drafts of the play set during the '08 US election, and eventually I realised I was writing a thriller.

I was over the moon when Lyndsey Turner agreed to direct it, and for more than a year she worked intensively on the play with me, visiting me in Norfolk and going as deeply into the research as I had. She is a peerless dramaturg and we value the same things, so her rigorous notes and questions were often hard but never painful, and always made the play better. Es Devlin agreed to design a year in advance, so the final drafts were entirely tailored to her sleek, protean design of a spinning cube. At the first reading it was four-and-a-half hours long and I felt despair. We changed a lot during previews, which was possible due to a talented and heroic cast and crew who understood with grace the complexity of the play's mechanics – it is down to all of them, and Lyndsey's holding of all our nerves, that it got to be performed in its best possible version.

At the time of writing, three years later, a ham-faced Donald Trump is whipping his supporters into a frenzy over China, and it occurs to me for the first time that *Chimerica* has more in common with

Tinderbox than any of the other plays in this book, being in part about the yielding of empire and identity, and the anxiety and ugliness that come with that. And as I am halfway through a new play about a comet, knee-deep in elliptical orbits, it seems right, somehow, that this body of work, spanning seven years of writing, should end up right back where it started.

Lucy Kirkwood
October 2016

I'd like to thank Mel Kenyon, Lucy Morrison and Ed Hime for their help in the writing of all of these plays.

TINDERBOX

or, Love Amid the Liver

To Pip, Ted, Kirk, Robert and Peggy

Tinderbox was first performed at the Bush Theatre, London, on 23 April 2008, with the following cast:

JOHN/JOHN JUNIOR JUNIOR/DIXON	Nigel Betts
JOHN JUNIOR/DOCK/ DETECTIVE PRAWN	Sartaj Garewal
PERCHIK	Bryan Dick
VANESSA	Sheridan Smith
SAUL	Jamie Foreman
Director	Josie Rourke
Designer	Lucy Osborne
Lighting Designer	James Farncombe
Sound Designer	Emma Laxton
Assistant Director	Tim Digby-Bell
Production Manager	Felix Davies
Company Stage Manager	Helen Reynolds
Deputy Stage Manager	Rebekah Kirk
Casting Director	Chloe Emmerson

I started making maps when I was small
Showing place, resources, where the enemy
And where love lay. I did not know
Time adds to land. Events drift continually down,
Effacing landmarks, raising the level, like snow.
I have grown up. My maps are out of date.
The land lies over me now.
I cannot move. It is time to go.

Alasdair Gray, Lanark

Characters

PERCHIK, *a tall and thin young man in his mid-twenties, Scottish.*
An Inverness cowboy.
SAUL, *a big, energetic man, sixties or older, old-fashioned*
Cockney accent. He walks with a stick supporting his right leg.
VANESSA, *tired-looking, pretty at one time but this isn't it, thirties*
or older. Noticeable scar down one side of her face.

DIXON
JOHN
WINSTON
JOHN JUNIOR JUNIOR

DOCK
JOHN JUNIOR
DETECTIVE PRAWN

DIXON, JOHN, WINSTON *and* JOHN JUNIOR JUNIOR *are to*
be played by the same actor; as are DOCK, JOHN JUNIOR *and*
DETECTIVE PRAWN.

The play is set in Bradford, Yorkshire, sometime in the twenty-first
century.

Note on the Text

(/) indicates the point that the next speaker interrupts
(–) indicates an abrupt interruption
(…) indicates a trailing off
(*) indicates two or more different characters speaking
     simultaneously

ACT ONE

'Dry Bones'

The end of a blazing afternoon. An old-fashioned butcher's shop.
Tiles, marble slabs, a display counter covered with a sheet.
A desiccated feel to the place. A yellowing blind on the window.
Straw on the floor. Three dead pot plants and a thriving cactus.
The sound of police sirens and dogs barking gets louder and
louder. Louder still when the shop door is opened. JOHN *enters.*
He looks around the empty shop, then calls:

JOHN. 'Livery!

He mops his brow. He has a stripe of zinc-oxide sunblock on his
face and a clipboard in his hand.

Mr Everard? Delivery!

No answer. JOHN *sticks his head out of the door.*

John Junior! You want to stir yer bleedin' stumps, lad?

Beat. Then JOHN JUNIOR *staggers in, dishevelled, and*
lugging a sack. He also wears sunblock. He dumps the sack and
stares accusingly at JOHN.

(*Innocently.*) What?

JOHN JUNIOR. You left me!

JOHN. I had to see a man about a dog.

During the following, JOHN *takes out a Cornetto and rolls it*
slowly over his face. He then peels off the wrapper, folds it, puts
it in his pocket, and starts to eat.

JOHN JUNIOR. They were kicking me and you said, 'I'll run
ahead and meet you there.'

JOHN. I thought they were your mates.

JOHN JUNIOR. They were trying to set fire to my shoes! (*Beat.*)
You know why they always go for me, don't you?

JOHN. You've just got one of those faces, I s'pose.

JOHN JUNIOR. No. It's cos it's always me carrying the bleeding sack!

JOHN. We've been through this, JJ. You carry the sack. I carry the clipboard. See?

He holds up the clipboard to demonstrate.

JOHN JUNIOR. S'like trying to carry a sugar cube through a sea of ants out there! Maybe if you had to be the human donkey once in a while, then – What's that?

JOHN *(still eating)*. What does it look like?

JOHN JUNIOR. It's an ice cream!

JOHN. To some extent.

JOHN JUNIOR. Where d'you get that from?

JOHN *(primly)*. Some of us don't fritter away our dairy rations on cheese omelettes, John Junior. Been saving up for weeks for this.

JOHN JUNIOR. Give us a lick.

JOHN. Not on your nelly.

JOHN JUNIOR. Aw, lemme have a –

JOHN. Get off –

JOHN JUNIOR. Just a quick one –

JOHN. NO!

JOHN JUNIOR. Alright, well, what about your wrapper then?

JOHN. What about it?

JOHN JUNIOR. Give us a little suck on it.

JOHN. Piss off.

JOHN JUNIOR. Alright, just a lick then.

JOHN. No. I'm saving it for my wife.

JOHN JUNIOR. I only want a taste, your wife's fat enough already. You're a feeder, you.

JOHN. John Junior! My wife is not fat. My wife has just –

JOHN JUNIOR. LET ME LICK YOUR WRAPPER!

JOHN. Pull yourself together, boy! What would Mr Womble say if he could see this exhibition, eh? Now come on. We've got four more drop-offs before we can –

JOHN JUNIOR *quickly leans in and takes a big bite of* JOHN*'s ice cream.*

You little – !

JOHN JUNIOR *runs out.* JOHN *exits after him. Silence once more. A beat. Another beat. Then the sack bursts open and* PERCHIK, *choking and spluttering, bursts out. He is blood-streaked. Feathers fly. He leans into the sack and pulls out a knapsack. Quietly, he crosses to the door. Opens it. The sound of a riot; angry crowds, sirens, dogs barking, glass smashing. He slams the door shut again. Suddenly,* VANESSA *comes running, weeping, through the shop from a door out to the back. She stops short as she sees* PERCHIK. *They both freeze. Beat.*

SAUL (*off*). Vanessa!

VANESSA *runs to the icebox door, heaves it open and slams it behind her.* PERCHIK *panics, jumps back into the sack.* SAUL *enters hurriedly. He limps on his right foot and carries a stick. He stops and looks at the sack.* PERCHIK*'s heavy breathing can be heard.*

(*Under his breath.*) Hmm… fresh.

He runs to the icebox door and bangs on it.

Little pig, little pig, let me come in!

He listens. No reply.

You can't hide in the icebox every time Sauly is naughty, Vanessa.

Pause.

Why won't you play with me?

VANESSA. Go away!

SAUL. But Vanessa! I'm having a heart attack!… Ow!

Pause.

OW. (*Beat.*) Really hurts.

Pause. He bangs on the door.

OPEN THIS DOOR!

VANESSA (*singing*). Oh, the toe bone's connected to the foot bone, the foot bone's connected to the –

SAUL. Vanessa!

VANESSA. – *ankle* bone, the ankle bone's connected to the leg bone, the leg bone's connected to the –

SAUL. Shut up!

VANESSA. – *knee* bone, the *knee* bone's connected to the –

SAUL. Open this door now!

VANESSA (*shouting now*). – THIGH BONE, THE THIGH BONE'S CONNECTED TO THE HIP BONE, NOW HEAR THE WORD OF THE LORD –

SAUL. You've left off the torso, you silly cow! If your toes freeze together again, I'm not taking you to the hospital to have them chipped apart this time. I'll do it myself and put the bits in a punch bowl and have cocktails on the bloody veranda!

He waits.

Vanessa?

No response. SAUL goes to the shop door, locks it, and exits. Beat. PERCHIK jumps out of the sack. VANESSA comes out of the icebox. They stare at each other. The power fails.

(*Off.*) I have turned the electricity off, Vanessa!

PERCHIK *and* VANESSA *panic*. PERCHIK *runs and throws himself down behind the counter*. VANESSA *runs to the door, finds it locked, looks around*.

VANESSA (*calling*). Don't be so stupid, Saul. The stock will spoil.

SAUL (*off*). Then you will have that on your conscience, wife.

VANESSA (*calling*). I didn't turn the power off, did I?

SAUL *approaches*. VANESSA *jumps in the sack*. SAUL *enters*. *Goes to the icebox*.

SAUL. You are behaving in such a naughty way that my hand was forced. Do you understand, wife? You left me no other option. No other option!

Pause. He opens the icebox door and peers in. Closes it silently.

No, no, Vanessa. You're quite right.

SAUL *turns to see the sack wriggling across the floor, towards the door. He sighs, goes to the sack and sits on it. It stops moving.*

The best thing for us to do is to sit quietly and Think About What You Have Done.

SAUL *hacks up some phlegm and spits it into a Union Jack handkerchief.*

I am a man of infinite patience. (*He suddenly turns to the counter.*) Whoever you are, I'd come out of there if I was you. The sound of your rattling pipes is getting distinctly on my breasts.

Pause.

I'm talking to you. Behind the counter. It's bloody sardines in here tonight. Come out.

Pause.

Tell you what. Make it sporting. I'll give you till ten. One… two… three… four…

PERCHIK *makes a dash for it.* SAUL *trips him, picks him up and sits him on a chair.*

Aha! Can I see your passport please, baggage?

PERCHIK. What? I've no' got a – What? Get off!

SAUL. Ah. You're a *foreign*! Splendid!

PERCHIK. No – I'm Scottish.

SAUL. Like I said. Foreign! Can I see your passport?

PERCHIK. This is an invasion of my civil liberties – What do you want tay see my –

SAUL. An Englishman's home is his castle, but an Englishman's shop is his Empire. We are short on staff at the moment so I am both monarch and border control.

PERCHIK. I don't –

SAUL (*shouting into the sack*). The First Lady has gone AWOL at present.

PERCHIK. I've no' got my passport wimme. I mean – I've no' got a passport.

SAUL. 'No' got a passport'! Dear me. What an untravelled young larrikin you must be. The marvellous crevices of this great turning world are of no interest / to you?

PERCHIK. What are you / on about?

SAUL. Never smelt the swamps of Venice or seen their silt of sunken city? Or watched the ice fields of Siberia melt into daisy-dotted washing-powder meadows?

PERCHIK. No, I've not!

SAUL. What! Never danced through the dusty kasbahs of In Salah picking mint leaves from your teeth, or observed the powdery course of the Milky Way as the bombs come down like windfalls on to Norwegian fjords? The blaze of a watery nation going up in flames. Tell me, have you *never* seen the Kalahari Desert lights, baggage?

PERCHIK. No. I told you, I've no' got a passport.

SAUL. Neither have I, I have an aversion to sand, but I am assured they are quite spectacular. I have never been to Scotland either, but I am assured that it is not. How did you get across Hadrian's Channel without a passport? Ferries wouldn't take you without papers, and you can't walk it at low tide any more.

PERCHIK. I swam.

SAUL. You swam?

PERCHIK. From Berwick to Newcastle.

SAUL. You swam from Berwick to Newcastle?

PERCHIK. Aye.

SAUL. You swam. He swam! Thirty-eight miles! That shows some gristle that does, shows some / bloody gristle.

PERCHIK. I should probably be / going.

He stands. SAUL *immediately forces him down again.*

SAUL. I underestimated you, er – what did you say your name was?

PERCHIK. I didn't. S'Perchik. Peter Perchik.

PERCHIK *holds out a hand in introduction.* SAUL *examines it.*

SAUL. Perchik? Not very Scottish, but that can only be a good thing. It will aid your integration into our native culture and value system. My name is Saul Everard but you may call me Mr Saul. More friendly, don't you think you're bleeding on my floor.

PERCHIK. What's that? (*He looks down.*) Oh. Yeah. Sorry 'bout that.

His knuckles are dripping blood. SAUL *silently passes an already bloody tea towel to him, and* PERCHIK *bandages himself.* SAUL *watches with detached interest.*

SAUL. It's a bit fighty out there tonight?

PERCHIK. Ay. A bit. Got lost in the Asian Quarter.

SAUL. The Asian Quarter? The whole city is the Asian Quarter, you dolt. Except for this shop. Do you want a job?

PERCHIK. What?

SAUL. A job. Do you want one? My last boy has just left me in the lurch and your low horizons and negligible intellect suggest you would be quite perfect for the role.

PERCHIK. But no one's hiring. There's nae jobs anywhere.

SAUL. On the contrary, there is one job in the whole of Bradford and you have had the serendipity to trespass right into it. So. What do you say?

PERCHIK. I dunno – what's the work like?

SAUL. Oh, awful.

PERCHIK. But the pay?

SAUL. Very bad. All round it's an excellent situation.

PERCHIK. Right. Well thanks, but no –

SAUL. Is it about the money?

PERCHIK. No, it's not about the / money.

SAUL. Because it's really quite distasteful / to haggle –

PERCHIK. I don't care about the money!

SAUL. Then don't look a gift horse in the mouth, little Perchik! Or it might eventually come to believe you are a sugar cube and *eat you.*

Pause. SAUL *crosses to the shop door and pulls the blind aside.*

Awful lot of coppers about tonight. Awful lot. You can say what you like about them, but they still have a tremendous sense of *pageantry*, don't you think? Tremendous *flair*. For example (I don't know if you read the papers but) it must take a certain amount of brute strength to physically *peel* an Irishman's kneecap off with just your bare hands – and just because he didn't have a passport! I mean, obviously unpleasant for the Irishman. But a real *spectacle*, nonetheless.

PERCHIK *crosses the shop and looks through the blind himself. He looks back at* SAUL.

PERCHIK. Mr Saul? I've bin thinking 'bout your offer.

SAUL. And?

PERCHIK. And I've decided to reconsider.

SAUL. Tremendous! (*He shakes* PERCHIK*'s hand.*) You know I was hoping you would!

PERCHIK. Sounds grand. Thank you. You, er, you get a lot of people coming and going?

SAUL *stops pumping* PERCHIK*'s hand.*

SAUL. People?

PERCHIK. Customers, ken.

SAUL. Customers, Perchik?

PERCHIK. Buying things?

SAUL. Oh! You mean 'The Wallets'! Not many, no. You couldn't call it many. The market has become awful hostile of late, what with times being not so much lean as anorexic. And of course it's very hard to get hold of good stock now, you know?

PERCHIK. Imagine it is, aye.

SAUL (*deadly serious*). You imagine? But I didn't ask you to imagine.

PERCHIK. Sorry?

SAUL. I didn't ask you to imagine. How hard it is to get hold of good stock, I mean. It wasn't open for debate. It *is* very *hard* for me to get hold of good stock. Understood?

Pause.

PERCHIK. Ye-ah. Right, Mr Saul. Very hard.

SAUL. Good. Good! And now, Perchik, you must tell me: what exactly are you doing in my shop? Naturally, you're on the hoof from someone. The question is, why?

PERCHIK. I'm a painter.

SAUL. Never mind.

PERCHIK. I was painting. On the palace. In London.

SAUL. A-ha. And what, Peter Perchik the Painter, were you painting?

PERCHIK. It was a… portrait. Of sorts.

SAUL. Of sorts?

PERCHIK. You'd mebbe call it an… erotic impression.

SAUL. Of who? The King?

PERCHIK. Nah. Of the PM.

SAUL. Aha. And what was the Prime Minister doing in this erotic impression?

PERCHIK. He wasnay really doing anything. Not that you could see.

SAUL. Not very erotic.

PERCHIK. But you know the Statue of Liberty?

SAUL. Intimately.

PERCHIK. Well, she was sitting on his face.

SAUL. Ha! Excellent. You're going to fit in nicely round here, Perchik, though I don't much care for your methods. Altogether too cerebral. Utopia will be born from the body and not from the mind. When the body is ordered, society follows. Do you see?

PERCHIK. No.

SAUL. Good! Now, my scrofulous whelp, just *one more thing*: do you know what a tinderbox is?

PERCHIK. Yeah – s'for fire-lighting and that.

SAUL. And that. Yes. Well, this shop is a veritable tinderbox. The walls are little more than parchment, and what you must remember is: who holds the matches, little Susan?

PERCHIK. My name's Perchik.

SAUL. I prefer Susan. It suits you better and brings out the blue in your eyes. Who holds the matches, little Susan?

PERCHIK. You do?

SAUL. Very good! Mr Saul holds the matches. You look a bit like a match, you know that? That swollen, scabby skull atop a stick of a body. Best not go rubbing your head on the walls, eh?

PERCHIK. Listen, can I stay here – just for tonight, I mean?

SAUL. No fixed abode, eh? Yes, very well. There's a mattress out back, you can bring it in here. Don't mind the stains. It's only blood. Now. Any questions?

PERCHIK. Ay. As it happens. What happened to your foot?

SAUL. My father fired an airgun at it during our annual family cricket tournament.

PERCHIK. Why?

SAUL. He said it was a joke. He had a funny sense of humour, my dad. Anything else?

PERCHIK. No. I mean yeah. Just one thing. What exactly do you sell?

SAUL. Dreams, baggage.

PERCHIK. What?

SAUL. The stuff dreams are made of. That is to say, meat.

He pulls the sheet off the display counter to reveal a pathetic show of sad-looking cuts. He pulls out the pocket watch and examines it.

(*Whispering.*) Now, zip your lip and do as I say. Quiet now.

He unlocks the shop door, then deliberately opens and closes it with a slam. SAUL gestures to PERCHIK to hide behind the counter. PERCHIK follows. After a moment, VANESSA tentatively pokes her head out of the sack. SAUL jumps up.

Vanessa! You've come out! Marvellous, it's like our honeymoon all over again!

She tries to get to the icebox, jumping as if in a sack race, but SAUL grabs her.

You're awful skittish today, my love, all this running about will be no good for your weak ankles. Give me a kiss.

VANESSA *shakes her head. He puts something in her hand.*

Give me a kiss.

She kisses him.

Thank you. And now, Vanessa *this* is a young man from *Scotland.* His name is *Perchik* which is rather ugly but at least it matches his face so we all know *where we stand.*

VANESSA. Hello, Perchik.

PERCHIK. Hello, Vanessa.

SAUL. That's right, that's right, get acquainted. Perchik, *this* is my wife.

VANESSA. I might just have a little smokey…

She reaches to a key hanging on a hook, tied to a long ribbon. The ribbon runs up through the floorboards to upstairs. Next to it is a small wall-mounted cupboard. VANESSA unlocks the cabinet and takes out a rumpled, nearly empty packet of fags.

SAUL. Common-law, but then she's a common girl. You've already had two today, wife.

VANESSA. Just to steady my / nerves…

She sticks a fag in her mouth, puts the pack back and locks the cupboard.

SAUL. Common, Perchik, is a politically correct way of saying vulgar. Vulgar is a refined way of saying trampy. Trampy is a slightly more coy word for sluttish. And by slut, Perchik, I mean, of course, that she puts it about, which is in itself an idiom dependent on a shared understanding between interlocutor and receiver of exactly what 'it', the great indefinite of our age, is.

He takes out a long box of matches and lights VANESSA*'s cigarette. As he talks,* SAUL *rummages in the sack* PERCHIK *arrived in, fishes out a few paltry bits of meat, wipes them with his hankie and slaps them straight into the display counter.*

No good if one of you thinks the term refers to apple strudel, now, is it? (Away from the *meat*, wife!) In the eighteenth century, she would have been a whorish orange-seller, you see, but in these days of bad health and halitosis skies, the orange trees spend their days gasping for breath and so she must say it out right. Say it out right, wife.

VANESSA. No –

SAUL. Say it out right.

VANESSA. Shan't.

SAUL. Say it out right or I shall smack your bottom in front of Perchik, and I think he might enjoy the spectacle a little too much.

VANESSA. Leave the boy alone.

SAUL. The boy wants to hear what you have to say, Vanessa. Say it.

VANESSA. No.

SAUL. This is my shop and Empire and while you're within her boundaries you'll do as I say! Or you will be put into jail at His Majesty's Pleasure.

VANESSA. You don't have a jail.

SAUL. Well, then I will put you in a sack. And post you.

PERCHIK. Where?

SAUL. What?

PERCHIK. Where will you post her?

SAUL. I don't know! Somewhere degenerate with an unfavourable exchange rate. (*Beat.*) France. Now say it!

VANESSA. I always thought that was a strange phrase. 'At His Majesty's Pleasure.' Imagine the King grinning at the thought of all the poor souls that he's locked up, away from the sky and the blossom and the stars blanking away in the indigo sky.

SAUL. I won't have poetry in this shop, wife, you know that. *Now say it!*

VANESSA. No.

SAUL. Yes!

VANESSA. NO!

SAUL. *Vanessa…*

Pause.

VANESSA (*quietly*). I'll give you a kiss for a quid.

SAUL. A kiss for a quid! Disgusting! Pity the morally cankered, innocent little Perchik, but mind you don't get too close. Whatever my wife has, it may be infectious.

VANESSA. Do be quiet, Saul.

SAUL. I remember the first kiss we had together, Perchik, it was on the night before the riots started and it tasted distinctly metallic.

VANESSA. Nonsense. Tell him the proper story.

She starts to wheeze.

SAUL. Never kiss a bought woman. All your food will start tasting like pennies.

VANESSA. You're getting me upset. You know it's not good for me. I better sit down.

PERCHIK *brings her a stool but she sits on the floor.*

SAUL. My wife has trouble breathing. Her tubes close up. Her body hates her. I don't hate her. I love her. Together we are waging a war against the enemy body. Watch.

He pushes her into a prone position, sits on her chest and holds her nose. He takes the cigarette from her and blows smoke into her mouth.

Show it who's boss, wife.

PERCHIK. Stop it. Don't do that.

SAUL. What? What was that, contraband? Did you say something?

PERCHIK. Nut. She's going to suffocate, s'all.

SAUL. Not if she knows what's good for her she won't.

VANESSA *is crying and wheezing.*

Show it who's boss, leather lungs! Relax the old pipes! Mind over matter!

She finally pushes him off, and moves onto her hands and knees.

See! Well done, wife, very *well done*!

VANESSA (*choking*). You're a bastard, Saul.

SAUL. On the contrary, Vanessa, unlike you, my mother was a saint and I am one hundred per cent legitimate. Ah, if you'd met Mother Everard, Perchik. She was really something. Put a live crab in her vest every morning to keep her on her toes and always a hot supper on the table. Now that's a woman. Not like Emphysema Annie here.

VANESSA. Could I have some water, please?

SAUL phlegms into his handkerchief. PERCHIK *pours her some water from a bottle into a pint glass.*

PERCHIK. You shouldn't smoke. It's bad for you.

VANESSA. Most of the things I love are.

She takes the glass from PERCHIK*, but* SAUL *snatches it away.*

SAUL. Ah-ah-ah! Think before you drink!

He bangs a poster Blu-Tacked to the wall, that reads 'THINK before you DRINK!' with a sad water droplet under it, then to a black line drawn around the pint glass like a WWII bathtub. He pours most of the water back. VANESSA *gulps down what's left.*

We are very careful of water in my Empire, Perchik, because we know its treachery. Once, we came home to find this very shop under two feet of the stuff.

VANESSA. When we were still in Barking, this was, Perchik.

SAUL. The arse-end of London proper, flooded so that more salubrious postcodes should be saved. Standing where you are now, we were, water up to our shins.

VANESSA. We began packing up, there and then. Everything we could take, we took.

SAUL. Took us eight hours to chisel the tiles off the wall.

VANESSA. This counter has travelled over two hundred miles, Perchik!

SAUL. Put the lot in the van and drove through the night.

VANESSA. And thank goodness we did! Because then –

SAUL. Because then, Perchik, the waters of Barking began to rise...

VANESSA. The River Roding spilled its banks!

SAUL. Just as the Tiber foamed with blood / before it!

VANESSA. Everything swimming in dirty water, kiddies crying on / rooftops –

SAUL. Within three months, all our friends and neighbours were dead.

PERCHIK. All of them?

SAUL. Well, either dead or very, very *damp*.

PERCHIK. But why here? Why Bradford?

SAUL. You recall, Perchik, that my Empire and I only narrowly escaped a drowning? And understand we were not anxious to repeat the experience?

VANESSA. Well, Bradford, you see, Perchik, is unusual for being one of the *only cities in England* to be built away from large bodies of water.

SAUL. See, baggage? (*He taps his head.*) Not just a hatrack!

VANESSA. Also, our petrol ran out, didn't it, Saul?

SAUL. Well, yes. That too.

VANESSA. By the time the drought was over, well, we couldn't face going through the whole palaver again. Saul was having funny turns as it was, weren't you, dear?

SAUL. I am not fond of *change*, Perchik. It disturbs my placid disposition. You'd do well to bear that in mind. Now, as Perchik will be staying with us, Nessa, I'd like you to make the place nice for him. Take your knickers out of the fridge, that sort of thing. Housewifery does not come easily to my wife. She was brought up in the lap of luxury and is unaccustomed to menial tasks such as the wiping of her bottom.

VANESSA. It was hardly luxury, Saul.

SAUL. Compared to what I had, it was. Compared to what I had –

VANESSA. I grew up on a council estate on the Roman Road.

SAUL. Stop trying to spoil the romance of our relationship! I'm your bit of rough! Isn't that exciting, Perchik?

PERCHIK. Do yous have any kids, like?

SAUL. What a question! No. We are not blessed with an heir.

VANESSA. No, but tell him, Saul.

SAUL. Tell him what?

VANESSA. Tell him about Enoch and Peggy.

SAUL. You tell him if you want it told. Come on, Perchik. Time to learn the drill.

He goes to the counter and starts slamming knives on to the surface.

VANESSA. We did have kids, Perchik. Two.

SAUL. All utensils must be thoroughly disinfected.

VANESSA. A boy and a girl.

SAUL. I am scrupulous in my regard for Health and Safety.

He coughs up some more phlegm into his handkerchief.

VANESSA. They died, Perchik.

SAUL. They didn't *die*, Perchik. They were *slaughtered*.

PERCHIK. Slaughtered? By who?

SAUL. By people like you. Immigrants with backpacks and accents. During the 2012 attacks on Stratford. Floor!

He hands PERCHIK *a broom.* PERCHIK *starts to sweep.*

VANESSA. That's how I got this. (*She points to her scar.*) Only went for the day.

SAUL. I warned her. I said to her, I said the whole shebang was just an open invitation to rabid ragheads. What did I say, Vanessa?

VANESSA. You said that the whole shebang was just an open invitation to rabid ragheads.

SAUL. See? Get right into those corners, Perchik!

VANESSA. But they were mad for the ice-dancers, you see. My little munchkins.

SAUL. I wanted to have more but Vanessa has failed us in that way – her uterus is now dryer than a dead camel's tongue.

My wife may be a fine actress but even she cannot emote a working reproductive system. (*He hands* PERCHIK *a bin bag.*) Chuck that.

PERCHIK *nervously opens the door. The riots are heard. He chucks the bin bag out.*

PERCHIK. An actress, ay? Will I have seen you in anything?

SAUL. You'll need an apron.

SAUL *crosses to* PERCHIK *with a number of blood-stained white aprons of varying lengths, and tries to find the best fit.*

VANESSA. Oh no. My career never really took off.

SAUL. Don't be so *modest*, wife! Vanessa here was the *star* of a series of short party-political pornographic films intended to broaden the appeal of the Conservative Party to the masses!

VANESSA. Featuring Great Englishmen of History, Perchik. All the big ones they did: Winston Churchill –

SAUL *puts the apron on* PERCHIK *and ties it, standing behind him.*

SAUL. *We Will Fuck Them on the Beaches* –

VANESSA. Francis Drake…

SAUL. *The Spanish Arse-mada* –

VANESSA. It was all proper. Lovely costumes. I played Lady Hamilton wearing silk skirts and a powdered wig.

SAUL. In *Fellatio Nelson*.

PERCHIK *stares at* VANESSA, *wide-eyed.*

PERCHIK (*whispering*). *Fellatio Nelson*?

VANESSA (*solemnly*). It was a bestseller.

SAUL. Yes, Vanessa was worth a good deal of money when I met her.

PERCHIK. How do you know?

SAUL. Because I bought her, didn't I! Bought her out of it!

VANESSA. Saved me.

SAUL. I can't stand to see a woman defiled. It was the same when I was younger and used to run an agency making flats in West London affordable to young Eastern European girls.

PERCHIK. How d'you do that then?

SAUL. By helping them sublet by the hour to businessmen from the Home Counties.

VANESSA. Ever so charitable you are, aren't you, Saul?

SAUL. It's just my character, dearest. Now, what about some supper for Perchik?

VANESSA. Um. There's your stew, Saul…

SAUL. Perfect! A fine introduction to our customs. The way to a country's heart is through its stomach. No, no, wife. *I* shall fetch it!

SAUL *exits with ceremony.*

VANESSA *(fondly)*. My husband is a very keen cook.

PERCHIK. Ay? What's his speciality then?

VANESSA. Well… he's very good at brown things. Not like me, I'm shocking, I'd burn a banana split! It comes of not having had a mum for very long I think, there's a certain kind of knowledge that gets passed down isn't there certain things like how to choose a good tomato and pricking sausages with a fork though that said I do make very good pastry, cold hands you see goodness listen to me banging on about myself! I'm sorry, er, Perchik, was it? Saul's right, it is a funny name, isn't it – I don't mean that in a horrible way – so what are you doing in our shop then, Perchik?

PERCHIK *(not missing a beat)*. I've come to fix your pianoforte, Lady Hamilton.

As VANESSA *spins round sharply,* SAUL *enters bearing a stockpot and ladle.* VANESSA *and* PERCHIK *break gaze as* VANESSA *rushes out to the back.*

SAUL. Ta-da! This'll put some strength in you, Perchik! Are you handy with a spade?

PERCHIK. Dunno. Never used one.

SAUL. You'll soon pick it up. Foundations must be laid!

PERCHIK. Foundations for what?

SAUL. For the extension! I'm expanding my Empire out back.

> SAUL *tucks his hankie into his shirt-neck.* VANESSA *enters with bowls and cutlery, and starts laying the table.*

And you are going to help me!

PERCHIK. Vanessa and I were just havin' a wee chat about –

> VANESSA *quickly holds out a salt-shaker and a pepper-grinder.*

VANESSA. Saul! Condiments to the chef!

> SAUL *stares at the salt and pepper for a moment, then they both roar with laughter.*

SAUL. Condiments to the – !

VANESSA (*giggling*). You will be careful, won't you? Out back?

SAUL. Of course we will.

VANESSA. Only, I wouldn't want Perchik to leave like Frankie.

SAUL. Not now, Vanessa.

PERCHIK. What happened to Frankie?

SAUL. Nothing happened to him. Who said anything happened to him?

PERCHIK. I just meant – why did he leave, like? Did he find another position?

SAUL. Yes. He found another position. At a more… grass-roots level.

VANESSA. But, Saul, he didn't –

SAUL. I'm trying not to frighten the boy, Vanessa.

VANESSA. But he should know…

PERCHIK. Know what?

SAUL. It's a sad story. A very sad story.

VANESSA. Oh, ever so sad, Perchik.

PERCHIK. What happened?

SAUL. Oh, I couldn't possibly say. No, it's too sad. I couldn't. No. I'd sooner die. Not even if you begged me on hand and knee I couldn't. Not in a million trillion billion –

PERCHIK. Please?

SAUL. He fell.

VANESSA. Into the cement mixer, Perchik.

SAUL. It was dreadful, I can't deny it, but entirely consonant with the laws of gravity, as I understand them. We were out back. Expanding the Empire. The boy was blind as a bat – he was a foreign as well, like you, no papers, barely spoke a word of English.

VANESSA. Saul is very socially minded.

SAUL. Thank you, wife. I appreciate that.

VANESSA. He's always taking people in, giving them a job.

SAUL. Even in these lean times, an Englishman must behave as an Englishman.

VANESSA. Oh, but so few do.

SAUL. Yes, so few do.

VANESSA. Go to the lengths you go to.

SAUL. I can't say it's not a daily struggle.

VANESSA. I mean, he's not a wealthy man himself.

SAUL. Never aspired to be.

VANESSA. But what he does for these poor foreign blind boys.

SAUL. Just a little education.

VANESSA. And don't they love him for it!

SAUL. They're like sons to me.

VANESSA. Like family.

SAUL. That's enough, wife. One lump or two?

> SAUL *starts to dish up stew for himself and* VANESSA. *It is indeed a stew of indistinguishable fleshy lumps* (*see* Delia Smith's Cookery Course (*1981*), *p.332*).

VANESSA. Little Francesco. Two please, Saul.

SAUL. Dig in, Perchik.

PERCHIK. I'm. Ah. I'm no' that hungry.

Pause.

SAUL. You're 'no' that hungry'?

VANESSA. But everyone is hungry, Perchik.

PERCHIK. I don't have a very big appetite.

SAUL. Do you know the lengths I go to to put meat on this table? You think it's easy? Essex underwater and Dorset dissolving into the sea like sherbet. There's no pasture any more, no grazing, and here I present you with a delicious stew and you turn up your nose!

VANESSA. Frankie never used to eat much either. The amount of work he did on the food you gave him, Saul. The boy was a real treasure.

PERCHIK. I don't want to seem ungrateful, but –

VANESSA. Actually, Perchik reminds me a bit of Frankie, Saul.

SAUL. If you don't mind me saying, you're being very short-sighted.

VANESSA. Ah, see, Frankie was long-sighted.

SAUL. How long do you think this heat can continue? Only those with enough food stores about their person have any hope of making it through the winter we will have.

PERCHIK. I'm just not –

As SAUL talks, he lifts out a ladle of stew. Sitting on top is a pair of NHS spectacles. VANESSA panics. SAUL and PERCHIK are oblivious.

SAUL. We must make ourselves into living larders, that is what we must do, for, to paraphrase the late, great / Charles Darwin –

VANESSA. Um… Saul –

SAUL. 'The human race will soon boil down to little more than survival of the / fattest.'

VANESSA. Saul –

SAUL. And you, you scrawny runt, won't last a minute!

VANESSA. *Saul!*

> SAUL *looks from her to the ladle. Sees. Starts. Chucks the ladle back into the pot.*

> On the other hand, nobody likes a fatso.

PERCHIK. Aw, go on then, just give us a few tatties. You're right, I should –

SAUL. No, I'm not.

PERCHIK. What?

SAUL. Don't listen to me! I've always had an unhealthy relationship with food!

VANESSA. He was chubby as a child!

PERCHIK. Och, now you're offended, I didnay mean – Just think my stomach must've shrunk, that's all, been that long since I ate properly –

SAUL. And how well you look on it! Doesn't he, Vanessa!

VANESSA. Oh yes. Very handsome.

SAUL. What?!

VANESSA. If you like that sort of thing, I mean.

PERCHIK. You're just trying to be polite.

SAUL. How dare you! I'd never dream of it.

PERCHIK. I'll just have a little taste – to show my appreciation, like.

SAUL. No – you mustn't.

PERCHIK. Why not?

SAUL. Because – because… because Vanessa spat in it! Didn't you, wife?

VANESSA. Did I?

> SAUL *whacks her with his stick.*

> Ow! Oh yeah. I forgot. I'm disgusting, I am. Spit in anything.

SAUL. One of her charming little habits.

VANESSA. Like a bloody llama, me.

PERCHIK *takes the ladle from* SAUL.

PERCHIK. Really, I don't mind. I wouldnay want to insult my hostess.

SAUL *snatches it back.*

SAUL. Ah, but you see, she spends an awful lot of time licking unpalatable objects in public toilets, so I wouldn't dream of asking –

PERCHIK *firmly takes the ladle back.*

PERCHIK. It's fine! I shouldnay've made such a fuss in the first –

PERCHIK *ladles out a spoonful of stew. The glasses are sitting on top. There is a pause as the three of them stare at the object.*

SAUL. The riots are quiet tonight, don't you think?

PERCHIK. Saul? Where did these come from?

SAUL. This blasted heat, I find it very draining. Don't you, Vanessa?

PERCHIK. Are they yours?

VANESSA. Saul has excellent vision.

SAUL. Shut up, wife.

PERCHIK (*to* VANESSA). They're no' yours, are they though?

VANESSA. I should think not.

SAUL. I don't care for what you're insinuating.

PERCHIK. I'm not insinuating nothing.

SAUL. I offer you my pot and you start fishing out bits of old junk.

VANESSA. Calm down, Saul –

SAUL. I will not! There's one thing I can't abide and that's fussy eaters!

PERCHIK. I just wondered what a pair of glasses was doin' in your stew.

SAUL. Waste not want not, Perchik. 'Dig for Victory' etcetera etcetera.

PERCHIK. Whose are they, Saul? Are they – They're not – Jesus.

The penny drops. Beat. VANESSA *suddenly sobs loudly.*

They're Frankie's. Aren't they, Saul? Saul? *Saul?*

SAUL. I did not ask for the Spanish Inquisition, Perchik! (*Beat.*) But seeing as you ask… I thought it a shame that such a… serendipitous bounty should go to waste.

Pause. SAUL *polishes his cutlery intently.* VANESSA *stifles her sobs.*

PERCHIK (*quietly*). How did he get in the cement mixer, Saul?

VANESSA. It was an accident. Wasn't it, Saul! A tragic twist of fate!

PERCHIK. Saul?

SAUL. I told you. He fell.

PERCHIK. Yeah, but *why*? People don't just –

SAUL. We were laying foundations. I stumbled over a spade young Frankie had carelessly left lying on the floor.

PERCHIK. And?

SAUL. And what?! And I may have knocked him with my elbow in my attempts to steady myself! Alright!

Beat.

VANESSA. But – you said that it was an accident. You said he *fell*.

SAUL. He did fall.

VANESSA. But… you pushed him.

SAUL. I… manipulated his centre of gravity, yes. Accidentally.

PERCHIK. And then he fell.

SAUL. I can't be held responsible for his trajectory thereafter.

VANESSA. But you pushed him.

SAUL. Don't be so naive, Vanessa. He had a terrible life. Terrible.

VANESSA. He was happy here, Saul.

SAUL. Worked his arse off –

VANESSA. We used to sing together –

SAUL. And for what? For a pittance! And you remember that disgusting acne –

VANESSA. It was characterful.

SAUL. It was pus-ful. His life was a waste of harvestable organs.

VANESSA. But you told me he fell.

SAUL. I was trying to spare your feelings. It wasn't my fault.

PERCHIK. But you pushed him.

VANESSA. He loved it here.

SAUL. Course he did.

VANESSA. Called me 'Mamma Vanessa'.

SAUL. Better than the godforsaken rathole he came from.

PERCHIK begins to edge away from the table.

VANESSA. Fitted in well.

SAUL. Forty degrees in the shade and women with hairy armpits.

VANESSA. Like it was his home.

SAUL. WELL, IT WASN'T HIS HOME, WAS IT!

Still looking at VANESSA, SAUL stabs his fork into PERCHIK's leg and holds it there. PERCHIK yelps then writhes in silent agony. VANESSA weeps quietly.

VANESSA. I thought… I thought it was an accident… Poor Frankie…

SAUL (*conversationally*). My wife has a very sensitive disposition. As a young girl she used to cry at compost heaps.

VANESSA. I did not. Last time I cried was when me mum died.

SAUL. You're awful talkative tonight, wife. Come here.

He lets go of the fork, grabs VANESSA's wrist and pulls her onto his lap. PERCHIK pulls the fork out of his leg with relief, and breathes deeply.

I think the pair of you are forgetting who holds the matches here. Discipline, Perchik, is the cornerstone of any Empire. I find the old methods remain the best, over time.

He turns VANESSA *over on his knee, pulls up her skirt and pulls down her knickers.*

VANESSA. Saul!

SAUL. Now, Perchik, give it a smack, she won't feel it, it's like donkey hide. The whole region is like donkey hide. The meaning of that simile is that my wife's nether regions have no sensation. The result of years of overuse, eh, my flower?

He smacks her, hard. She struggles, trying to cover herself.

VANESSA. Ow! Saul, stop it, not in front / of him, please – Saul!

SAUL. Have a go. It's great fun.

PERCHIK. No, thanks all the same.

SAUL. No?

PERCHIK. … Nah. You're alright.

SAUL. Do you have any testicles, Perchik? Or do you just view them as useful if inconveniently located paperweights?

PERCHIK. I jus' don't think it's – appropriate.

SAUL. Nonsense! Come over and give her a smack now! Plant it right *there*.

He smacks her again to indicate the spot. PERCHIK *crosses to them. He stands for a moment, raises his hand, then leans over and softly kisses* VANESSA*'s bottom.*

Eh? What's all this? Who said you could kiss my wife's arse?

PERCHIK. You did.

SAUL. I did not!

PERCHIK. I must have misunderstood. You should give your invitations more clarity in future.

SAUL (*disbelieving*). I should what? You little –

PERCHIK. A slip of the tongue, a flawed e-nun-cia-tion. Can send the whole meaning of your sentence into chaos.

SAUL. You… you… get in the van. We're going for a drive.

Beat. SAUL *throws* VANESSA *off his lap and grabs* PERCHIK.

PERCHIK. Ay? Where we going?

SAUL. Calais.

PERCHIK. I don't want to go to Calais.

SAUL. No one *wants* to go to Calais. Even people who *live* in Calais don't *want* to go to Calais. It's a stinking grey mudbank reeking of pilchards. It would be like wanting to wear a syphilitic streetwalker's knickers as a sunhat. But nonetheless, we're going.

VANESSA. Don't hurt him, Saul, he didn't mean anything by it.

SAUL. Who said anything about hurting him? I didn't.

VANESSA. But you said you were taking him / to Calais.

SAUL. Yes. Calais was mentioned, hurting him was not. Vanessa's confused, Perchik, perhaps my enunciation was flawed.

PERCHIK. Perhaps it was.

SAUL. Are you trying to be clever?

PERCHIK. No. Not trying.

SAUL. You ungrateful little – !

Suddenly there's a banging at the door. All three start.

DETECTIVE PRAWN (*off*). This is Detective Prawn. Open up!

VANESSA. They know, Saul! About Frankie! Oh God! I can't – I / can't breathe!

SAUL. Don't get hysterical, wife.

DETECTIVE PRAWN (*off*). I can hear you in there!

SAUL (*panicking*). Just coming, Detective! Get the door, Perchik. Quickly!

PERCHIK. You've got to be kidding?

SAUL. Oh yes! I look like I'm in a puckish mood, do I?

PERCHIK. What I meant was, if I do, that they'll come in here and – you know.

SAUL. Of course they won't.

PERCHIK. Oh no? And what makes you think that?

SAUL. Because I won't tell them who you are, you fetid little arse-kisser! Now get the blasted door before I decide to introduce you as Colin the paedo cop-killer!

PERCHIK *flings open the door. As he does,* VANESSA *notices Frankie's glasses.*

VANESSA. The spectacles, Saul!

SAUL *panics, then puts the spectacles on. Gravy drips down his face.* DETECTIVE PRAWN *enters.*

DETECTIVE PRAWN. Who's in charge of this establishment?

SAUL. Hello. This is my shop. This is my wife. And this is… Um…

VANESSA. *Francesco.* Frankie.

SAUL. Yes! Very good, wife. This is Frankie, my – Frankie. He's Italian.

PERCHIK *throws a panicked look at* SAUL*, then smiles.*

PERCHIK. Er… Ciao, bella!

DETECTIVE PRAWN. I've not got time for 'Ciao, bellas'! A dangerous painter is on the loose!

SAUL. The worst kind! Perhaps we can help. What does he look like?

DETECTIVE PRAWN. He looks… like a painter.

VANESSA. Which one?

DETECTIVE PRAWN. All of them.

VANESSA. All of them?

DETECTIVE PRAWN. What I mean to say is that he has a generic artistic *countenance*. (*Beat.*) You know. Shifty.

VANESSA. But why would you think he's here?

DETECTIVE PRAWN. We have intelligence to suggest that he hitched a lift from London and arrived at a landfill site here in Bradford at around four-thirty this afternoon.

VANESSA. How do you know it was him?

DETECTIVE PRAWN. The car that he flagged down was an unmarked police car driven by my Superior, DCI Swann. It seems this 'artist' is an exceptionally stupid character.

VANESSA. But why didn't DCI Swann arrest him?

DETECTIVE PRAWN. He's not too bright either.

SAUL. I'm sorry, Detective. We've not seen anyone of that description, but of course we'll let you know if... What?

SAUL *stops*. DETECTIVE PRAWN *is staring at him*.

DETECTIVE PRAWN. Umm... there's gravy on your face, sir.

SAUL. Sorry?

DETECTIVE PRAWN. There's gravy.

SAUL. Where?

DETECTIVE PRAWN. On your face.

SAUL. Oh.

Beat.

DETECTIVE PRAWN. Why is there gravy on your face, sir?

SAUL. Why is there gravy on my face? Why is there gravy on my... What an *excellent* question, the reason is – The reason, I mean to say –

PERCHIK. It's our custom, Officer.

DETECTIVE PRAWN. What?

PERCHIK. Er – I mean... it'sa oura customa! Ciao, bella!

SAUL. Yes! Very good, P... Frankie! Our custom! A silly little custom of ours. If we've had an exceptionally good meal, to, ah – show our appreciation we put – um –

DETECTIVE PRAWN. Gravy on your face, sir?

SAUL. Exactly!

DETECTIVE PRAWN. I see. You must waste a lot of gravy.

SAUL. Not really. My wife is a very mediocre cook.

DETECTIVE PRAWN. I'm sorry. You, er – You mind if I have a taste?

He picks up the ladle, VANESSA *swipes it off him.*

VANESSA. Won't you spoil your dinner, Detective?

DETECTIVE PRAWN. Oh no. Mrs Prawn has recently become
a freegan.

VANESSA. A freegan?

DETECTIVE PRAWN. She'll only eat food out of skips.
Ecologically it's very sound, but I can't say it's not damaged our
standing on Bradford's dinner-party circuit. You mind?

He takes the ladle from VANESSA *and ladles out some stew.*

SAUL. No!

VANESSA. No!

PERCHIK. No... -a!

Sitting on top of the ladle is a flip-flop.

DETECTIVE PRAWN (*staring down*). *What the hell is this?*

SAUL. It was an accident!

VANESSA. He fell!

Silently, SAUL *takes a cricket bat from behind the counter,
creeps behind* DETECTIVE PRAWN *and raises it. But*
DETECTIVE PRAWN *isn't looking at the flip-flop. He produces
a pair of tweezers, then lifts something from the floor. It's a
cigarette butt. He rises with a nasty grin.* SAUL *chucks the
cricket bat behind him.*

DETECTIVE PRAWN. Oh-ho-ho. You are *for it*, mate.

SAUL. Is there a problem, Detective?

DETECTIVE PRAWN. Tell me – is this your shop?

SAUL. Yes. It's my shop. And Empire, Detective.

DETECTIVE PRAWN. And so, sir, does this – *cigarette butt*
belong to you?

SAUL. No. I've never seen it before in my life. But if I had to
make a guess, I'd say it belonged to the unruly gang of sado-
masochistic asthmatics who use my property for their 'Wine,
Wheeze and Cheese Evenings', every last Sunday of the month.

DETECTIVE PRAWN. Don't try and be *funny*, fella. Tobacco and its derivatives are designated a Class-A drug, and the purchase and consumption of their associated products is a serious offence. You're looking at five to ten in a prison full of Estonian gangsters and kiddy-fiddlers with dubious personal hygiene and I've heard bathtime can get a bit friendly, so why don't you just ANSWER THE FUCKING QUESTION!

Pause. PERCHIK *picks up the cricket bat. Then suddenly* DETECTIVE PRAWN *grins.*

Aaahhh! Only kidding! I've got six rapes and an identity theft to write up tonight! Last thing I want is fourteen hours of paperwork over this! But I got you, didn't I!

He starts to wander again, poking his head round doors, then approaches the icebox.

SAUL. Oh yes, Detective! Yes! You got me!

All three relax and laugh matily along.

DETECTIVE PRAWN. The look on your face! Priceless! Well, you've got to laugh, haven't you? What have we got here? (*He opens the icebox door, looks in.*) What I'm always saying to my colleagues, in a job like ours, you really have got to laugh...

SAUL. Oh yes, Detective! You've got to laugh!

DETECTIVE PRAWN. Otherwise you'll... (*He turns suddenly.*) Hang on. Was that – a *flip-flop*?

Quick as a flash, PERCHIK *chucks the cricket bat to* SAUL, *who brings it down on* DETECTIVE PRAWN's *head. He collapses into the icebox.*

PERCHIK. Here.

PERCHIK *helps* SAUL *manoeuvre* DETECTIVE PRAWN *into the sack that* PERCHIK *arrived in.* VANESSA *opens the shop door and peers out.*

VANESSA. Quick! There's a lorry backing up!

SAUL *and* PERCHIK *carry the sack out of the door. The sound of an engine starting up is heard as they re-enter, exhausted.* VANESSA *collapses with relief.*

Well! I think that could have gone a lot worse. Don't you?

SAUL *chucks the spectacles in the pot, then marches on*
PERCHIK. *He's spoiling to lamp him. At the last moment,*
SAUL *takes out his hankie and phlegms into it.*

SAUL. Nicely done, baggage.

PERCHIK. Thanks. Listen, sorry about before. I shouldn't / have –

SAUL. Vanessa?

VANESSA. Yes, Saul?

SAUL. Tell Perchik the next time he considers kissing my wife's
bottom, he should remember which one of us has papers and
which one does not.

SAUL *exits.* VANESSA *turns to* PERCHIK.

VANESSA. My husband said to tell you the next time you consider –

PERCHIK. I heard.

VANESSA *pulls out her workbox. She sits and starts to sew.*
PERCHIK *watches her intently. The muffled sound of 'Pomp
and Circumstance' starts up above them.*

VANESSA. I'm glad you came, Perchik. I think we're going to be
good good friends. Only, you must try not to upset Saul. He's an
old man, you see. He's a bit stuck in his ways but that's only
natural can you stop staring at me please?

PERCHIK (*embarrassed*). Sorry. I just… Sorry. (*Beat.*) What's he
doing up there?

VANESSA. Oh, you know. Blueprints. For the revolution.

PERCHIK. For the revolution. Right. If you don't mind me saying,
your husband – he's a little bit… (*He taps his head.*) Isn't he?
What's it, senile dementia?

VANESSA. No, it's bloody not! He's just… past his prime. Knows
a lot of stuff though.

PERCHIK. About bloody what? Lamb chops and mince?

VANESSA. No. Like, history. Culture and that. He gives me
classes. You'll probably have to do them too. Frankie did. And
Klaus. Only, they never understood much.

'Pomp and Circumstance' gets louder.

PERCHIK. Can't stand that racket. Can't we put something else on?

VANESSA. Don't have nothing, do I? Used to. Used to have loads. Tammy Wynette. She was my favourite. And Edith Piaf. I loved them two. Had all the albums. But they got lost during the move. I swear I put them in at Barking… but when we got here… they were gone. Saul says they must've fallen out of the van. Or been stolen by Gypsy DJs. Or something. I miss my records. Don't get nothing but bloody Elgar now. Hold these.

She hands PERCHIK *a pair of shears to hold as she rummages in her workbox.*

PERCHIK. What you making?

VANESSA. Just some curtains. For the cottage.

PERCHIK. The cottage?

VANESSA takes a scrap of paper out, gives it to PERCHIK, and continues sewing.

VANESSA. S'in the country somewhere. By the sea. I forget where. Up north though. More north than Bradford, I mean. Where it still snows. This is just – what d'you call it – *an artist's impression*. S'not finished yet, see. We're building it slowly. 'Brick by bastard brick,' Saul says. (*Confidentially.*) It's got a room *just for boots*, Perchik!

PERCHIK. It's nice, in'it? Pretty.

VANESSA beams at him. She looks beautiful.

VANESSA. It's our dream house! We've waited ten years but it won't be long now. S'taking longer than expected. What with business being so bad. But things'll pick up soon. You could come with us, Perchik! I'm going to paddle in the sea every – ow!

PERCHIK. Are you okay?

VANESSA. Yeah. Just pricked myself.

PERCHIK. Let's see.

VANESSA holds her finger out.

It's bleeding.

VANESSA. Only a bit.

PERCHIK puts her finger in his mouth and sucks the blood from it.

What are you –

PERCHIK. You're a very beautiful woman.

VANESSA. What?

PERCHIK. I said. You're a Very. Beautiful. Woman.

Pause. They stare at each other. Then:

VANESSA. Shut up.

PERCHIK. I've always thought so.

VANESSA. Don't be daft, we've only just met.

PERCHIK. I knew it was you. They say the camera adds ten pounds, but I could spot you a mile off.

VANESSA. You mean – before. When you said. I mean… You've seen *Fellatio Nelson*?

PERCHIK. Seen it?! You made me come like a train twice a day for five years!

VANESSA. You're just saying that.

PERCHIK. No, I'm not! Used to steal me da's mags and films from under his bed, didn't I? Stacks of 'em, he had.

VANESSA. Including those made by the Conservative Party?

PERCHIK. 'Specially those made by the Conservative Party.

VANESSA. I should've thought your father was a Labour man.

PERCHIK. He was blue-curious.

VANESSA. I've never met a fan before.

PERCHIK. You look just the same.

VANESSA. Apart from Saul of course.

PERCHIK. Just as beautiful, / I mean it.

VANESSA. Imagine you sat there / at home.

PERCHIK. Watching you / on the telly.

VANESSA. Watching me / in my powdered wig.

PERCHIK. I can remember it off by heart.

VANESSA. Really?

PERCHIK *puts one hand inside his shirt, then gallops up to her.*

PERCHIK (*porn voice*). 'Hello, Lady Hamilton. I've come to fix your pianoforte.'

VANESSA. Oh no, Perchik. I can't!

PERCHIK. Aw, go on!

VANESSA. I mean, I shouldn't. That's all in the past, that's – I mean... no.

PERCHIK. Alright then. Suit yeself.

PERCHIK *shrugs and walks to the blind. Looks through.* VANESSA *bites her lip.*

VANESSA. Well. I suppose it wouldn't –

PERCHIK (*quickly*). Yes?

VANESSA. If it was just –

PERCHIK. Of course –

VANESSA. And no one has to –

PERCHIK. No!

VANESSA. What was that you said?

PERCHIK. About your pianoforte?

VANESSA. Yes.

PERCHIK (*grins*). I've come to fix it!

VANESSA. 'Oh Lord Nelson! You've caught me tinkling my ivories in my scanties! How shameful!'

PERCHIK. 'Your scanties are divine, Lady Hamilton. Now that I've seen them, I must have you now, here in this very drawing room!'

VANESSA. 'It's not a drawing room, it's a library.'

PERCHIK. 'Nonetheless!'

VANESSA. 'Oh, but I can't! I mustn't! I won't!'

PERCHIK. 'But England expects that you do, Emma!'

VANESSA. 'Then in the name of England and her outlying lands, I demand that you jizz on my tits, Lord Nelson!'

PERCHIK *seizes* VANESSA *and leans her over his knee.*

PERCHIK. 'Lady Hamilton! I declare you are a pedigree saucepot!'

PERCHIK *suddenly kisses her.* VANESSA *slaps his face. She runs into the icebox.*

Vanessa…

VANESSA (*indistinct through the door and tears*). I'm a married woman, Perchik.

PERCHIK. What?

VANESSA *opens the door. It's quite an operation.*

VANESSA. I said, I'm a married woman!

VANESSA *slams the door again.*

PERCHIK. I'm sorry, Vanessa. Vanessa?

VANESSA (*singing, off*). Oh, the toe bone's connected to the –

PERCHIK. Vanessa. Open the door.

VANESSA (*off*). – *foot* bone, the foot bone's connected to the –

PERCHIK. OPEN THE DOOR!

VANESSA (*off*). – *ankle* bone, the ankle bone's connected to the knee bone…

PERCHIK *sighs and sits. He takes a banana out of his bag.* VANESSA *continues to sing.* SAUL *enters, and makes an OTT show of searching the shop for something.*

SAUL. Where are they then?

PERCHIK (*nervously*). Who? There's nobody here but me, Mr Saul.

SAUL. Oooh! I'm sorry! I'm so – It's just, I assumed from the noise that someone was *trapping cats* down here! (*His smile vanishes.*) If you don't mind I'm trying to – WHAT THE HELL IS THAT?

He gestures at PERCHIK's *banana.*

PERCHIK. It's a banana.

SAUL. I won't have fruit in the shop.

PERCHIK. What the – Why not?

SAUL. It upsets the meat.

PERCHIK. That sausage looks perfectly happy to me.

SAUL. Well, it's crying on the inside. Do you know how many *Phoneutria Fera*, or Brazilian wandering spiders, enter this country illegally in banana crates? By thinking only of your own potassium levels, you are throwing our national ecology into turmoil.

PERCHIK. Potassium levels?

SAUL. I mean, if you *must* indulge the appendix, there are plenty of good *English* fruits you might try. The Cox's orange pippin! The Victoria plum! All fine varieties. But a *banana*, Perchik. A banana? Of all things.

PERCHIK. It's just a banana.

SAUL. It was just cake to Marie Antoinette, my friend.

VANESSA (*off*). NOW HEAR THE WORD OF THE LORD!

SAUL (*irritably*). Shut up, wife!

SAUL *slams his stick against the icebox. The door opens and* VANESSA *creeps out.*

(*Beaming at her.*) Ah! Hello, piglet. Hiding in the icebox again?

VANESSA (*irritably*). Had to cool down, didn't I? Can't stand this bloody heat. Makes my fingers itch.

VANESSA *starts to sew.* PERCHIK *watches.* SAUL *pulls his face round by the chin.*

SAUL. Oi. Goggle-eyes. I don't love her for her brains and she's not much to look at but she's mine and if you touch her I'll feed you your own kidneys.

PERCHIK *laughs nervously.*

What are you laughing at?

PERCHIK. I'm not sure.

SAUL *starts to exit, then turns back and surveys* PERCHIK.

SAUL. I mean. A *banana*.

End of Act One.

ACT TWO

'At the Meat of Things'

We discover SAUL *busy with some paper and glue.* PERCHIK *is leant over a ledger and a calculator at the counter. He taps his pencil. Sighs. Looks up.*

PERCHIK. Mr Saul? These accounts – they're no' very / healthy.

SAUL. Ah-ah-ah!

SAUL *points to what he's doing and puts his finger to his lips.*

PERCHIK. I'm not joking. They're in a really bad way.

SAUL. Yes yes, *later*, Perchik. First: I've made you a present. (*He holds it up.*) A passport, Perchik! To identify you as a citizen of my Empire.

PERCHIK. Oh. Well. Ta.

He goes to take it from SAUL*'s hand, but* SAUL *snatches it back.*

SAUL. No, no, not yet. You haven't *earned* it yet.

PERCHIK. But –

SAUL *holds up a hand: 'quiet'.* PERCHIK *wanders, bored.*

It's hot, ay? I'm hot. Where's everybody? Where's all the customers?

SAUL. Making the most of a blazing February afternoon, I imagine. To some, the melanoma is infinitely fascinating. They may as well enjoy it while it lasts.

PERCHIK. You mean, for ever?

SAUL *snorts in laughter.*

Wha'? You mean you don't believe in climate change?

SAUL. I've told you, I don't believe in any kind of change at all.

PERCHIK. Aw, but come on, Mr Saul – what about the heat? The floods!

SAUL. Nothing but an excuse for the English to carry on doing what they love best.

PERCHIK. And what's that then?

SAUL. Talking about the weather.

PERCHIK wanders to the door and looks through the blind.

PERCHIK. Come on! Someone! Someone come in!

SAUL. Don't hold your / breath.

PERCHIK. Wait, wait! There's someone coming. Yes! He's definitely… he's at the door.

He runs behind the counter. Long pause. A solitary letter slips through the letterbox.

The postman. It was just the postman.

Deflated, PERCHIK goes to pick the letter up.

SAUL. DON'T TOUCH IT!

PERCHIK. S'just a letter.

SAUL rushes over and pulls PERCHIK away.

SAUL. Don't be so *naive*. We live in an age of biological warfare. This *letter* could be dripping in anthrax. Or truth drugs!

PERCHIK. And is it?

SAUL gingerly picks up the envelope and sniffs it.

SAUL. … No.

PERCHIK tuts and goes back to the blind. SAUL opens the letter.

PERCHIK (*under his breath*). Who knew the end ay the world would be this fuckin' borin'.

SAUL. Aha!

PERCHIK. Well? Who's it from?

SAUL. Apparently I may have won a substantial cash prize.

PERCHIK looks back through the blind.

PERCHIK. We've not had a customer all morning. Not one.

SAUL. Business as usual.

PERCHIK. Why don't you *do* something? You can't survive like this.

SAUL. I have fingers in many pies, Perchik. Only one of them is meat.

PERCHIK. Your fingers or the pies?

Beat.

SAUL. Both.

PERCHIK. Yeah, well, maybe if you worked on your customer service –

SAUL. And what would you know about my customer service?

PERCHIK. I know by looking at the state of these books!

SAUL. Don't you cheek me, ragamuffin! I treat every customer that walks through that door like I would a minor Royal!

WINSTON *enters. He's a flustered English gentleman. He wears a suit similar to* SAUL*'s.*

What the hell do you want?

WINSTON. H-h-h-hullo. I was wondering if you had a spot of h-h-him?

SAUL. Him?

WINSTON. Yes. H-h-h-him. You know. (*Beat.*) As in 'him sandwiches'.

SAUL. Ohhhh! 'Aaaam! Sorry, no pig today. Goodbye.

WINSTON *starts to exit.* PERCHIK *rushes to block the doorway.*

PERCHIK. How about a lovely sausage, sir? I'll bet a man of your impeccable tastes would appreciate a good sausage, sir?

WINSTON. Well, that's very kind of you, but I don't think my tastes are especially –

PERCHIK. Oh, but look at your suit, sir! Look at the gentleman's suit, Mr Saul!

PERCHIK *violently nudges* SAUL *with his elbow and waves the ledger at him.*

WINSTON. This old thing? Do you like it, do you? It was my father's, h-h-h-actually. Terribly old now, I'm afraid. Practically an / antique.

SAUL. Not at all, sir! I admire a man who wears his inheritance on his back! Little hot spell like this is no excuse not to make an *effort*. My dad never went out with a bare head or an empty buttonhole. Immaculate, he was. Compare him to Perchik. Looks like a washing machine vomited, don't he? Do you remember, sir? / The old days?

WINSTON (*chuckles*). Oh yes –

SAUL. When the summers went by in a golden haze –

WINSTON. Gorgeous summers –

SAUL. We never had it so good, did we, sir?

WINSTON. H-h-h-halcyon days.

SAUL. When you could leave your car keys in the ignition and your front door on the latch!

WINSTON. Well h-h-h-actually that's a bit / before my –

SAUL. Or take a girl to the pictures and get change for a thruppenny bit?

WINSTON. I really don't remember / that far…

SAUL. Cockles from the fishman's barrow on a Sunday night and Gracie Fields singing 'The Largest Aspidistra in the World' on the wireless –

WINSTON. I'm only forty-two!

An icy pause.

SAUL. Alright, sir. No need to get testy. I was only speaking *figuratively*.

WINSTON. I'm sorry, I didn't mean… Oh dear me, how embarrassing. You must excuse me, I'm just – I'm a little *fraught*. The thing is, I'm terribly worried about my sister.

PERCHIK. Your sister, sir?

WINSTON. We've just arrived in town, you see. And since we left the old pile of bricks –

PERCHIK. Old pile of bricks, sir?

WINSTON. Oh, er – Bootlebum Hall. In Gloucestershire.

PERCHIK. Bootlebum Hall, sir?

WINSTON. Yes.

PERCHIK. In Gloucestershire, sir?

WINSTON. Yes! Do you know it?

PERCHIK. No. Nice place, was it?

WINSTON. Oh yes. It broke poor Constance's heart to leave, but after we had to have the gamekeeper put down, well – there really wasn't h-h-any other option. Connie's been an absolute brick about it, only, since we arrived in Bradford, she's been…well, she's not been tickety-boo.

PERCHIK. Not tickety-boo, sir?

WINSTON. Not tickety-boo at *all*. Pale. Won't eat a scrap, though she says she might manage a little h-h-him, if it was very thinly sliced. I can't think what's caused it.

SAUL. Mark my words, it'll be the water, sir, did you boil it before you drank?

WINSTON. Boil it? Of course we didn't boil it, this isn't *Africa* for goodness' sakes!

SAUL. Ah.

WINSTON. You mean… you think it's – some sort of stomach bug? Delhi belly?

SAUL. I'd say so, sir. Something like that. A stomach bug. Delhi belly. Cholera.

WINSTON. Cholera!

SAUL. I don't mean to upset you, sir, that's merely a worst-case scenario.

PERCHIK. Probably just needs feeding up a wee bit. How about a nice sausage?

WINSTON. Well, that sounds –

SAUL. Put a bit of colour in her cheeks, will a nice sausage. Made fresh this month.

WINSTON. Pork or beef?

SAUL. Hard to say.

PERCHIK *whisks a sad little bird body from the counter.*

PERCHIK. Or what about this pigeon, sir?

SAUL. Oh, now you cannot underestimate the palliative power of a pigeon, sir!

WINSTON. What are those black marks?

SAUL. Don't worry about that! That's only tyre tracks, that'll come out in the cooking!

WINSTON. I'm not sure… I can't / risk –

WINSTON *starts to exit.* SAUL *shrugs. Quickly,* PERCHIK *calls after him.*

PERCHIK. Is she very pale, sir?

WINSTON *turns back, worried.*

WINSTON. I, er – Rather pale, yes. Except for a sort of… green tinge.

PERCHIK. Only, sounds like she's got what my poor sausage-starved Auntie Bernice had.

WINSTON. Really?

PERCHIK. Started off pale, she did, couldnay keep nuthin' down. Kept asking for 'him'. Then came the green tinge. Then the bloating.

WINSTON. The bloating?

PERCHIK. Ay. Round like a melon she was. Then the next day, she exploded.

Beat.

WINSTON. Exploded?

PERCHIK. Ay. Exploded. All over ma father's collection of pornographic films.

WINSTON. But… that's terrible.

PERCHIK. I know. Some of them were collector's items.

SAUL. And all for the want of a bit of protein, sir…

WINSTON. I see. Well. In that case. I'd better take the lot.

PERCHIK. *Very* good, sir!

   PERCHIK *starts chucking all the meat into a plastic bag.*

SAUL (*whispering to* PERCHIK). Not the chop.

PERCHIK. Wha'?

SAUL. That chop came all the way from Barking with me. I even gave her a name.

WINSTON. Would you mind awfully h-h-hurrying up?

PERCHIK. Hold your horses, sir. There's still the question of payment.

WINSTON. How much does it cost?

PERCHIK. Well, how much have you got?

WINSTON. Um… fifty?

   SAUL *and* PERCHIK *suck in their breath.*

PERCHIK. Sterling is that, sir? Cannay do nuthin' with sterling. What about your suit, sir?

WINSTON. My suit?

PERCHIK. It's a nice suit. Call it fifty sterling and the suit. Cannay say fairer than that.

WINSTON. Well, I…

PERCHIK. *Kaboom!*

   PERCHIK *does a slow-motion mime of Auntie Bernice exploding.* WINSTON *hurriedly takes off his suit, and swaps it with* SAUL *for the meat.*

WINSTON. The money's h-in the h-inside pocket. Thanks very much.

   He rushes out, clutching the meat. SAUL *calls after him.*

SAUL. Not at all, sir! A pleasure to serve you!

   The door slams.

   Toffee-nosed git.

   He turns and stares at PERCHIK.

PERCHIK. What?

SAUL. She *exploded*?

PERCHIK. I was improvising, wasn't I! And it worked, didn't it?

SAUL. Oh *yes*, it worked alright. And now muggins here has to spend the rest of the day restocking! In the meantime, what have we got left to sell? Bugger all!

PERCHIK. There's that lamb chop for a start.

SAUL. You leave Danielle out of this! I've told you how hard it is for me to get good stock! Could be days before we get another delivery!

JOHN enters.

JOHN. Delivery!

PERCHIK. Ha! – Ow!

SAUL has smacked him round the head.

JOHN. Good morning, Mr Everard!

SAUL. Good morning, John! (*He looks for a sack.*) Where is it then?

JOHN. Oh, for Christ's – (*He calls off.*) JOHN JUNIOR! You great lump of –

JOHN JUNIOR enters, lugging a sack. He dumps it centre stage.

SAUL. And what do we have here?

JOHN. You're in luck today, Mr Everard! Articulated lorry hit a Gypsy caravan on the outskirts of Ilkley Moor! Sign here please.

JOHN JUNIOR pulls a saddle out of the top of the sack and holds it up.

JOHN JUNIOR. Will you be wanting to keep this, Mr Everard?

SAUL (*signing*). Just leave it out back with the others, John Junior.

JOHN JUNIOR exits to the back, with the saddle. Suddenly, SAUL, JOHN and PERCHIK are hit with a foul stench.

JOHN. Listen, you might want t'shift it quick, like. It's, er, on the turn a bit.

SAUL. 'On the turn a bit'!

JOHN. It's this bloody heat. Encourages the growth of bacteria.

SAUL. I paid in advance! I want my money back.

JOHN. I'm sorry, Mr Everard, my hands are tied. You'll have to take it up with the boss.

SAUL. At least take this filth away!

JOHN. Oh no no no, Mr Everard.

JOHN scribbles on some documents on his clipboard.

SAUL. What do you mean, 'no no no'? This is fetid. It's crawling with maggots!

JOHN. More than my job's worth, Mr Everard. And where would I put it?

SAUL. Oh, I don't know, John, up your capacious rectum perhaps?

Beat. JOHN looks up at SAUL, who smiles at him. JOHN JUNIOR enters from out back.

JOHN. What?

SAUL. What? (*Beat.*) How's the little one, John?

JOHN JUNIOR. Not so little, Mr Saul!

JOHN JUNIOR gestures the size of a leviathan baby.

JOHN. Shut up, lad. (*Beat.*) He's fine, Mr Saul. Baby's fine. (*Beat.*) Listen, I'll tell you what I'll do. JJ? Run back to Mr Womble and express Mr Everard's dissatisfaction. Mr Everard is a loyal and valued customer. He deserves better.

SAUL. Well, thank you, John! I appreciate that.

JOHN. Come on then, lad! Mush! Mush! Mush!

JOHN JUNIOR starts and scampers from the shop.

PERCHIK. Your boss will replace it, will he? The meat?

SAUL. Don't pester the man, Perchik.

PERCHIK. But what will we do? Look at these books, the accounts are a *joke* –

SAUL. Profit and loss, Perchik, profit and loss. The Empire must absorb. And find ways to balance both.

JOHN. I'll be off then.

SAUL. Would you care to inspect our expansion out back, John?

JOHN. I'm a bit pushed for time, to be honest.

SAUL. It really has come on a long way. The foundations are all but completed.

JOHN. Really, I better be –

SAUL. I think you'll be especially impressed with the ground beams…

Beat. PERCHIK *is staring at* SAUL, SAUL *at* JOHN.

JOHN. Yeah. Alright then. Why not, eh? That'd be grand.

SAUL. Excellent! Perchik, run along and make John a nice cup of tea.

PERCHIK. Wha'?

SAUL (*elaborately miming*). MAKE. JOHN. A. CUP. OF. TEA.

PERCHIK. Right. Yeah.

PERCHIK *exits*.

SAUL. You'll have to excuse Perchik, John. He's Scottish. Shall we?

JOHN. Been thinking of building a patio myself. Bit of a suntrap. Get myself a tan.

SAUL. Mmm. Crackling.

JOHN. What?

SAUL. Nothing, nothing. Step this way, John. Only, watch out for the cement mixer. It's a little… precarious.

SAUL *and* JOHN *exit to back.* VANESSA *enters by the front door, pushing a pram.*

VANESSA. Shop! (*Beat.*) Sho-op!

No reply. VANESSA *shrugs, then produces a cardboard box with 'Cottage' written on it. She pulls item after item out of the pram into the box; twee decorative things – windchimes, china figurines, etc. Finally, she looks round, then brings out a banana. She unpeels it.* PERCHIK *arrives in the doorway in time to watch as she crams it into her mouth. Lovely. He smiles. Then he hears* SAUL *approaching. He disappears as* SAUL *enters, breathless, with a builder's bucket, which he sets down by the doorway.*

SAUL. Ah, wife, you're home. Good.

VANESSA hurriedly swallows and holds up a novelty teapot to distract SAUL.

VANESSA. Look! For the cottage, Saul! Amazing, ain't it? It's a *teapot*. But it's shaped *like a cat*!

SAUL. Good God! And yet they still haven't found a cure for cancer!

PERCHIK enters at a pace, carefully balancing a cup of tea.

PERCHIK. I've done John's tea, Mr Saul.

SAUL winks at him and puts his finger to his lips with a grin. He picks up the passport and waves it at PERCHIK, who freezes. He downs the tea.

VANESSA. Oh. Is John here? Only, I made these for him.

She takes a pair of knitted baby's booties from the pram. SAUL takes them and scrutinises them, brow furrowed. A long pause. He looks up.

SAUL. But, Vanessa! These are far too small!

VANESSA. Silly! They're not *for John*! They're for his *baby*!

VANESSA and SAUL laugh their heads off at SAUL's japery.

(*Through giggles.*) Well? Where is he then?

SAUL (*still laughing too*). John? Oh, he was here. Yes. But he had to… head off.

SAUL picks up the bucket and plonks it on the counter. PERCHIK stares at it.

VANESSA. Oh. Never mind. I'll pop 'em down here for next time, eh?

VANESSA bends behind the counter. SAUL stares at PERCHIK, nods at the bucket.

SAUL. You might take another look at those accounts, Perchik. Ahem. (*He coughs into his hankie.*) Got anything for me, princess?

VANESSA straightens. SAUL sits and leads her round the counter and on to his lap.

VANESSA. Few bits and bobs. Too hot to carry on.

SAUL. Let's have a look then.

VANESSA. Couple of wallets. Nice cigarette lighter...

She starts to unpack the items from the pram. SAUL *snatches the lighter off her.*

SAUL. Naughty!

VANESSA. ... three fags. And a lovely white loaf.

PERCHIK. Bread?

SAUL. She got bread! *Clever* gel!

He kisses VANESSA*'s cheek over and over.*

PERCHIK. Where d'you get all this?

VANESSA. Riots stopped for lunch. Lot of big queues about. (*Giggles.*) Get off, Saul! Dodgy Julio was up in Little Germany with a barrowload of old Christmas cakes. Easy to lift stuff during a scramble.

PERCHIK. You stole them, Vanessa?

SAUL. It's all by the book, of course. In the grandest of traditions.

VANESSA puts the cigarettes in the fag cupboard.

PERCHIK. What tradition would that be?

SAUL. She will only rob from the rich and only give to the poor.

PERCHIK. Oh. Right.

SAUL. Conveniently, we are the poor. Give him his watch back, Nessa.

PERCHIK. What? When did you – I never –

SAUL. She's extremely dextrous, ain't she? Taught her myself. Hours of training. I fully endorse women in the marketplace. Never let it be said I am not a feminist.

VANESSA. Saul is an excellent teacher.

SAUL. Now, wife, you'll have me blushing beetroot. Pop those in the safe, chop-chop.

VANESSA takes the wallets and exits out back.

PERCHIK. She's – That was incredible.

SAUL. Thank you. She's my greatest achievement.

PERCHIK. What d'you mean by that?

> SAUL *coughs up some phlegm and spits it into his handkerchief.*

SAUL. Excuse me. The body must eject what it cannot entertain.
Ha ha ha.

PERCHIK. Saul?

SAUL. I *mean*, Perchik, that I have *made her what she is*.

PERCHIK. And what's that then?

SAUL. One: the best pickpocket in Bradford. Two: more stupid
than you could imagine. And three: not to be trusted.

PERCHIK. Is that not a bit daft? Making someone untrustworthy?

SAUL. Of course *I* can trust her. She's very loyal to *me*. Basically
a labrador in a dress.

PERCHIK. Yeah, but who wants to marry a complete dog, right?

> *He laughs feebly.* SAUL *stares at him.*

SAUL. A little… *conditioning* is very potent. Only through it will
people accept your ways, clasp them to their odd little bosoms
and, in time, become as you are.

PERCHIK. And what exactly is 'as you are'?

SAUL. Why! Culturally elite! The shop in which you stand, my
dear little retard, is the last bastion of the greatest cultural
machine the world has ever seen. We have civilised whole
continents! Barbarous peoples and arid lands have been tamed
by our touch!

PERCHIK. And modest with it, eh, Mr Saul?

SAUL. I couldn't expect you to understand, you porridge-sucking
little Pict. Well, put this in your pipe and smoke it: do you know
what 'poor Vanessa' did before I began work on her? She soaked
her parents' sheets in kerosene and burnt them in their beds.

PERCHIK. Don't be daft.

SAUL. I don't think she realised what she was doing. Vanessa has
always been one sausage short of a barbecue. That must be

taken into account. But it was down to my testimony that her
sentence / was suspended.

PERCHIK. Shut up –

SAUL. *I* rehabilitated her! If it weren't for my jurisdiction you'd
have 'pyro' to add to the klepto-nympho-maniacal mix that is
Vanessa's / psyche!

PERCHIK. I don't *believe* you!

SAUL. *Immaterial!* The gel is a fire hazard! That is an *empirical
fact*. Why d'you think she's not allowed to light her own
cigarettes, eh? You ever smelt burning flesh? It's not fragrant.

PERCHIK. She couldnay. They must've –

*VANESSA skips in, jauntily singing 'Blue Moon of Kentucky'.
She takes the key and starts unlocking the cigarette cupboard.*

Ahhh!

SAUL. You're being rather cavalier with the fags of late, wife. Tell
you what.

*VANESSA comes to him for a light. SAUL takes out his
matches.*

You may have one if you can tell me what the adjective
'cavalier' means, Vanessa.

VANESSA (*sulkily*). I don't know, do I?

SAUL. It means 'showing a lack of proper concern'. See Perchik?
To coin a phrase, '*Education, education, education.*' It's very
important. She'd know that if she had it.

*He lights a match, then blows it out and catches hold of her
arm. It's bandaged at the wrist.*

What's this, Nessa?

VANESSA. Oh that. S'nothing. Atifa again. What's-his-name, Mr
Quasim's daughter. Said I was on her patch. That's never bloody
her patch.

SAUL. Burn or cut?

VANESSA. Burn.

SAUL. It hurt?

VANESSA. Yeah. Stings a bit.

SAUL. You get her back, sweetheart?

> VANESSA *shakes her head.* SAUL *kisses the bandage and puts the matches away.* VANESSA *is crestfallen.*

Never mind.

VANESSA. But –

SAUL. Run and fetch my hat and we shall pay a little visit to Miss Quasim.

> *He gives her a coin. She kisses him. He pats her on the bum and she exits to back.* SAUL *takes a knife from the rack and sharpens it.*

PERCHIK. Hang on – What's goin' on?

SAUL. An eye for an eye, a tooth for a tooth. Or, for the secular audience who prefer the newest testament of all and hold the science of matter as their godhead, for every action, there is an equal and opposite reaction.

PERCHIK. Wha'?

SAUL. Revenge, Perchik! Nobody burns my wife and gets away with it!

PERCHIK. Except you, / ay?

SAUL. Except m – shut up.

PERCHIK. But you're no' leavin' me here on my own?

SAUL *(chuckling).* Let me tell you something, little Perchik. I have a dream. A dream – that one day, everything will be *exactly as it is now*.

PERCHIK. Well, you're an ambitious man, that's only natural.

SAUL. But I'm old, Perchik.

PERCHIK. Nonsense, Mr Saul. You're only as old as the woman you feel. Right?

SAUL. Well, she's old too. And when I'm gone I expect she'll do the decent thing.

PERCHIK *(hopefully).* Remarry, you mean?

SAUL. No, die. It would be unseemly for her not to. And then where will my Empire be? I need an *heir*. Do you see where I'm heading?

PERCHIK. Ay. Do you want to adopt me?

SAUL. Don't be disgusting. No. I have a better plan. This afternoon, little Perchik, you shall enter the world of commerce – not as a dogsbody... but as a *store manager*!

PERCHIK. An' that's good, is it?

SAUL. Yes.

PERCHIK. Oh.

SAUL. I knew you'd be excited! You are now In Charge, Perchik. I am *handing over the reins*! As my father did to me! The future of his Empire is in your hands!

PERCHIK. You want me to mind the shop? On my own? But we've no stock.

SAUL. No stock? Nonsense! We've got enough to last us a week! (*He bangs the bucket with his stick.*) Think what I'm offering you, Perchik! Promotion! Power! Prestige!

PERCHIK. Prestige?

SAUL. Well, no, not prestige, exactly. And not really power, actually. But certainly promotion! At least on a trial basis. Don't bugger it up.

VANESSA *enters.* SAUL *chucks* WINSTON*'s suit at* PERCHIK, *who catches it.*

Make yourself respectable. (*He bangs the bucket again.*) And don't sell all that at once! Come on, wife. If you're very good I'll pinch you a Christmas cake on the way home.

SAUL *takes his panama hat from* VANESSA, *puts it on and exits.*

PERCHIK. But, Mr Saul! You don't want me to... I mean, I don't know how to...

VANESSA *follows* SAUL, *but drops her shawl.* PERCHIK *darts forward and picks it up.* VANESSA *takes it from him, flustered, and exits.* PERCHIK *surveys the shop.*

A store manager, eh? A *Store*. *Manager*.

He puts the suit on. It's too big for him. He pushes up his sleeves, and tentatively lifts a lump of meat out of the bucket. He drops it with a grimace on the counter. Raises the cleaver.

Bloody hell.

He brings the cleaver down with force and splits the meat in two.

Scene Two

Sundowner time. PERCHIK *is counting yen. The sack remains onstage.*

PERCHIK.... Fifty, sixty, seventy, / eighty, ninety, a hundred –

VANESSA *enters, cooling herself with the fan, nibbling on a Christmas cake.*

VANESSA. Phew. I'm sweating like a – Perchik? Where d'you get that from?

PERCHIK. I got it from *paying customers*, Vanessa!

VANESSA. You never! (*Beat.*) What they pay for then?

PERCHIK. For meat, my darlin'! Where's Saul?

VANESSA. He's just bringing the petrol in from the van. What meat?

PERCHIK. Oh, er – just some bits and bobs that came in with John.

VANESSA. You clever boy! The cottage'll be done in no time at this rate! Pack your bags, Perchik! We're off to the seaside!

She seizes his hands and they polka madly. PERCHIK *pulls away.*

PERCHIK. Vanessa? I, um – I got you a present. On my lunch break.

He gives her a newspaper-wrapped parcel. She unwraps it. It's a book.

VANESSA. What's this? *Lady Hamilton and Horatio Nelson: Behind Closed Doors.*

PERCHIK. Thought you might, you know… be interested.

VANESSA. Oh, it's *lovely*, Perchik.

She flicks through. Then looks up. A guilty smile. Faux nonchalance.

Did you… um… Did you happen to see the sequel, Perchik?

PERCHIK. You mean the sequel to –

VANESSA. Yes.

PERCHIK *grins. He puts his hand inside his shirt. They fall into position.*

PERCHIK. 'I've come to fix your pianoforte, Lady Hamilton.'

VANESSA. 'Again, Lord Nelson?'

PERCHIK. 'Your G-string is a disgrace to the Empire and demands to be tuned.'

VANESSA. 'Oh! You've caught me in my scanties again! Once might be considered a mishap, twice is simply *asking* for a raping!'

PERCHIK. 'I make it my duty never to refuse a lady's request.'

VANESSA. 'Lord Nelson! Your britches are bulging like billy-o!'

PERCHIK. 'Well observed, you come-hungry wench! They were designed by Princess Caroline of Brunswick herself to show off my every contour!'

VANESSA. 'Then God bless Princess Caroline of Brunswick!'

PERCHIK. 'And all who sail in her!'

PERCHIK *leans* VANESSA *over his knee as before.*

VANESSA (*whispering*). Perchik, don't –

But PERCHIK *leans in closer. This time,* VANESSA *does too.*

(*Whispering.*) You smell of the snow, you know. Cold has this – *scent* of its own. Like lemons squeezed over turpentine… I miss snow. Don't you…?

PERCHIK *nods. Their faces move closer.* SAUL *enters, carrying a petrol can.* PERCHIK *drops* VANESSA *on the floor with a thud.*

SAUL. Could you be more careful with my wife, Perchik? Her head may look like it is carved from a lump of igneous rock, but I assure you it will sustain only the lightest of batterings.

PERCHIK. Mr Saul! Look! Smell it! Smell that money, Mr Saul!

VANESSA. For the cottage, Saul!

SAUL. Yes, dear. For the cottage.

VANESSA. How many bastard bricks is that, Saul?

SAUL *surveys the empty counter. Picks up a book from on top.*

SAUL. What is this?

VANESSA. I bet it's loads!

PERCHIK. It's a book, Mr Saul.

SAUL (*incredulously*). *The Beginnner's Guide to Halal Butchery*?

VANESSA. I don't think I've ever been happier than I am right now.

PERCHIK. I just thought – you need to appeal to your core market.

SAUL. Perchik, could I have a word please? Over here?

PERCHIK. Yes, Mr Saul?

SAUL. I'm not quite sure how to put this, but… where is all of the meat?

Beat. PERCHIK *falters.*

PERCHIK. Well… I sold it. Didn't I? That's how I got the money. See?

SAUL (*trying to hold his temper*). But I told you not to sell it all at once, Perchik.

PERCHIK. But – I thought you were / joking –

SAUL. How am I supposed to expand my Empire if I've got to be tending to this scrawny little concern the whole time? That was s'posed to last us the week! You know how hard it is for me to get good stock! How did you shift it anyway?

PERCHIK. Ah! Now I know you're gonna love this, Mr Saul! I realised, what you need, is *publicity*! So I created an *advertising campaign*!

SAUL. Advertising campaign, Perchik?

PERCHIK. Well – I made a banner.

He unfurls a tatty banner, beautifully painted in an art-nouveau style, reading: 'MEET (for sale)'.

SAUL. Are you trying to tell me how to run my business?

PERCHIK. No! No, I wasn't trying to – I thought you'd be pleased!

SAUL. This is mutiny! You're trying to disrupt the equilibrium of my Empire!

PERCHIK. No, Mr Saul – I'm just trying to change – to improve –

SAUL. 'Improve'? On my father's legacy? I've got an idea, Perchik, let's you and me put on our Sunday best, drive to his resting place and have a good old dance on his grave together! Let's you and me do the bloody Macarena over my dead dad's body! Shall we? You little locust, I'll – *What the hell is this?*

SAUL *picks up a small round object from the counter. A haggis.*

PERCHIK. Umm. It's a haggis, Mr Saul.

SAUL. I beg your pardon?

PERCHIK. A haggis. Thought you could broaden your product range. Cater to new markets.

SAUL *advances on* PERCHIK.

SAUL. CATER TO NEW –

The telephone rings. All heads turn in that direction. A long pause. Then:

VANESSA. Shall I get that?

SAUL. Does anyone ever telephone you, wife?

VANESSA. No, Saul.

SAUL. Then is there any point in you getting it?

VANESSA. No, Saul.

SAUL. No, wife. There is not. I'll take it upstairs. This (*He shakes the haggis at* PERCHIK.) is an *outrage*. Stay where you are. Don't move a *muscle*.

SAUL *exits. After a moment, the phone stops ringing.*

PERCHIK. What's his fucking problem!

VANESSA. He just likes things done his way.

PERCHIK. But his way's *shite*!

VANESSA. He used to be a great man, Perchik. He just finds it difficult to *adjust*. He's shrunk a bit, you see. But men do shrink as they get old, don't they?

PERCHIK (*surly*). Yeah. They do. (*Beat*.) Except for their ears.

VANESSA. What?

PERCHIK. Well, they've always got really big ears, haven't they? Old men. Cos they carry on growing when everything else stops. So their ears are just *massive* –

SAUL *enters, fired up*.

SAUL. All the better to hear you with!

VANESSA. Saul!

SAUL. They've done it! They've finally gone and done it. Bastards!

VANESSA. Oh, Saul! Was that –

SAUL. Yes. Vanessa?

VANESSA. Yes, Saul?

SAUL. The map!

VANESSA. The map!

PERCHIK. What map?

SAUL. *The* map!

VANESSA *pulls down a huge roller blind*.

PERCHIK. WHAT MAP?

SAUL. THIS MAP.

On the blind is an enormous world map, like those found in Victorian schoolrooms. Britain is a small lozenge-shaped pink blob with two protrusions at the bottom right (Central London) and left (Cornwall). The rest of it is either eroded by sea (blue) or shaded in a different colour. Scotland is an island separated from England by Hadrian's Channel. SAUL examines it wistfully.

I remember when all this was pink.

PERCHIK. What's going on?

SAUL. Shut your mouth, garbage.

VANESSA. There, there, darling. Don't upset yourself.

SAUL. Oh, I know, I know. It had to happen. It had to go.

PERCHIK. What had to happen?

SAUL. But I still can't believe it. Gone. Just like that.

PERCHIK. Can someone tell me *what* exactly has gone?

SAUL. Cornwall. Bring me my pigments, Vanessa.

> VANESSA *fetches them.*

PERCHIK. What do you mean, Cornwall's gone?

SAUL (*imitating in a whiny voice*). 'What do you mean, Cornwall's gone?' – Sold! I mean, it's been sold, you little tumour!

PERCHIK. Sold? *Sold?* Who have they sold it to?

SAUL. Who d'you think! The septic tanks and the Chinese got into bed together!

> SAUL *colours in Cornwall on the map with a black pencil.*

It's not right. Remember that glorious holiday, yachting in Penzance, wife?

VANESSA. Camping, dear. In Torquay.

SAUL. We paddled in the sea and ate fish and chips.

VANESSA. It rained for a week. Lovely.

SAUL. There. Now, wife. If you wouldn't mind?

> VANESSA *nods solemnly, and pulls out a bugle. She stands to attention next to the map and plays a mournful 'Last Post'.* SAUL *salutes. He notices* PERCHIK *slouching.*

Have you no respect?

> *He forces* PERCHIK*'s arm up and watches* VANESSA *play, transported.*

She may be riddled with herpes but her omberture is magnificent.

> VANESSA *finishes, and chokes back a sob.*

No tears, wife. No tears. We shall fight the good fight. Even as the lights go out all over Truro, we shall keep the home fires burning.

He hands out black armbands to each of them.

VANESSA. It *was* a lovely service, wasn't it?

SAUL. It was, wife.

VANESSA. What Cornwall would have wanted.

SAUL. Yes, wife.

VANESSA. Don't you think, Perchik?

SAUL. Leave the boy, wife. He's in a state of mourning.

PERCHIK. No, I'm not.

SAUL. Yes, you are.

PERCHIK. No. I'm not!

SAUL. Yes, you are. I say you are!

PERCHIK. NO, I'M NOT!

SAUL. WELL, WHY NOT!?

SAUL *grabs a large knife and stabs it into the haggis and pushes it against* PERCHIK*'s throat.* PERCHIK *grabs the haggis off the knife and throws it at the map. It bursts. The contents of a sheep's stomach slither down the Empire.* VANESSA *inhales sharply.* SAUL *stares at the map. He slowly turns to* PERCHIK.

PERCHIK (*trying to divert the storm*). Oh, now, Mr Saul, I didnay mean to… Let's all just calm down, take a deep breath and –

SAUL (*quietly*). Get out.

PERCHIK. What?

SAUL. GET OUT!

PERCHIK. You cannay chuck me out! It's murder out there! Or prison, Mr Saul!

SAUL. You wet your own bed. You can lie in the damp patch.

PERCHIK. Please, they'll peel my kneecaps off – I didnay mean –

SAUL. I am not a *charity*.

PERCHIK. I spoke wrong, I *am* upset about Cornwall, I'm –

SAUL. I will not be *disrespected*.

PERCHIK. I'm proper devastated! And what about my wages?

SAUL. What wages? Do you know how much you cost me? It all adds up. And you don't care about money. / Remember?

PERCHIK. Please, Mr Saul!

SAUL. The matter isn't up for debate!

VANESSA. Please, Saul, let him stay! Please let him –

SAUL. Fine! One last chance. Sing 'Jerusalem', Perchik. Sing it all the way through.

PERCHIK. I can't – I don't / remember…

SAUL. SING!

PERCHIK (*singing*). 'And did those feet, in ancient times, walk upon England's pastures green… and did the – and did the – AND DID THE…'

SAUL. Wife.

PERCHIK. No, wait, I know it, it's ' – and did the – '

SAUL. Wife?

VANESSA. No, Saul, please –

PERCHIK. 'Countenance divine'? S'that it? 'Countenance divine'!

SAUL. *Wife*.

He smacks his stick against the counter. VANESSA *runs behind the counter, returning with a bottle of chloroform and a cloth. She puts it over* PERCHIK*'s mouth.*

VANESSA (*whispering*). I'm so sorry, Perchik.

PERCHIK *passes out.* VANESSA *opens the shop door. She and* SAUL *drag* PERCHIK *out.* SAUL *grabs* PERCHIK*'s bag and slings it. He slams the door and locks it behind him.* VANESSA *is weeping.* SAUL *pats her with the end of his stick.*

SAUL. There, there, wife. You mustn't get so *attached* to these boys.

VANESSA. How many has it been now? Is it seven? Or eight?

SAUL. You just can't get the staff.

VANESSA. We have such bad luck, don't we, Saul? Either they have to leave. Like Perchik. Or Stavros. Or they have an accident. Like Frankie. Or Klaus.

SAUL. I told you, wife. Klaus didn't have an accident. Klaus was headhunted by the International Monetary Fund.

VANESSA (*wailing*). He couldn't even add up on his fingers, Saul!

SAUL. The International Monetary Fund are admirably committed to a policy of equal opportunity, Vanessa.

SAUL *suddenly bangs his stick in frustration.*

Why don't people *listen* to me any more? Why won't they do as they're told!

VANESSA. Calm down, dearest.

SAUL. I'm sorry, wife. It's just – I liked that one. I really. I really quite liked that one.

VANESSA. Then let him stay! It's not too late.

SAUL. Yes, it is. He has betrayed my trust! I mean, there are *rules*, Vanessa. Protocol. An order of things. (*Beat.*) I'm so tired, wife. I feel like I'm being eaten at.

VANESSA. Poor Saul. (*She suddenly bursts into tears.*) Oh, I'm sorry, love. S'just, sometimes I think I'm being punished. For being such a wicked girl.

SAUL. Oh, *Vanessa.*

He chuckles fondly and puts his arms round her. He sighs.

You probably are.

VANESSA *bawls harder.*

Come on, wife. Buck up. Give me a kiss.

He puts a coin into her hand and she kisses him, still sniffing a bit.

All better?

She nods. He gives her the handkerchief. She blows her nose. He takes it back again.

Goodnight, wife.

He starts to exit. Then turns.

Vanessa? Do you think. Do you think I'm. Out of date?

VANESSA (*snottily*). Out of date, dear? Like a yogurt, you mean?

SAUL. Yes, wife. Like a yogurt. I sometimes wonder – no. Never
mind.

SAUL *exits.* VANESSA *calls after him, drying her face.*

VANESSA. I don't think city living is good for you, my love.
You'll feel better when we move to the cottage. Where it's nice.
By the sea. Quiet. Just you and me. And Perchik.

SAUL (*off*). Not Perchik!

VANESSA (*sadly*). No. Not Perchik.

VANESSA *sits. She takes out the picture of the cottage. Traces
a finger over it. Then puts it away, unlocks the fag cupboard and
takes one. Realises she needs a light.*

(*Whisper to back.*) Saul? Saul? Are you there? Saul? Please?
I need you to –

The letterbox creaks open and PERCHIK*'s hand appears
through it, holding a lighter. He sparks it.* VANESSA *turns to
see it, then runs to the door and leans into the flame.*

(*Whispering*). Perchik! What are you doing?

PERCHIK. Bleeding internally.

VANESSA. I / meant –

PERCHIK. I left something. In the icebox. For you.

VANESSA. For me?

PERCHIK. Yeah. It's a portrait.

VANESSA. Of me?

VANESSA *goes to the icebox.*

PERCHIK. Aye of you, you daft girl. Behind the bacon slicer!

*She returns with a canvas. It's a portrait of a luminous version
of* VANESSA*'s genetically superior – if imaginary – sister.*
VANESSA *examines it.*

VANESSA. Oh, Perchik…

PERCHIK. Do you like it?

VANESSA. It's lovely, Perchik. Only…

PERCHIK. Only what?

VANESSA. Only. It doesn't really look like me, does it?

PERCHIK. Let me in? I want to say goodbye. Proper, like.

VANESSA. I can't.

PERCHIK. Please?

VANESSA. No. Go away.

PERCHIK (*loudly*). 'Lady Hamilton! Your pianoforte is – '

VANESSA. Shh! Alright! Alright.

> VANESSA *opens the door.* PERCHIK *bursts in.*

PERCHIK. Come with me.

VANESSA. Don't be stupid.

PERCHIK. Why? This place is a dump! Why would you want to stay here –

VANESSA. Maybe… because I'm just too stupid to leave.

PERCHIK. No, you're not. You just act like you are.

VANESSA (*smiles*). Well. There are certain advantages.

PERCHIK. To what?

VANESSA. To people thinking you're stupid.

PERCHIK. And what would those be then?

VANESSA. They're more surprised when you steal the watch off their wrist. (*Beat.*) I can't leave him, Perchik. He's –

SAUL (*off*). Vanessa!

> VANESSA *hides her fag.* PERCHIK *ducks behind the counter.* SAUL *enters.*

Are you coming up, Nessa?

VANESSA. In a minute.

SAUL. Your breathing doesn't sound too good tonight, love.

VANESSA. Just a bit tight. Nighty-night, Saul.

SAUL. Turn the lights out before you come up, eh?

SAUL exits. VANESSA breathes a sigh of relief, before, a second later, his head appears round the door again. She freezes.

By the way. Um. I forgot. What with all the upset, but…

Beat.

Happy birthday, wife.

Beat. VANESSA rises and kisses SAUL on the cheek. He grabs her, needily rather than violently, and kisses her on the mouth. She lets him. As they part, he puts something into her hand. It's a tacky snow globe. She shakes it.

It's, ah. It's for the cottage.

VANESSA (*touched*). Thank you, Saul. It's lovely.

SAUL (*embarrassed*). Wasn't very expensive.

VANESSA. It's *lovely*. Go to bed now, eh? I'll be up in a minute.

SAUL nods, exits. PERCHIK emerges. VANESSA clamps a hand over his mouth and listens till she hears the bedsprings creak overhead. She moves her hand.

See. He needs me. And I couldn't get by without him.

PERCHIK. That's just what he's told you. You said it yourself. You're not stupid.

VANESSA. Oh, but I am. Awful thick.

She holds up PERCHIK's belt, which she's managed to steal without him noticing. He grins.

PERCHIK. You thieving little –

VANESSA. You have to go now.

PERCHIK. He's never going to leave here, you know. (*Beat.*) I said, he's never going to –

VANESSA. You don't know what you're talking about, shut up –

PERCHIK. F'this place was mine I'd sell it tomorrow. You could be waiting another ten years. Longer. You could be stuck here / for the rest of your –

VANESSA. I'm sorry, Perchik. I've made up my mind. Goodbye.

PERCHIK. – life, no – *no*. Stay there. I've – I've got a – present.
For you.

VANESSA (*new interest*). A present?

PERCHIK. Ay. A present. Y'never said it was your birthday.
Dinnay move.

VANESSA. Perchik, I've got to –

PERCHIK. Close your eyes. Tight. (*Beat.*) Do it!

*She sighs and closes her eyes. He's stumped for a moment. Then
he spots his pillow. He peels off her shawl.*

Right. Right. Okaaay. So. Imagine it's the past. Imagine it's the
year… 2008. It's, um – Christmas Eve. You're on a train from
Glasgow to Oban. When you get out at the –

VANESSA. How did I get to Glasgow?

PERCHIK. What?

VANESSA. I just like to get the details straight.

PERCHIK. I dunno. You hitched.

VANESSA. Hitched! For goodness' sakes, Perchik! A woman on
her own! Hitching! I'd be dead in a ditch before Carlisle!

PERCHIK. Hitched a lift with a minibus full of nuns can I continue?

He guides VANESSA *in front of the counter and climbs onto it
with the pillow.*

When you get out at the station you taste the sea straight away
and the wind whips off the water and slashes at your face, it's
that cold. From there you get on this huge ferry. As the boat
travels onwards, the tide looks like it's made of tar because dusk
is already falling and by the time you reach an island called
Colonsay it's pitch black. And it's freezing now, you can't feel
your feet in your boots so you hitch a lift in a truck driven by an
eighty-six-year-old man with a tattoo of Johnny Cash on the
back of his neck. He's playing a cassette tape of Tammy
Wynette songs –

VANESSA. My favourite!

PERCHIK. Exactly – and singing along in a voice like cracked
leather as he slugs whisky from a tartan thermos.

VANESSA. Cracked leather?

PERCHIK. I'm on a roll, don't interrupt. He drops you off outside a wee brick cottage on the edge of a white cliff –

VANESSA. Does the cottage have a room just for boots?

PERCHIK. It does. You don't go inside the cottage, not just yet, instead you scramble down the steep stony path to the shore below, and you stand on the beach, and hurl off your shoes to dip your toes in the icy Pacific, and the Northern Lights play in the sky, and the seaweed slimes under your feet and your ears pound with the cold, and you close your eyes to remember the feeling better when suddenly, then, at that moment, the chill in the air drops another half a degree, and from the clouds hanging over the ocean, something very strange, and very beautiful, and very cold, starts to happen...

> PERCHIK *rips open the pillow. It's full of white down. He takes* VANESSA*'s electric fan and throws handfuls of feathers into the air, blowing them with the fan.*

And you open your eyes...

> VANESSA *opens her eyes and gasps in delight. The feathers are falling. A clear, pure tone cuts through the air like a tuning fork.*

VANESSA (*whispering*). It's snowing. Perchik...

> VANESSA *grins and shuts her eyes tight again.*

It's snowing.

PERCHIK. Are you cold?

VANESSA. Oh yes. I'm freezing. I'm absolutely...

PERCHIK. Really, really cold?

VANESSA. Yes! Yes!

PERCHIK. Can you smell it?

VANESSA. Yes!

> PERCHIK *jumps down from the counter. She grabs him.*

Have you got a pound, Perchik?

> *He shakes his head. She pulls him to her.*

Never mind. You can start a tab.

She kisses him. They kiss again, and again, their embrace getting more and more heated, an itch being scratched. PERCHIK lifts her up and sits her on the counter.

(*Dreamily.*) Do you know what I'd like? I'd like for this whole shop to just disappear as if it was never there in the first place. Imagine it.

PERCHIK. The blaze of an Empire going up in flames, ay?

VANESSA. And then we could live in the cottage by the sea… you and me… in the cottage by the sea… and Saul can be a snowman…

They fall back to kissing. There's a creak overhead. VANESSA looks up.

Come on. Let's go.

PERCHIK. Now?

VANESSA. Yes, Perchik. Now.

SAUL (*off*). Vanessa?

VANESSA jumps off the counter and runs to the icebox. Her shawl catches in the door. PERCHIK jumps behind the counter. SAUL enters. Goes to the icebox door.

Vanessa? Please come to bed. I. I can't sleep.

He waits. No answer. He sighs. He looks small, sad and tired. He exits out to the back. A beat, then PERCHIK creeps out. He spots the painting, picks it up.

PERCHIK (*whispering*). Vanessa? Vanessa?

He waits. Looks searchingly round the shop. Then spots the shawl trapped in the door of the icebox. He smiles. Goes over and whispers through the door.

Vanessa, I'm going now. But I'll come back tomorrow. Promise. Won't be long now. We'll have you paddling in the sea before pancake day, ay? Vanessa?

SAUL enters from the back, silently. He is holding a raised shotgun that is pointed at PERCHIK's head. He stalks towards him with glee.

The thing is… I think – I might – sort of – be in love with you.

As SAUL *speaks,* PERCHIK *starts and spins round.*

SAUL. That's very flattering, Perchik. But you're really not my type. Can I see your passport, please?

PERCHIK. I – I – I don't have a passport, Saul.

SAUL. No?

Beat. SAUL *cocks the gun and grins.*

Oh dear.

Blackout. Gunshot.

End of Act Two.

Interval.

ACT THREE

'Evacuation'

PERCHIK *has been hung upside down from a butcher's hook by a rope tied round his ankles. He is gagged and writhing. The gunshot at the end of Act Two was aimed at his right foot, and this is now a bloody bundle.* SAUL *sits, reading a newspaper.*

PERCHIK. Mmmmrggrhh!

SAUL. How many times, Perchik? Like this: The rein in Spein falls meinly on the *plein*. It's not *hard*. Now try *agein*.

PERCHIK. Mmmmmmmrrrgggghhh!

SAUL. Better! Much better! We'll make a newsreader of you yet.

PERCHIK. Mmmmmmmrrrrrrrrrrrggggggggghhhhhhh!

SAUL. On the contrary, I don't think I'm being at all unreasonable. You've put my business in jeopardy. You've trespassed on my property. And now this monstrosity!

He produces the painting of VANESSA *and holds it up.*

PERCHIK. Ret ri row!

SAUL. Stop mumbling, Perchik, it's tiresome. What? What's that?

He pulls the gag off PERCHIK*'s mouth.*

PERCHIK. Let me down!

SAUL. No. You have hurt me greatly with this tomfoolery. You come in here, stealing my jobs –

PERCHIK. You *gave* me the job.

SAUL. Semantics, Perchik! Say you're sorry.

PERCHIK. No! I think I need a doctor.

SAUL. Where are your manners?

PERCHIK. You shot me in the foot!

SAUL. It was just a joke, Perchik! You have to *laugh*, don't you? Now say you're sorry.

PERCHIK. Fuck off!

SAUL. Oh dear. I think I'll make a telephone call.

He goes to the phone and lifts the receiver.

Let me see. Nine. (*He dials.*) Nine – (*He dials, then pauses.*) Now, what was the last bit?

He goes behind the counter, pulls out a telephone directory and looks it up.

Ah yes. (*He returns to the phone.*) Nine. Yes, hello, police please. (*Beat.*) Ah, hello, yes, I'm calling with information regarding a dangerous artist who is On The Loose.

PERCHIK. Saul…

SAUL. Yes. Yes – armed, dangerous *and* Scottish. Yes, his name is –

PERCHIK. Okay!

SAUL (*to* PERCHIK). I'm on the telephone. It's very rude to interrupt.

PERCHIK. I said okay! I'll say it.

SAUL surveys him for a second, then turns back to the phone.

SAUL. Oh, I *am* sorry. I've made a mistake. I was trying to get hold of my mother but I've just remembered she's dead. Goodbye. (*He hangs up.*) Well?

PERCHIK. I'm – sorry.

SAUL. Good! And I forgive you! See how simple that was? And to show there are no hard feelings, I've cooked you a special dinner. A pork chop, Perchik!

He brings a plate out from behind the counter.

PERCHIK. I can't eat that.

SAUL. Oh, but you can. The dental plan of the human mouth is perfectly equipped for you to eat it. Eat it.

He cuts it up for PERCHIK *and puts the fork to his face.*

PERCHIK. Don't make me.

SAUL. Who holds the matches, Perchik?

PERCHIK. You do, you do, but please, I'll be sick –

SAUL. Don't make Sauly hold your nose.

SAUL forces a forkful into PERCHIK*'s mouth and waits for
him to chew.*

Chew.

Pause.

Chew and be grateful.

PERCHIK *chews, gagging as he does.*

Now swallow.

He swallows. SAUL *claps his hands in delight, then starts to
cut* PERCHIK *down.*

It's terribly clever, don't you think, for the human body to allow
the bolus – that is, the chewed sustenance – to contradict physical
science. The swallow is an action that should by rights be
impossible when suspended upside down. And yet the contraction
of the muscles in peristalsis propels it upwards in flagrant
defiance of the universal laws of gravity. It wants to get to the
stomach so very much, you see. It's almost enough to make you
believe in God, isn't it? Was that good? Bearing in mind the
trouble I took, would you say that it was a very tasty dish?

PERCHIK *is finally down. He nods.*

Good! Good, I'm so glad.

SAUL *spits into a handkerchief.* PERCHIK *makes a painful run
for the door.*

No you don't.

He grabs PERCHIK *and perches him on the counter.*

You can't just run away from your responsibilities. Come on
now, you've barely touched your chop.

PERCHIK. I'm full.

SAUL *feeds him another mouthful.*

SAUL. Here comes the aeroplane into mouthy airport, wooo…

> Now, what would you say if I was to tell you that this juicy pork chop had come from a very *special* sort of pig? It is the kind of pig that the natives of the Marquesas Islands of Polynesia refer to by the name of 'long pig', but which civilised society – people who have trains and washing machines and a ninety-nine per cent literacy rate – the kind of pig that they refer to as… Vanessa. What would you say to that, eh?

> PERCHIK *spits it out.*

> Don't waste food! Don't waste my wife! Remember her with your stomach. The memory in the brain is unreliable, it paints in black and white. If you want the truth of the woman that was Vanessa, see what she does to your duodenum!

PERCHIK. What've you done to her? You're disgusting. You sick old –

SAUL. Don't say that! I loved her! Even if she was common and trampy / I still –

PERCHIK. I'm gonnay call the police.

SAUL. – *loved her* – no! You mustn't, promise me you won't – it was an accident. She must've still been in the icebox. I locked the door but I didn't know she was still in there, I swear. And then, when I came down this morning – the *shock*, Perchik. Later, when you were still unconscious I mean, I thawed her out. Her lashes were all crystalled with frost and her skin – alabaster, that's what they call it, isn't it?

PERCHIK (*sourly*). I thought you didnay allow poetry in the shop.

SAUL. Allowances are made on days of mourning, Perchik! Allowances are made!

PERCHIK. Oh God. Poor Vanessa…

SAUL. Why are you getting upset? She was my wife! Do you know what I did next?

PERCHIK. I don't want to know.

SAUL. I laid her on the marble and performed the last rites.

PERCHIK. You're no' religious, Saul. You're a hypocrite as well as a murderer.

SAUL. Not the last rites of the soul. The last rites one might perform on a hundred-pound pig. I laid her on the slab and I butchered her.

PERCHIK. No...

SAUL. *Yes.* I took my sharpest knife and slit her, throat to belly. Then I removed the head with my saw, such care I took, except the blood, Perchik. The blood was awful – Vanessa's juices all over my hands. I made the slits behind the Achilles tendons, inserted the gambrel – the gambrel, Perchik, is a frame from which we hang the beast – and up she went. I removed her arms. And then I skinned her.

PERCHIK. I'm think I'm going to be sick.

He runs behind the counter and heaves.

SAUL. An incision through the belly to remove the guts, being especially careful with the intestines for they can contaminate the meat and render it unfit for eating.

PERCHIK. You're lying, aren't you? I mean. You couldn't do that. Not even you, this is –

SAUL. I did it, Perchik! Believe me, I did it! And I put the radio on and listened to *The Archers* omnibus *while* I did it!

PERCHIK. Animal!

SAUL. I was mad with grief!

PERCHIK (*sarcastically*). Is that right?

SAUL. Of course! Otherwise I would never have been able to skin my wife or listen to *The Archers* omnibus! (*Beat.*) It was sawing the feet off that was hardest, Perchik.

PERCHIK. Oh God.

SAUL. I always loved my wife's feet, her breeding showed in her feet, but I had to do that so that I could deal with the rear ham, didn't I? Then I separated ribs from chops and trimmed the loin, cutting out the bundles of muscle with my smallest knife. And with love, Perchik. With such love.

PERCHIK. You didn't love her, you killed her! Don't pretend to me that you loved her!

SAUL. Of course I loved her! I lived with her, didn't I? She was my best chum... It was an accident, Perchik, I promise. I wanted her

inside me, so I could remember her. Physically. I ate her heart.
Fried it and ate it with my fingers and I felt so warm inside. You
know how I hate seeing food go to waste. Oh God. Vanessa.

SAUL *breaks down, wretched, and lies heaving, sobbing on
the floor.*

PERCHIK. Saul?

Pause. PERCHIK *pulls off the restraints on his hands.*

Saul? Get up! You disgusting piece a... I'm gonnay fuckin' kill
you – I'm gonnay –

VANESSA *hurriedly enters the shop.* SAUL *sits up slowly,
enjoying the look on* PERCHIK*'s face, and his sobs transform
into laughter, relishing his trick.*

Vanessa? You – But he told me he'd –

SAUL. He thought I'd *eaten* you! Ha! He actually thought I'd
eaten you, old girl! / He's awful gullible!

PERCHIK. You bastard. You sick, inhuman –

SAUL. You stupid goose! I wouldn't waste the good knives on her!

VANESSA. I did it. I said I would and I did. I went to the police
and I told them.

SAUL (*laughing*). Eh? What d'you tell 'em then? You mad old
sow. I bet they had a good old laugh at you, didn't they?

VANESSA. Yes. They laughed at me. At first. But then I told them
some other things and they stopped laughing and they turned
a little tape recorder on and asked if I'd like a cup of tea.

SAUL. And what you did tell them?

VANESSA. I said yes please. Two sugars.

PERCHIK. He meant –

VANESSA. I know what he meant. I told them how he sits on my
lungs and how he boxes my ears and how he tattooed his name
on my bum and it went septic and how he put Frankie in the
cement mixer and how you put Detective Prawn in a sack and
how you don't have planning permission for the extension / of
your Empire –

SAUL. You little bitch. You ungrateful slut. Telling everyone our business. That's our private, secret business!

VANESSA. I just want things to *change* around here – cos I warned you, Saul. I warned you to let him go or I would and you didn't *listen*, / so you've only yourself to blame.

SAUL. I didn't think you'd actually do it, did I?!

VANESSA. Maybe they'll give you a talking-to you'll take mind of, / cos God help us you don't listen to me any more.

SAUL. After all I've done for you, telling people things like that! Our secrets, state secrets, this is *treason*, you know what happens to traitors? Is this your idea, Perchik?

VANESSA. No! It wasn't him. It wasn't his idea. Don't –

SAUL. Remember who holds the matches here, you two. I could burn you both in your beds. This shop is a tinderbox, the walls in here are little more than parchment.

VANESSA. It wasn't him!

SAUL. I don't believe you.

VANESSA. It wasn't!

SAUL. Well, who was it then? Who's the dozy sod who'd put up with you for –

VANESSA. He's a poet. He lives in a big house that looks like a bride cake. He imports tropical fruit, he hates Elgar, his mum's a Hindu, he doesn't eat meat and – and – he's *French*.

SAUL. You lying little *bitch*.

He punches her in the stomach. She doubles over. PERCHIK *jumps on* SAUL*'s back.*

PERCHIK. Don't touch her! You touch her again and I'll kill you!

SAUL. You? You couldn't maim a monkey.

PERCHIK. Don't touch her!

VANESSA. It's alright, Perchik, leave off.

SAUL. I wouldn't sully my hands with her! She's no better than that sack of old horse. Past her sell-by-date and reeking of rot.

He throws PERCHIK *off, runs to the counter, grabs his cleaver.*

Do you know what they do in the Arab lands to promiscuous women who can't keep their knickers on? They cut off their hands! Think what a saving you'll make on gloves, wife!

VANESSA. No, Saul, please, put it down, put it down. PUT IT DOWN!

PERCHIK. Saul, calm down, please, come on now, let's just –

SAUL. Mr Everard! To people like you my name is Mr Everard! Get me a pen, Perchik. I want to write a label for my wife. I'm posting you to France, girl. Get in there.

He drags VANESSA *towards the sack.*

VANESSA. No! Get off!

SAUL. Bon voyage, you little cow!

DIXON (*off*). Open up.

SAUL. Who the bloody hell is that?

DOCK (*off*). It's the police!

PERCHIK. It's the police.

VANESSA. They must have followed me here. I didn't think...

SAUL. Well, that makes a change, doesn't it? You *silly* stupid mare. You really have surpassed yourself this time! Your mistakes have already cost me the best years of my life and two kids, was that not enough for you, eh –

VANESSA (*whiplash venom*). Oh, I hope you rot in a windowless cell, you vicious grasping nasty old *cripple*.

SAUL *gasps then freezes as if he's been slapped.* VANESSA *freezes too, both surprised by what she has said. Finally* SAUL *makes a tiny, frail noise.* VANESSA *runs to him and cradles his head, trying to soothe him. He whimpers as she rocks him.*

Saul, I'm *sorry.* I'm sorry, love. I didn't / mean –

SAUL. You hurt my feelings!

VANESSA. I spoke without thinking –

SAUL (*whining*). You're not playing *nice* tonight, Vanessa!

VANESSA. I got carried away. Shh... it's alright... shh...

PERCHIK. Vanessa…

SAUL. You're not playing *nice*.

There's more banging on the door.

PERCHIK. Vanessa, he was gonnay cut your hands off!

DIXON (*off*). We have here a warrant for the arrest of a Mr Saul Everard –

DOCK (*off*). – regarding the disappearances of Detective Derek Prawn, John Grimmup, Francesco Mancini, and various other charges of a serious nature.

SAUL. They're going to arrest me? But this is my Empire. They can't arrest me.

VANESSA. I think they can, my love. Help him, Perchik!

PERCHIK. You've got to be kidding!

VANESSA. Please? *Please?*

PERCHIK *sighs*.

PERCHIK (*gesturing to the sack*). Hide in here, Saul.

SAUL. No!

PERCHIK. Get in the sack. Quickly, or do you want to go to prison?

SAUL. I can't! It's full of maggots. You'll tell 'em, won't you, Nessa, tell them it was lies and I never did none of those things? You'll tell them, sweetheart, won't you?

VANESSA. Course I will, I'll tell them it was all lies.

PERCHIK. Won't matter if she does. They all heard her. They had a little tape recorder.

VANESSA. Oh, what have I done? I'm sorry, my love. I didn't mean –

DIXON (*off*). Mr Everard? If you don't open this door we shall break it down.

SAUL. Pigs!

PERCHIK. Get in the sack, Saul.

SAUL. Can't. Sick.

PERCHIK. I'm sorry?

SAUL. I'll be sick.

PERCHIK. So be sick. Get in the sack.

SAUL. I see your game! You want to pack me off to France! Well, I won't go! I won't!

PERCHIK *tries to guide* SAUL *to the sack.* SAUL *sobs helplessly. All defences down.*

Please... please don't make me... I can't. I'm frightened.

PERCHIK. Of what?

SAUL. ... I don't know.

VANESSA (*softly*). It's for your own safety, Saul.

DIXON (*off*). I'm going to give you from the count of ten...

VANESSA. Come on, Saul. Quick!

DOCK (*off*). This is your last warning. Get ready, Dixon. / Ten, nine, eight, seven, six, five, four, three, two, one...

PERCHIK. Get in, Saul.

As DOCK *counts down,* PERCHIK *manhandles* SAUL *in.* SAUL *is dazed. He grabs hold of* PERCHIK'*s hand desperately.*

SAUL (*faintly*). Your fingers, Perchik... or the pies?

PERCHIK *pushes* SAUL'*s head in and closes the sack.* SAUL'*s stick clatters to the floor.* DOCK *reaches 'one' and the* POLICEMEN *burst in.*

PERCHIK. Hello, gentlemen.

DIXON. Is this the residence of Saul Everard?

DOCK. That's my line, Dixon.

DIXON. Does it matter?

DOCK. No, it doesn't matter, it's just, you know, you have your lines and I have my lines, but whatever. You've said it now.

DIXON. Well, you can say it again.

DOCK. I'm not going to say it aga –

DIXON. Fine. Is this the resi –

DOCK (*very fast, to get it out first*). IsthistheresidenceofSaulEverard?

PERCHIK. I've never heard of a Mr Everard. Have you, Tammy? (*Beat*.) Tammy?

VANESSA. No. I've never heard of nobody.

DIXON. Excuse me, ma'am, but you *were* the lady down at the station this morning?

PERCHIK. What an idea! Imagine, my wife – common-law, mind – in a police station! Sat amongst a load of junkies and gigolos! She's been here with me all day. Building a coal shed. For our coal. I'm afraid you've had a wasted trip, but while you're here, this is a sack of black-market offal. I'd take it away and incinerate it if I was you.

VANESSA. Perchik, no.

PERCHIK. Crawling with maggots. It's a public-health disturbance.

VANESSA. I said *no*, Perchik.

DOCK. Well, that's quite an order, sir, but it begs some questions, don't it.

DIXON. It certainly does beg some questions.

VANESSA. Please, Perchik. *Please*.

DOCK. Such as, how did you come by this *offal*, if I may ask?

DIXON. And he may.

PERCHIK. Don't threaten me. It was got –

VANESSA. Don't say anything.

PERCHIK. It was procured on the request of your Chief, but he failed to collect it. If you take us down we'll take half the West Yorkshire police force with us and you won't be very popular at the Christmas party. Think of the media frenzy, Officer. A very black picture it would paint of the boys in blue. I can see it now. 'Maggotgate.'

VANESSA. Perchik –

DOCK. 'Maggot – '?

PERCHIK. Gate.

DIXON. Are you attempting to blackmail us, sir?

DOCK. Be quiet, Dixon. 'Maggotgate.' Dear me. Not a pretty picture. Our apologies, sir, we'll be getting along now. Dixon.

DIXON. Dock!

DOCK. *Dixon.*

They face each other off. DIXON *breaks first.*

DIXON. Right. If you say so. My apologies.

The POLICEMEN *start to move the sack. Coming to,* SAUL *starts to shout.*

SAUL. Put me down! I'm not going to France! You hear me, I won't go!

The two POLICEMEN *freeze and exchange a look.*

DIXON. The offal appears to be – talking. Sir.

PERCHIK. Well, they are very highly evolved maggots, Officer.

Pause.

DIXON. Very good, sir.

He tries to proceed, but DOCK *stays rooted to the spot.*

DOCK. Big?

DIXON. Come on, Dock.

PERCHIK. Sorry, pal?

DIXON. He's not your pal.

DOCK. I'm not your pal. These maggots. Are they big?

PERCHIK. Big? Oh yeah. They'll have your arm off.

DOCK. Hmmm.

Beat. Then DOCK *thoughtfully pulls out his gun and shoots the sack. It goes quiet.*

There's a long silence, finally broken by DOCK.

As you were, Dixon.

DIXON. What's all this, 'as you were'?! You're not in the army, how many times?

DOCK. Could be in the army. Just don't want to.

DIXON. Oh yeah. I forgot. They were just playing hard-to-get when they turned you down. Twice. Your feet are flatter than your sister's chest and you can't shoot for shit.

DOCK. I shot that alright, didn't I?

DIXON. That's the other thing, always shooting everything, bang bang bang. You've got to hold your *fire*, mate.

DOCK. I'm not your mate.

DIXON. All I'm saying is, you didn't have to shoot a sack of meat what's already dead.

DOCK. Did you want to listen to that racket all the way to the municipal dump? It was giving me gip, Dixon. Much like you are now. Can we go?

PERCHIK *holds the door open, and* DOCK *and* DIXON *exit with the sack.*

DIXON (*exiting*). You're trigger-happy, that's what you are.

PERCHIK *slams the door after them. He hobbles excitedly to* VANESSA.

PERCHIK. Did you see me? Did you see that, Vanessa!

VANESSA. Perchik –

PERCHIK. They were all, 'Are you trying to bribe us, sir?'

VANESSA. Perchik –

PERCHIK. And I was all, 'Take that, pigs!' And – And – Vanessa?

VANESSA *starts to bawl.*

Hey hey hey, what's this? Come on darlin' – shhh.

He puts his arms round her and kisses her on the head.

It's alright. Don't cry, pet. It's all over. He'll not hurt you any more.

VANESSA. You put him in a sack!

PERCHIK. I was just trying to help him. You asked me to –

VANESSA. Do you think they'll – I mean, they can't. They won't –

PERCHIK. Oh, I think they will, darlin'. They will. This country is lucky to be served by the most efficient police force in the world.

VANESSA. If I go after them, it might not be too late.

PERCHIK. Say what you like about them but they *get the job done*.

VANESSA. He should have a proper burial.

PERCHIK. It's too late, darlin'.

VANESSA. Decent. In the ground. With flowers.

PERCHIK. They'll be miles away by now.

VANESSA. Singing 'Jerusalem'.

PERCHIK. And it's not safe out there.

VANESSA. I'd like to mourn him properly. In a traditional fashion.

VANESSA goes to exit by the front door.

PERCHIK. Vanessa…

VANESSA. It's not right.

PERCHIK. I said *no*, sweetheart.

He slams the door. VANESSA *runs to the icebox.*

Come on, darlin'. I know you're upset but – Aw, *Jesus*.

VANESSA *stops, closes the door.* PERCHIK *flinches in acute pain as he stands on his bad foot. He spots* SAUL*'s stick on the floor. He picks it up and tries it. He likes it.*

VANESSA. You should see a doctor about that foot.

PERCHIK. Yeah, yeah. I know. Jus' – give us a minute to think, okay, love? Would you like a banana?

VANESSA. What?

PERCHIK. *Would you like a banana?*

VANESSA. Oh. Yeah. Ta.

He gets two bananas from his bag and they eat quietly.

You know, I never wanted to marry a butcher. I hate this shop.

PERCHIK. I know what you mean.

VANESSA. Really?

PERCHIK. I'm a vegetarian.

They look at each other. A beat. Then they laugh. Another pause.

VANESSA. See, this is nice, isn't it? This is nice. Quiet. Bananas. I mean, I wish you hadn't done it, Perchik. He didn't have long left in him, you see. I was just going to let him go gently. Fade away. I wouldn't have jumped the gun myself.

PERCHIK. So to speak.

VANESSA. But now he's gone anyway… we can start again, can't we? Do it properly. A new era.

PERCHIK. Yeah, that's right – a new Empire.

VANESSA. That's not what I / said –

PERCHIK. You don't really mind, do you, darlin'? About Saul?

VANESSA. Oh yes. I do. I feel awful.

VANESSA goes to open the cigarette cupboard.

PERCHIK. Well, you shouldn't, my love. 'The body must reject what it cannot entertain', eh? What just happened was just the evacuation of a toxin. Speaking of which – maybe you should lay off those a bit, eh? Apparently they're no' very good for you.

VANESSA. *But, Perchik –

PERCHIK. *New start, Vanessa! Chance to get rid of all those bad old habits, eh? (*He picks up the painting of* VANESSA.) Tell you what, you give up that and I'll give up painting monstrosities like this, eh?

He laughs. Then VANESSA *does too. She takes a deep breath. Then she smiles.*

VANESSA. Yeah. Yeah. Okay. Deal.

She picks up PERCHIK*'s knapsack with purpose, and hands it to him.*

Come on then. Let's go.

PERCHIK. Give us a minute, darlin'! I'm beat. And there's no rush is there?

JOHN JUNIOR enters, empty-handed.

JOHN JUNIOR. 'Livery!

PERCHIK. John Junior! What a treat. Come in, come in.

JOHN JUNIOR. Meat.

PERCHIK. I'm sorry?

JOHN JUNIOR. I have with me here a delivery of meat.

PERCHIK. Ah! (*Beat*.) Where?

> JOHN JUNIOR *looks round. Then he leans out the door and yells.*

JOHN JUNIOR. John Junior Junior! Stir your stumps, boy!

> JOHN JUNIOR JUNIOR *enters, hot and sweaty, carrying a sack.*

JOHN JUNIOR JUNIOR. What about this weather, eh?

PERCHIK. What about it?

JOHN JUNIOR. John Junior Junior, this is our esteemed customer, Mr Everard.

PERCHIK. Ah, Mr Everard's not – I mean, he isn't – I, er –

(*Beat*.) Call me Saul, John Junior. Thank you. Just put it down there.

JOHN JUNIOR JUNIOR. Meat.

JOHN JUNIOR. Compliments of the boss.

PERCHIK. Ay. I should think so.

> JOHN JUNIOR *pulls out a letter and clears his throat.*

JOHN JUNIOR. He give me something to read: 'Dear Mr Everard comma please accept my apologies for the recent customer product interface error full stop the ano – ano – '

> JOHN JUNIOR *holds the paper out for* JOHN JUNIOR JUNIOR *to read.*

JOHN JUNIOR JUNIOR. Anomaly.

JOHN JUNIOR. '– was the result of a systems failure and the problem has now been rectified.' So that's that.

PERCHIK. Tell your boss that... Tell him that his sentiments are appreciated and I look forward to continuing our longstanding commercial relationship.

JOHN JUNIOR. Er. Yeah. Same time tomorrow, Mr Everard?

PERCHIK. Ay. Same time tomorrow, fellas.

They exit. PERCHIK *opens the sack.* VANESSA *stares at him.*

Now that's fresh, Vanessa!

VANESSA. They thought you were –

PERCHIK. This'll fly off the shelves!

VANESSA. You said you were –

PERCHIK. Turn this place around in no time.

VANESSA. But we don't need it now, do we?

PERCHIK. Well…

VANESSA. We're not staying. You didn't think… We're not staying.

Pause.

PERCHIK. See, I've been thinking, Vanessa, and what it is, is I've come to the conclusion that leaving the shop would not be a financially sound decision.

VANESSA. But that's what you said! This place is a dump, / you said!

PERCHIK. Only needs a lick of paint, a few… cosmetic enhancements.

VANESSA. But what about your story? The sea, the cottage –

PERCHIK. We could make a killing.

VANESSA. Our plans?

PERCHIK. I've got responsibilities now.

VANESSA. But you *said* –

PERCHIK. I've never been a man of property.

VANESSA. We could start again.

PERCHIK. The expansion out back's nearly finished.

VANESSA. Start differently –

PERCHIK. I've got big plans for it.

VANESSA. Evolve.

PERCHIK. No.

VANESSA. Yes!

PERCHIK. Darlin' –

VANESSA. We were s'posed to *leave*. We were s'posed to go to the cottage.

PERCHIK. I don't think you fully / understand our –

VANESSA. Go to the cottage in the country –

PERCHIK (*exploding*). THERE IS NO COTTAGE, YOU STUPID – !

Beat.

VANESSA. What?

PERCHIK. There's no cottage. He cut the picture out of a magazine.

VANESSA. Out of a… No. No, I don't think…

VANESSA *takes the picture out and unfolds it slowly.*

PERCHIK. Ay. Out the *Sunday Times* Style section.

PERCHIK *takes the picture out of her hand and flips it over.*

D'you never think why there was an advert for pain-free leg-waxing on the other side, ye daft girl? Jesus, hon. You really are thick, aren't you?

VANESSA. I don't know. I never… And you knew this? All along?

PERCHIK. Didn't want to piss on your bonfire, did I? It was a nice idea, like.

VANESSA. So we're stuck here.

PERCHIK. Not stuck, darlin'! Look at this place! Why would we want to go somewhere new when we have all this?

PERCHIK *pulls down his banner, clears the books, and chucks the haggis remains.*

VANESSA. Why go somewhere new when…

PERCHIK. Just need to clear this rubbish and we'll get ourselves back to normal, ay?

VANESSA. *I want to paddle in the sea, Perchik!*

PERCHIK. There's time for paddling, darlin'! Once things have calmed down a bit. Give it a couple of months, a year or two. Be patient, eh?

VANESSA. I've been *patient*. / For ten years I've been very, very –

PERCHIK. Let's vote on it, ay? All those in favour say yay.

VANESSA. – PATIENT. Nay. I'm sorry, Perchik.

PERCHIK. Yay. Motion carried. What for?

VANESSA. I'm not staying here. I can't. I'll go mad.

PERCHIK. Aw, you're jus' tired, lamb.

VANESSA. And I told you not to do it. It wasn't right.

PERCHIK. He was a toxin, Vanessa!

VANESSA. One mustn't bite the hand that feeds one, 'ticularly in this day and age.

PERCHIK. Vanessa!

She spins to face him – furious, frustrated.

VANESSA. And now I'm *stuck* here. With nothing but a load of old meat and *you*!

PERCHIK. But – I *love* you.

VANESSA. Yes. I dare say you do.

Pause. VANESSA *examines* PERCHIK.

(*Brightly.*) Never mind, eh? I'm really doing you a favour. You wouldn't last a minute where I'm going. You're a vegetarian.

PERCHIK. What?

VANESSA. Survival of the fattest, love. There's just not enough substance in a banana.

PERCHIK *puts his arms around her and kisses her neck. Wheedling.*

PERCHIK. But… Lady Hamilton… if you leave me, who's gonnay fix your pianoforte?

He puts a hand under her skirt.

VANESSA. Stop it. I read that book you gave me, Perchik. I read the whole thing. You know what happened to Lady Hamilton? She *died*. In prison. In Calais, Perchik. Her skin went all yellow and she lost her memory and her hair fell out and then she *died*. She never had a powdered wig or nothing. Poor cow.

PERCHIK. Vanessa, what the fuck are you talking about?

VANESSA. Meanwhile, old Horatio Cyclops gets a state funeral! Well, no thank you. (*Beat. Idea.*) I'll tell them you was a hero, Perchik.

She starts to undress, calmly, down to her slip.

PERCHIK. Tell who?

VANESSA. A martyr. I'll say you rescued me from my bed, averting your eyes as you carried me down so as not to hurt my modesty, dressed as I was in only my *scanties*.

PERCHIK. Stop talking shite.

VANESSA. And then, *cavalier* in regard for your own young life, you plunged yourself back into the raging fire to attend to the old man who was still snoring while his Empire went up in flames, before finally choking to death on the *fragrant smoke* of his burning flesh, as it drifted up into the big brown canopy of Bradford's *halitosis skies*.

PERCHIK. I've had enough ay this. I'm going to bed. You comin'?

VANESSA. *These are the new rules, Perchik.* You better pay attention. I'm going to paint the pictures from now on. And I'm not playing any more silly games.

She swiftly produces a pair of handcuffs, locks one end on PERCHIK*'s wrist and locks the other end onto the counter. He tries to pull them off. He can't.*

PERCHIK. What the – Where d'you get these from?

VANESSA. Dixon. Or Dock. Can't remember which.

PERCHIK. Okay. So joke's over, get 'em off me. Now!

VANESSA. He was a great man. Once. It's a shame you had to pick up only his worst habits. Do you see?

PERCHIK. No, I fuckin' don't!

VANESSA. Well. Never mind. I'll tell them you were a hero.

PERCHIK. Ay, and I'll tell them you're a cracked bitch. Get 'em off me!

VANESSA rummages in PERCHIK*'s bag. Pulls out a half-litre bottle of clear liquid.*

VANESSA. Oh, I don't need speaking for. I've got a tongue of my own. What's this?

PERCHIK. S'white spirit. Turps. For my brushes. / Vanessa –

VANESSA. Lovely.

She starts to douse the area behind PERCHIK *with the contents of the bottle, singing a few bars of 'Blue Moon of Kentucky' as she does so. He strains to see.*

PERCHIK. What are you doing? I swear, darlin', I'm gonnay count to ten –

VANESSA. The thing is, Perchik, this shop… it's a veritable tinderbox…

PERCHIK. Don't start that again. Give us the key. S'cutting into / my wrists –

VANESSA. A tinderbox, Perchik. The walls are little more than parchment.

She pulls out a matchbox and shakes it.

PERCHIK. Vanessa – eh, Vanessa, no!

VANESSA. I stole them from his pocket.

PERCHIK. Vanessa! You dare – / *you dare* –

VANESSA. I'm sorry, Perchik. I can't understand what you're saying. I'm ever so stupid.

VANESSA *takes a pair of scissors and cuts the ribbon on the key. She unlocks the cupboard and takes a cigarette, sticks it in her mouth.*

PERCHIK. Vanessa, darlin', please, whatever you're – Please. *Please!*

VANESSA. Poor thing. Look at you. You're terrified.

VANESSA *lights a match and uses it to light the cigarette. Takes a drag.*

Good.

She throws the lit match. Blackout.

PERCHIK. VANESSA!

Tammy Wynette's 'Stand by Your Man' plays.

The music stops. The lights come up. The sounds of waves breaking and gulls calling. VANESSA is at the seaside. She takes off her shoes and socks, tucks her skirt into her knickers, and steps forward into the cold water. She smiles. The light fades as she paddles up the shore.

The End.

it felt empty when
the heart went
at first but it
is alright
now

it felt empty when the heart went at first but it is alright now
was first produced by Clean Break at the Arcola Theatre,
London, on 7 October 2009, with the following cast:

DIJANA   Hara Yannas
GLORIA   Madeline Appiah

Director   Lucy Morrison
Designer   Chloe Lamford
Lighting Designer   Anna Watson
Sound Designer   Becky Smith
Production Managers   Ali Beale,
                                    Rachel Shipp

Company Stage Manager   Helen Gaynor
Deputy Stage Manager   Rebecca Carnell
Casting Consultant   Amy Ball
Accent Coach   Elspeth Morrison
Publicity Designer   Richard Scarborough
Assistant Lighting Designer   Sunghee
Production Electrician   Crin Claxton
Costume Supervisor   Nicola Fitchett
*Trainee Assistant Production   Renee Ge
    Technician*
Design Assistants   Cecilia Carey,
                                    Alison McDowell,
                                    Helen Quinn-Goddard
Marketing Consultants   The Cogency
Press Consultant   Nancy Poole PR

Author's Note

This play was created in close collaboration with the director and design team of its original production. We had a large warehouse space at our disposal, and the stage directions reflect this – I think it would be just as possible to produce the play simply in a single studio space. The stage directions are metaphorical provocations not literal instructions.

The sections in which Dijana speaks in her native language can be done in any tongue you deem appropriate – but it may be of interest to know that in the original production, Dijana was Croatian, and that is represented in the text here.

Whilst elements of *it felt empty when the heart went at first but it is alright now* are inspired by real-life events, all characters, their names and incidents portrayed are entirely fictitious. Any resemblance to the name, character or history of any person is coincidental and unintentional.

Characters

DIJANA, *Eastern European*
GLORIA, *West African*

Note on the Text

A forward slash (/) in the text indicates the point at which the next speaker interrupts.

Part One

You pay some money. You wait your turn. You are led into a room.
You are given a letter. The letter is written by somebody who dots
their 'i's with little hearts.

You are reading the letter when everything goes completely black.
You cannot see your hand in front of your face. You hear bird wings
flapping. The sound is all around you. It gets more and more frantic.

A scream. A loud, repeated thwacking sound. The flapping cuts out,
and the lights come up.

You are in a modern, sparsely decorated flat. There is a copy of
Cosmopolitan *magazine. There is a mug with a smiley face and the*
word 'Happy' on it. A pair of kicked-off pink high heels. A small
fridge.

DIJANA *is standing on a bed with a rolled-up newspaper. She is*
dressed in a miniskirt and a strappy top. She breathes sharply and
deeply. Frozen like a child caught doing something naughty. There
is a dead bird lying on the floor. She has just killed it with the
newspaper.

DIJANA. It wasn't me.

Beat. She scrambles down off the bed.

Don't be mad, shit, but, no but it flew in at the window and then
it was flapping was frightened

THIS IS SO NOT WHAT I NEED RIGHT NOW it

could not go out again. Stupid bird. Sorry. You should not say
bad of the dead but

I try! Try to push it out with newspaper try to HELP IT, hello!
but then it *fly*, it fly right at my face and so I

panic and I

hit it and now is

dead. Is dead is dead on my floor and I am so so sorry. I am so
sorry. But he should look where he goes!

*She throws the newspaper in the bin and squats on the floor.
Peering at the bird.*

His beak… is broken. I broke it. I didn't mean.

Her face crumples. She starts to cry.

I think is a baby. It is so small. Oh shit. Oh God. Poor baby.
Poor bird. I wish you did not see this.

*She starts to brush at her arms, as if sweeping off invisible
insects.*

I am so sorry baby. This is horror to see. I wish you did not –

*She stops suddenly. Shakes her head. Takes out a mobile phone
and dials, pacing, one eye on the bird. Waits.*

(*Muttering.*) Babac is not answering.

Hangs up. Rubs her head.

Shit FUCK.

She stares at the bird.

I am so glad I am out of here soon. I cannot fucking wait I tell
you.

*She picks up the bin, finds a plastic bag and starts counting out
used condoms.*

One, two

Three four five

Six seven

Eight nine ten eleven twelve thirteen fourteen fifteen

Sixteen

Seventeen eighteen nineteen

Twenty twenty-one

Beat.

Today is quiet. Usually, Saturday, special so close to Christmas,
thirty maybe. Today? Only twenty-one.

Her phone beeps. A text. She looks at it.

Twenty-two. Ten minutes.

So twenty-two including next one, yes. Not so bad twenty-two.
Maybe enough, twenty-two.

Beat. She takes out a small notebook and a pencil.

My maths it is very good. I have a head for numbers. Babac
always say, You have a head for numbers Dijana Polančec. So.
Twenty-one. Not including next. All fucks. So twenty-one times
thirty is...

She writes the sum and works it out.

sixty hundred thirty UK pounds.

She pencils this figure in.

Plus two times fifteen for blowjobs plus five times ten for
handjobs is

eighty add to six hundred thirty minus fifty for rent today and
ten pounds for tissues and one hundred for maid is five hundred
fifty profit, take this from monies outstanding...

*She works it out, then writes in her calculation. Holds up the
notebook.*

I keep account. I keep account of money I earn very careful
because when this number reaches twenty thousand UK pounds
then I will have earned all the money I owe to Babac and he will
give me my passport and I can stop.

I have earned already... nineteen thousand nine hundred and
seventy pounds. So when I have earned thirty UK pounds more
I can stop. That is the deal. When Babac tell me the deal I am like
Oh! Yeah! Sure! Like I am gonna fucking trust you! Do I look
like some IDIOT?! But I make it proper. We have a contract.
I draw it myself and I make him sign it so yeah. It is all on paper.

I need only thirty UK pounds.

After next client I will have earned this.

So next client he will be my last.

Beat.

The next is the last.

Beat. This is a momentous thing to absorb.

So tomorrow I come to find you.

The first thing to do is to buy you chips and a swimming suit.

We are going to swim in the sea. I am going to eat chips in a car and swim in the sea with my baby. In Brighton.

She takes out a dog-eared, folded ultrasound image. Examines it.

I promise you. Can you hear me?

Knock once for yes and twice for no!

I wish I had other photos of you. Look how I have rubbed your face off. And you are so small here. You look like a fucking Heinz Baked Bean!

She laughs. Puts the print away. Then looks at her phone.

I better get ready.

She ties her hair up. We see there is a letter 'B' branded into the back of her neck. She picks up a foundation compact, wipes it round her face. Puts some lipstick on. Picks up a thong from the bed.

Babac gave me this. It is bit small for me, the girl before she must have been so thin. It's clean, I wash it really hot with soap. I have two others and also a bra.

She puts the underwear on under her skirt. She takes a big tub of Vaseline from under the bed and wipes some inside herself. Picks up two bottles.

Look. Babac did not give me these I took them by myself from bootsthechemist.

L'Oréal shampoo. And conditioner too. Because I'm worth it!

She pulls her hair out of its ponytail like she's in a shampoo advert and shakes her head in slow motion.

See.

But she doesn't laugh.

This is extra funny because I know exactly how much I am worth. How many people can say this! I am worth one thousand euros because that is how much Babac pay for me.

To put this in easy language, that is like two-and-a-half iPhones.

She puts the bottles back carefully, arranges them on the chest of drawers. Tidies the bed. Then sits on it. She stares at the bird. Thinking.

Something strange happen this morning also. This guy, he come and we fuck. Just normal him on top once then in my mouth and he come on my tits but after he go something weird, he go

Ummm... do you want me to call someone?

And in my head I am like Yeah do you have number of a dentist cos your breath stink.

But I do not say out loud. I do not say nothing.

But this guy he is still standing there and my next client he is coming and the guy he is looking all red and English like meat and he go Ummm you don't have to do this if you don't want you know.

And in my head I'm like Uh, okay it is like none of your business! Shit! Like I don't do what I want you know? I am fine. You think I stay here if I am not fine? I am fucking great mate! And anyway it is not like there are so many things I could do you know! It is not like I went to Oxford University or something!

Anyway I tell him, Today is my last day, *actually*. That shut him up!

He go, Oh.

Yeah I say, Tomorrow I will not be working here no more, which actually is true, I say I am starting new job in an office in the Canary Wharf, which is a small lie but who give a fuck right. I say Where do *you* work? We are not sposed to ask stuff like that but I am just like Fuck it today is my last day and he is been so nosy to me and tomorrow I am out of here so I say What is your job?

And he says I am a supplier.

And I am like Yeah. And I yawn, to show how boring he is. Of what?

And he says Pigs.

She raises her eyebrows.

Okay. And what do you supply to these *pigs*?

No, he say, I supply pork. I am a pork supplier.

And I start to laugh cos I think it is a joke, right? Like a shit joke, but a joke, but he don't laugh. He say

My business partner has a farm. In Glaus-ter... in Glauster. It is beautiful place. The pigs can go anywhere. It is open fields. There is apple trees. They eat. They sleep. They have long life.

And then you slit their throat! I say. I just try to piss him off now, I don't like him. It is right he makes pigs, his eyes are like a pig's they are small and close together and he blinks like there is flies in them.

The meat is so good he say. You should taste it. You would not believe. The difference in taste.

How much it cost I say. And he say a number and I laugh, I have a head for numbers and that is a fucking stupid price to pay for some bit of pig you can get it so cheap in Kingsland Road.

And he look sad then, and he go Our customers can afford it. Our customers believe to pay for quality.

Who your customers, I am shouting now I don't know why, What shop you sell this in!

Waitrose, he go. And then I am quiet so he say, It is a supermarket, and *that* make me MAD so I go YEAH I KNOW. And I am bored of this now and his time is over so I put my bra on and that tells him.

Good luck with your new job, he go, as he walk out.

I see he has forgot to do up his flies.

Beat.

Prick.

Usual the men I see are better than him. Usual they are very rich and high-class. And sometime famous.

And the *experience* is real high-class too. V... *exclusive* yeah? I make more money this way.

For example, when a man comes to see me, he must first allow me to wash his penis.

I know, it sounds not so nice!

But I do it very sensual. In the bathroom with rubber gloves on. And in this way we know the man is clean.

I am clean too. Babac take me to get tested in a clinic every month. By Pamela. She is so funny. She make me lie, like this...

She lies on the floor with her knees bent and together.

And then she say FLOP.

She flops her legs open, feet still together.

And then she say to me always, Dijana does this hurt? Every time, Dijana, does this hurt?

And I am like, What do you think? You have got big piece of plastic in my pussy!

She does not laugh at this but I know she finds it funny. Cos she keeps saying it like every fucking time.

Pamela is so nice but she is so *old* like about fifty years old so it make me laugh so hard when she says the word 'anal'! I always pretend I have not heard so she have to say it again.

So yeah I am pretty high-class.

She turns round and pulls her top off, leaving just her bra. Across her back are a number of large, violent, spreading bruises. At the base of her back is a tattoo reading 'Angela'.

I am like, what is her name, I am like – *Billie Piper*. High-class! She has a Secret Diary, it is so funny! So yeah, I guess I am like Billie Piper the most.

She pulls on a different top and turns back to us.

Sometimes I go to nice hotels. Four star! Or five. With minibar and small soaps you can take home.

I have even been with film stars!

Well. Men from the television, I do not know if they have been in the movies.

But definitely TV. Definitely famous.

I can't tell you who.

She bites her lip, tempted. Then shakes her head.

No! I must not say! Not even to you, little clown!

Pause.

I think Babac has new girlfriend.

I don't care or nothing. I am done with men! I just really like sex you know. That is why is okay this. I love it so much, sex. I am so modern. Babac can fuck who he wants. When I meet him for first time I think Oh man I am so in love. But I go off him now. And I am out of here tomorrow anyway! He can fuck who he wants. Is my choosing not his. I won't cry.

She shrugs. Brushes at her arms again. Sweeping invisible pests away.

I don't cry too much. It does not help fucking no one. I cry when you go. Sure I cry then.

Beat.

But since that time? (*Shrugs.*) I cry like… never. No, wait, shit, I cry once.

Cos what is was yeah this guy he come and we fuck and then he die. On top of me my face is squashed on floor by how heavy he is. Was horrible.

And Babac he sort it out, like he make the body go but in time I wait for him to come I just sit here with dead man. And it make me sad cos I see his wedding ring and I think of his wife and it make me cry. Thinking about police when they go to her, and say her man is dead. Questions she will ask.

Like, How he die? Was it car accident?

No.

Was he pushed under a train?

No.

Was he shot with a gun?

(*Shakes her head.*) No.

Well what his wife will say! You must tell me how did my husband die?

And they would say

Your husband die in Dalston fucking beautiful prostitute in
the ass.

Beat.

It probably made the funeral a bit difficult for her.

But maybe they say something different. The truth it is very
strong for some people.

It was strong for me! I cry then. When I sat there waiting.

Believe it or not my ass has never killed a man before!

Sorry. Is not funny.

Beat. She puts her hand to her mouth, and looks at the bird.

I just had such bad thought. Like if this bird was not a bird but
a person that looked like a bird like a little boy or a girl and it
was lost and flew in here and then I and then I and then I and
then I and –

*She starts to hyperventilate. She brushes at her arms. Frenzied,
purposeful activity as she goes to the bin. Pulls out the
newspaper. Spreads it on the floor, tips the bird onto the
newspaper and wraps it up quickly, gagging, picks up the
bundle at arm's length, marches to the fridge, puts the bird in
and slams the door. A shudder – the feel of feathers on her skin
– then she rummages in her handbag, can't find what she
wants, she tips it upside down, the contents spill onto the floor
– make-up, perfume and shampoo bottles, her notebook,
a hairbrush, condoms, deodorant, cigarettes, tissues, and,
falling in a flutter, many pictures cut out from newspapers
and magazines of little girls. She ignores these, grabs the
deodorant, sprays herself, then scrabbles for her lighter and
cigarettes, lights one. She checks her phone for the time.*

Shit. He is here soon.

*She briskly starts repacking her handbag. Gathers the scraps of
paper. Stops on one. Holds it up.*

Look at this girl! She is seven years old!

She is youngest person in the country to have her heart
transplant with another person's! They took out her heart and
they put another one in because hers did not work properly.

She is really brave she is only seven. I bet you would not be so brave. But this little girl, she has her whole heart taken out and still she smiles for the camera and talks to journalists and when they ask How does it feel? she says

It felt empty when the heart went at first but it is alright now

Tubes up her nose she says something beautiful like that! If a journalist tried to talk to me when I had tubes up my nose I would tell him to go and fuck himself.

But maybe they gave her chocolate or something.

Beat. DIJANA *looks round at the fridge.*

I hope it does not come alive and start to fly round the fridge when client is here.

She shudders. Then looks at her phone. Busies herself tidying the bed.

A knock at the door. She quickly sits on the bed. The door swings open.

He is here! Twenty-two. The last man.

She waits as the client, invisible to us, enters. The door swings shut again. We hear footsteps.

He is old this one.

But he wears nice suit. Maybe Dolce Gabbana or River Island. That was nice of him, to wear a nice suit for such special occasion.

DIJANA'*s eyes follow him across the room as he walks to the bed.*

His legs are like a lady's, almost no hair at all.

The mattress indents with his invisible weight. Some banknotes drop on the bed.

He does not want to talk.

She lies down on the bed. Opens her legs. Turns her head to look at us as she starts to be fucked by the client. Her body jolts with his invisible movements.

His skin smells. Not aftershave. Not bad.

Just smells.

He keeps his eyes closed.

I hope he has a strong heart.

Pause. The fucking gets harder, faster.

What do I think about?

I think about tonight.

I think about if when I see my passport I will recognise my face.

I think about who is the girl who will be in this room tomorrow when I am in Brighton with you.

I think about the cracks in ceiling.

Harder, faster. She looks right at us. The sound of bird wings flapping from the fridge.

I think about washing my hair with L'Oréal because I am worth it.

I think about the pig man and shopping in Waitrose.

Harder, faster. DIJANA *closes her eyes. The flapping gets louder.*

I think about the wife of the dead man crying her heart out.

I think about how scared must have been the bird, to fly inside and not know how to leave again.

She is thrown onto all fours as the client fucks her from behind.

And then I can't stop it I think about you I think about you I think about you and how I have been waiting for this day for seem like always and now is here I don't believe I don't believe it ow.

And I think about how I will be in Brighton tomorrow and buy you chips and a swimming suit and then we are going to go swimming in the sea.

I think about what colour swimming suit is best.

I think about tomorrow ow.

I think about tomorrow and

I think about

I think about...

I think about nothing.

Her hair has been grabbed, her head is yanked back, her neck stretched.

Is better to think about nothing.

I think about nothing

and count to twenty-two.

Harder. Faster. Harder. Faster. Harder –

The bird wings suddenly stop. DIJANA *flops onto her front, her face against the bed, looking at us.*

Thank you. Have a nice day.

She lies there. Quiet. The door opens and closes. The man has left. She pulls two ten-pound notes and two fivers out from under her. She counts them.

Ten. Twenty. Twenty-five. Thirty. (*Beat. Again:*) Ten. Twenty. Twenty-five. Thirty. (*Beat. Again:*) Ten. Twenty. Twenty-five. Thirty.

She writes the number neatly in her account book. She checks her sums. She closes the book. She puts the book and the money in her handbag. Beat.

The enormity of this spreads through her. DIJANA *stands. She pours vodka into the 'Happy' mug. She downs it, staring at the fridge. Takes a deep breath. Gathers herself. Goes to the fridge. Takes out the bird. She walks to the window. She opens the window. She throws the bird out as if releasing it. She closes her eyes.*

Tonight that is me. Tonight I fly away. And in the morning I will be in Brighton. By lunchtime I will find you. For lunch we will eat chips in a car and then I will buy you a swimming suit. I wish you could hear me, little clown. I wish you could hear that tomorrow I will be with you but I hope you know more that I was always with you even when I was not I was always with you like when I wake in the night and I can't sleep sometimes I hear you breathe small sounds you make and then I could sleep then I could sleep because I think if I can hear you like this you can hear me too and if you can hear me you will know, you will know that I am coming and I have said this before but now is *true* –

Suddenly a vent falls from the wall. Wind whistling through it. The smell of the sea. A dark chasm big enough for a person to disappear into. DIJANA opens her eyes. She goes to the vent. Puts her hand in. Takes it out. Sprinkles a handful of sand to the floor. Smiles.

See?

I told you.

I told you I was coming. I don't think you believe me.

But now you see.

She picks up her bags. She climbs into the vent. And then she is gone.

The room is quiet. Then...

* * *

BA-DOOM BA-DOOM BA-DOOM BA-DOOM a heartbeat pulses in the air and GO GO GO GO you are pushed out of the space the building is being raided the police are coming up the stairs and their sirens wail and lights flash and you find yourself moving quickly and you notice that above you DIJANA is scrambling through a tunnel, moving faster than you, speeding ahead through time and space –

– and then you lose her but you keep moving and soon you find yourself in –

– a corridor. Doors on either side. It is lit above by electric bulbs but there is sand under your feet.

You come to a desk and there is a policewoman sitting at it and she doesn't seem to understand you but she shows you a child's swimming costume in a clear Ziploc bag. It still has the price tag on. And then she wants you to press your fingertips into a pad of ink and you don't know what you've done wrong but you do it anyway and she takes your hand and she presses your fingers to the walls –

– and soon fingerprints cover the wall and the policewoman guides you on past her desk and now the sand is deeper but there's something else mixed with it, it looks like –

– hair and you can hear the sea, the waves crashing against the shingle beach. A breeze rolling up the corridor towards you. The smell of salt. Then –

A security alarm going off in the distance. And someone panting. Running. Breath getting quicker and quicker as they run faster and faster and then with one last gasp of air –

End of Part One.

Part Two

It is suddenly dead quiet. You are in a long, long narrow room.
The size of things in here seems all wrong. The walls are lined with
doors of all sizes, too-big doors, too-thin doors, too-small doors.
Exits all over the place but no feeling they go anywhere. Some
things in the room seem larger than they should. Others smaller.
It is a sterile, impersonal place. You are not meant to feel at home.
DIJANA *sits on the floor.*

DIJANA. So Brighton is a dump huh.

When I am there it is pretty grey most time and the shops they
are so expensive like three UK pounds for fucking cup of shit
coffee and arcades of games I didn't like it.

But it was good when I found you. Then it was good.

I was so scared I cannot tell you, that you would not know me.

But you was so happy to see me! You would not let go my hand
you was so happy. And how much we talked.

Not at first, you was quiet at first but then! You are a real little
motormouth.

We did not get to swim in sea though.

I wish we had got to swim in sea. That is really annoying that
we did not get to do that.

I did get you swimming suit though so maybe one day when
I stop being here.

Beat. DIJANA*'s right hand starts shaking. She holds it still with*
her left hand. Waits for it to stop.

When I earned twenty thousand UK pounds I showed Babac
my account book and my sums and the contract and he laughed
at me.

And I watch him laugh for some time and it is weird like I am
outside my body, like I watch me watching Babac laughing like
I am on the ceiling not in my body at all and then scream I don't

know for how long but I scream and I bite him, I am hitting and
biting Babac

And then pain at my head and everything go funny again, like
underwater, like sounds get loud then quiet again, loud then
quiet, and my hair catch in something and then I see what my
hair is catch in is his hand Babac's hand and just after this is
when I see Babac is bashing my head on the wall.

Everything go black then and I guess I go to sleep cos when
I open my eyes later it is morning but early still dark and I hear
a bird sing and I listen to him and I think about you because
I always think about you when I wake up and I wonder how
I am going to do it and what is more quick the pills or the razor.

Beat.

But you would not believe then what happened then.

There is a doorbell

and I pull myself to the window. And I see outside two men.
And I guess Babac answer the door because then he is there on
the path and they have his wrists in the cuffs and Babac is
shouting and kicking but they hold him push down his head and
into the car and then Babac is gone.

Later someone tell me they come cos he was doing fraud with
credit cards. It is so weird how you can live in a house with
someone and not know things they do.

They have gone so fast they have not locked the door.

I just walk out.

I just walk out.

I just

walk out.

And it is so scary for a minute.

I just stand in the street. On my own. In the street. Then I see
the Christmas tree in the windows and remember I am cold so
I go inside and take a big coat of Babac's from the hook and
also my bag and then I go and then I am gone and I start to run
and I keep running and I stop only when I get to the canal and
I sit on a bench and light cigarette and the sky is no colour and
I take deep breaths.

The coat smells of him and I am sick on the path.

Beat.

Last night I drive for so long in a car with three women and also some men. But there was cages to keep us apart so was okay. I did not have to touch them or nothing. And then in the morning I was here.

Beat.

In Brighton we ate chips, I had enough money for chips. Not enough money for swimming suit because it was like fifteen UK pounds but it was big shop and I know what I am doing and Babac's coat have big pockets and the swimming suit it is so fucking pretty and I know you would look so beautiful in it and what am I supposed to do put you in the sea in your fucking underwear?

It really is a big shop and part of a famous chain.

At police station, they were shits. Question they ask. The worst was woman police, she talk for like hours and I tell her everything again and then she go

You say you wanted the item for your daughter, Miss Polančec? And the man, he whisper something in her ear like I am not sitting right there, and *then* she go

Oh.

But she still say it again she say You claim you take the item for your daughter.

And I know she's got it there right there on the paper fucking, in front of her so what a stupid fucking question but I just say Yes.

Then there is a big quiet. And then she go You understand Miss Polančec, that you are against UK law?

Beat.

I say I don't know.

She say You don't know?

I say No.

Beat.

After I am sick I sneak in bendy bus and I sit outside Victoria Train Station with a cup and because I am pretty and cry sometimes I make thirty UK pounds about.

Then I got on another bus they call it Megabus but apart from that you can get on it for five UK pounds it is really not so great. And then I am in Brighton.

And for three days I am walking walking all day long and looking but no good.

And I start to feel bad like I have been so fucking stupid. To think I could just get on Megabus to Brighton and find my baby all so easy.

You cannot imagine.

You really cannot.

I am looking for so long and not finding you.

I am so tired I walk up the pier but my feet they are just dead meat and even though it is blue skies and sun I am feeling very black.

So you cannot imagine

You really cannot.

The surprise.

When I look down and you are standing next to me, up on the rail.

I am searching for three fucking days and there you are on the pier all the time!

Careful, I say to you, you are leaning over rail. You will fall in the sea and a fish will eat you.

You shake your head, No.

No what I say! You do not think the fish would be happy to find a tasty little dish like you? He would gobble you like that!

I click my fingers and you laugh. You have a bad haircut, like they put a fucking bowl on your head or something but your hair it is dark like mine.

I want to smell it.

You don't say nothing and I pretend not to be bothered with you no more and this upset you, you do tumbles on the floor, check with your little sly eyes if I see or not – yes I saw you! and I want to watch you so much but I stop myself till you roll at my legs and this is when I turn and I look at you and I gasp

My God, little clown I say. Where did you learn such amazing cool tricks?

You just laugh again and get back up on the rail.

We stand like this for a while and the wind comes off the water and it makes me feel so nice.

I look down, you are pulling a face

Careful I say, the wind will change and you will be stuck ugly like that for ever.

You don't stop so I pull a face back.

She pulls the face.

The sun go down now and the sky is pink and a man's wheels squeak as his wife push him up the pier.

And when I look down again my baby lies on the floor pretending to sleep!

You make little snores.

And that make me cry, cos you look like I always imagine.

And then you put your hand

into my hand

DIJANA's *face crumples.*

And it's so small, you know?

And then it is quiet for a long time

and then I say

Little clown?

Little clown?

I lean down and whisper in your ear my nose in your hair I can smell it

Little clown? I say.

How would you like to go swimming in the sea?

And you nod your head. And I take from my bag a packet of chips. The paper is still warm and your eyes go so wide. And I say to you Stay here. Eat. And by the time the bag is empty, I will be back. And I will have a present for you.

Beat.

It really was a massive shop.

They had a whole floor of new underwear.

Beat. DIJANA *looks down. Then* DIJANA *cries. An animal howl. Sobbing into her chest.*

I don't want you now.

Go away.

GO AWAY PLEASE.

I SAID GO AWAY I AM SORRY OKAY I AM SO SORRY BUT YOU CAN'T BE HERE ALL THE TIME I am so tired just

looking at me GO AWAY! Goawaygoawaygoawaygoaway I CAN'T SEE YOU! I can't see you no more please go away!

GLORIA. Who are you talking to?

DIJANA *spins round. Freezes.* GLORIA *is sitting up in bed. Nigerian. Far away up the other end of the room, on a ledge high on the wall. We have not noticed her before.*

DIJANA. Nobody.

GLORIA. If you do not shut up, I am going to stamp on your head.

She climbs from the bed. Stares at DIJANA. *Stamps hard on the floor. It echoes.*

DIJANA *stares at her, terrified. Then* GLORIA *starts to laugh.*

Only joking! Oh my life, your face!

GLORIA *moves up the room towards* DIJANA.

DIJANA. You said –

GLORIA. I did not mean it! Look at your face! I got you!

DIJANA *sinks to the floor.*

DIJANA. Yes. You got me.

GLORIA. I got you so *good*! HA! Do not sit on the floor there, that is where I piss.

DIJANA *leaps up.* GLORIA *laughs again.*

I got you again! You think I do that! Oh shit, you think I am an animal or something!

DIJANA. No. Please. / No –

GLORIA. It is okay. Chill. Hi. I am Gloria.

Beat.

You are Dijana right? This is your first day?

DIJANA *nods.* GLORIA *takes out a little plastic box from her pocket.*

Yeah I thought so. Me? One hundred twelve. Do you want a Tic Tac?

DIJANA *shakes her head.*

Take it. I am not being funny but

you got *breath*.

DIJANA *takes a mint. Puts it in her mouth. She feels in her pocket. Pulls out a coin. Holds it out.* GLORIA *looks at it.*

What is this?

DIJANA. Pay.

GLORIA. Pay?

DIJANA. For Tic Tac.

GLORIA *kisses her teeth.*

GLORIA. You do not got to pay. It is a *mint*! You do not got to pay!

Beat.

DIJANA. Thank you.

GLORIA *nods. Knocks back a handful of Tic Tacs.* DIJANA *takes out the small notebook from Part One and starts to write in it.*

GLORIA. What is this?

DIJANA. I keep account. I keep account because the lawyer say ninety/-six days –

GLORIA. They send you a lawyer already?

Beat.

DIJANA. Today.

GLORIA. Today? Oh shit. You are *lucky*. I have been waiting time. They never send me one yet. They send you one already? What did he say?

DIJANA. She say. When ninety-six days are over I maybe leave here and go somewhere else. I have been here one day.

She writes this in the notebook.

So in ninety-five days I can stop being here maybe.

She closes the notebook.

I have a head for numbers.

GLORIA. Is it?

DIJANA. Yes. Why are you here?

GLORIA. I chop off my auntie's head with a cleaver. She died.

Beat.

Shit, got you again! No, I am joking. I am the same as you yes. No passport.

DIJANA. I do have... I do have passport.

GLORIA. You just left it in your other bag right? Me too.

GLORIA *laughs.*

DIJANA. I DO HAVE PASSPORT.

Beat.

GLORIA. Okay. Chill. Where is it then?

DIJANA. My boyfriend. Somewhere. I dunno.

GLORIA. Oh right. Your boyfriend is it? My auntie has got mine. That is what I say to the police, I have not lost my passport, I have lost my auntie. They didn't laugh though.

Pause. GLORIA *takes a hairbrush and pulls it through her hair. Watching* DIJANA.

DIJANA. I am... sorry if I wake you.

GLORIA. You did not wake me.

DIJANA. You try to sleep.

GLORIA. I don't really sleep any more.

I have got... problem sleeping. Do you get me?

DIJANA *nods*.

Yeah.

Beat. DIJANA *takes a scrap of paper from her pocket, gives it to* GLORIA.

DIJANA. Can you tell me please. What does this mean? I ask the doctor to write it for me.

GLORIA. You see a doctor already? Oh shit you are so lucky!

DIJANA. Please. I don't know.

GLORIA. I'm just saying, you don't know how lucky you are! (*Reading.*) 'Cervical abnormalities.'

She looks up at DIJANA. *A recognition. Then hands the paper back.*

Yes. I got this too. It is your downstairs. Your privates. They did not explain it to you?

DIJANA. Babies?

GLORIA. No. Not babies. We have got enough problems without babies, right! Wait.

GLORIA *suddenly races back towards her bunk, climbs up to it, rummages under her mattress and runs back to* DIJANA *with something in her hand. She hands* DIJANA *a well-loved greetings card. It has a cartoon of a large pair of breasts in a pink bra on it.*

Here. My friend Nkoyo send it to me. She is in a town now called Nottingham. She send this card to me at my auntie's and I keep it in my knickers drawer. I look at it every day.

When I first read it, I laugh so hard some urine came out of me.

DIJANA *stares at the card.* GLORIA *continues, pointing out the words as she reads.*

I will read it to you. It says: 'A good friend is like a good bra. They both give you a lift.'

Beat.

It is a joke.

DIJANA. Funny?

GLORIA. Yes. So funny.

Beat. Then DIJANA *looks up at* GLORIA. *Smiles.* GLORIA *smiles back.* DIJANA *starts to laugh.* GLORIA *laughs too. They become almost hysterical together.*

Oh man, it is so nice to meet you! I am not just saying that, it actually is so nice to meet you. I don't like the others they put here before. They are all Somalian bitches. But we are going to get along so good! There were four of us at my auntie's. By six months, we were all getting our bleeding at the same time. Like the nuns!

DIJANA *laughs again. Then* GLORIA *takes the card back. Finds a pen in her pocket and scribbles on the card. She hands it back to* DIJANA.

Take it. It is yours now. I give it to you. See how I have changed the names? Do you see?

I have crossed out 'To Gloria, from Nkoyo' and written here instead, 'To Dijana, from Gloria'. And I have put one kiss after only because we are friends but we do not know each other very well yet. Maybe I will add more kisses tomorrow once I know you more.

Beat.

DIJANA. We are

friends?

GLORIA *beams at her.* DIJANA *is overcome. A pause. Then:*

Thank you.

A long pause. They look at each other.

GLORIA. They don't believe anything I say here. They think I lie. Ask me why I did not run away.

But it is only on maps Africa is a big country. People find you. My auntie could find me.

Like that, she could find me. And then...

They smile when I say the word.

JuJu. Little smile at each other. Like I do not see.

They think it is hocus-pocus. But it is real. There, a market there. You can buy what you want. Anything. A heart. Some hair. A breast.

Anything. Fresh tongue is one hundred thousand naira.

That is about four hundred pounds. A lot of money people can make from you, you see.

So it is not funny. JuJu. They should not smile.

I like my tongue to stay in my mouth, thank you.

DIJANA. Today is my birthday. I am twenty-two years.

GLORIA *beams at her. Then gently guides* DIJANA *to the floor.*

DIJANA. What are you –

GLORIA. Your hair it look like something die in it. I am going to brush it for you! Relax girl please!

DIJANA *tenses, her back rigid.* GLORIA *brushes her hair.*

See. It feels so nice doesn't it?

DIJANA (*quiet*). Yes.

GLORIA. Did he bring you here?

DIJANA. What?

GLORIA. Your boyfriend, did he bring you here? To England?

Beat.

DIJANA. No. Babac was not who bring me here.

GLORIA. My auntie was who brought me. She not my real auntie, you get me? I just call her that.

GLORIA *has pulled away quite a bit of hair. She looks at it.*

Oh shit girl! You are shedding like a dog.

Hey, it is okay. It will grow back right? Hey! You can have some of mine!

Gloria will take care of you. Gloria is here now. Gloria will be your momma.

Oh shit, this is so strange for you, yes? Yesterday you were – where were you yesterday?

Beat.

DIJANA. Brighton.

GLORIA. Right, yesterday you are in Brighton and today you are in this place with strange African lady. Talking about the selling of breasts! Yes well. Welcome to England! You don't need to be scared any more please. The Albanians next door will try to steal from you, and the Somalians, the Somalians are pigs do not talk to them. And the lady across the hall keep trying to hang herself from her tights, but most times she put it on to get attention so do not be scared. And if anyone gives you a problem. Gloria will sort them. Anyone touch you. Gloria. Anyone say something. Gloria. Anyone – anything. Gloria. Okay?

DIJANA (*quiet, but smiling*). Okay. Gloria. Okay.

GLORIA. That's right! That's right! Gloria is your momma! And what is this? A smile! That is better! Look at your pretty face when you smile! Look at it! I could eat it you know!

GLORIA *wraps* DIJANA *in a fierce hug.* DIJANA *tenses. Starts to struggle. Murmurs of discomfort. But* GLORIA *holds her there until she calms, quietens. Then slowly,* DIJANA'*s arms creep up round* GLORIA'*s back, until she is holding her tightly too. Clinging on to her. They stand there like that for a moment. Then* GLORIA *gently pulls away.*

Lights out now.

DIJANA. But... no.

GLORIA. But yes. You are tired little one. And I am here.

DIJANA. No. Lights on.

GLORIA. It is not allowed. I promise it is not so bad. And I will sing you a song to sleep to.

GLORIA *turns off the light. The following occurs in the darkness:*

See? Not so scary.

DIJANA. Lights on.

GLORIA. Shhhhh...

DIJANA. I don't like.

GLORIA. I sit with you till you sleep okay? / Come lie down.

DIJANA. LIGHTS ON.

DIJANA *starts to cry, panicked, scrabbling for an escape.*

GLORIA. I put the covers over you. Shh. It okay. / Gloria make you safe. Gloria your momma now.

DIJANA. Please I don't like *lights off* I don't want I want

In the dark the sound of a struggle.

GLORIA. Stop now / you will hurt yourself –

DIJANA. Sići mene, ne popipati mene ne popipati mene to mise ne svida – [Get off me don't touch me don't touch me I don't like it don't –]

GLORIA. Shhh. / The wardens will come you must calm

DIJANA. Žao mi je na taj način žalostan ugoditi siči – [I'm so sorry I'm so sorry I'm so sorry get off please get off –]

GLORIA. You must let your eyes get used to the dark. Let me hold your hand –

In the dark, the sound of a struggle. Animal noises. Canine barking and growling. Two separate, non-English languages, competing with each other. GLORIA, surprised, screams in pain. DIJANA, frantic, hyperventilating. GLORIA turns the light on. Blood on her cheek. A little around DIJANA's mouth. She has bitten GLORIA.

What is wrong with you! Huh? What is the matter with you?

Silence. DIJANA *wipes her mouth and brushes the ants from her arms.*

Hey! I said WHAT IS WRONG I ASK YOU A QUESTION WHAT IS WRONG WITH YOU?

DIJANA. I don't trust you.

Pause. GLORIA *stares at* DIJANA. *Then she snatches back her greetings card, and walks back to her own bed. Once she's under the covers:*

GLORIA. Yes, well. I don't trust you either.

The moment I saw you, I did not trust you.

Beat. DIJANA *is sobbing quietly again.*

You better stop crying now. Pissing me off.

Sort yourself out before I turn off the light.

I got to sleep sometime you know.

Silence. DIJANA *stops crying.*

DIJANA*'s right hand starts to shake again. It gets more and more violent. She cannot control it. She holds her arm to steady it. She lets go of her arm. It shakes more violently. She waits for it to stop. Eventually it does. She is exhausted by it. She stares at the bed covers as she speaks.*

DIJANA. I am not sposed to talk to you no more.

The doctor says it's not healthy.

DIJANA *suddenly starts to choke, coughing. Eventually she brings up a tiny golden key. She stares at it. Then looks up. There is a tiny door in the opposite wall, the only one with a keyhole. She runs to it, unlocks it, it swings open.* DIJANA *kneels, crawls head-first into the space. And disappears.*

* * *

BING BONG BING!

The lights come on brightly and you hear the bustle of a busy airport terminal.

ANNOUNCEMENT (*in a variety of languages*). LADIES AND
GENTLEMEN PLEASE MAKE YOUR WAY TO GATE
SEVENTEEN, FLIGHT 793 IS NOW BOARDING!

And now GLORIA *is marching down the long thin room
towards you dressed as an air hostess with a big air hostess
smile and you are led by* GLORIA *along another corridor lined
with clocks –*

*– and you notice that the clocks are going backwards rather
quickly and you go through passport control where they check
your ticket and then you are ushered onwards –*

– and there is a light at the end of the tunnel!

*– and suddenly your shoes are wet and there are birds singing
and you realise that you are in –*

End of Part Two.

Part Three

A wide-open corn or wheatfield. The sense that we are in a huge space of freedom and light. Dark green, lush hedgerows, and a clear blue sky. There is a door in the horizon.

There is a standard lamp in one corner of the field. An armchair. A small side table. A TV. A stereo.

Downstage there is a line of stuff, laid out, like one does when packing for a holiday. A little wall. DIJANA's *suitcase, upright and ready. Bottles and tubs and tubes of suncream, hairspray, deodorant, insect repellent. Books, mainly tourist guides. Toothbrushes, hairbrushes, phone chargers, coat hangers, a frisbee, items she's added to over a period of days, like careful packers do.*

DIJANA *is hoovering the field. She is pregnant. Five months gone. She wears a white smock-like dress.*

Music plays from the stereo. She sings along. Dances a little. Then: the sound of a plane roaring overhead. DIJANA *turns off the hoover, drops it and switches off the music. She runs to the window, watches the plane go overhead. She feels her stomach. Then points upwards. Excited.*

DIJANA. Did you see that! Shit. Did you hear it? That will be me tomorrow! On a plane NEEEEEEEEEEEOOOOO – OOOOW flying away! (*She puts her hand to her belly.*) That will be us baby!

We are going on holiday tomorrow! Babac and me and you!

We are going on a holiday.

On our holidays VACATION! I am a celebrity get me out of here!

Babac take care of everything. Your daddy is so smart.

He book the hotel

He book the flight

He say Give me your passport, and I will take care of everything!

And he has! He has taken care of everything!

It is so easy. I just give him my passport and I leave all to him.
I am a lazy bitch yes!

BUTOHMYGODIAMSOEXCITED!!!

Babac has not done no packing yet. MEN! What can you do!
I tell him, I won't do it for you just cos –

Beat. DIJANA *looks down at her stomach. Rubs her hands
over it.*

Do I sound weird? To talk out loud? Just... I want your English
to be so good when you come out from there! And the doctor
say I should talk to you... she say you can hear me and –

Can you hear me?

Knock once for yes and twice for no!

She laughs.

Okay. I am gonna think you can hear me. And so if you can,
when you come out, you will know my voice and speak English
like Princess Diana. Except not be in a car crash! Or make love
with a Arab.

And if you can't hear me I am just mad fucking fat lady talking
to herself!

You are gonna love the plane. I love the plane even when my
ears go pop I love the plane. Last plane I go on, OHMYGOD,
when I get off at London Heathrow, my cousin waits for me.
I don't know him so well but he is so nice his name is Goran
and he take me to his small house in Leytonstone and his wife
make me instant cappuccino and say, Welcome to England!

She has many tea towels with cats on them.

And later Goran say Do you want to go out tonight? So we go to
this club and inside at the bar already is Goran's friends and
they say, Welcome to England! and Goran is friend with this one
guy name Babac and he say, Welcome to England! I shake his
hand and he kiss me on my cheek and then I am shy and sudden
so tired.

Can you think how far I had come in one day!?

Music starts to fade in.

But soon the music is strong and I am dancing, I love to dance
and the beats are good OH MY GOD I LOVE THIS SONG!
And Babac buys me a drink and with a girl in the toilets I take
a pill –

The music cuts and DIJANA *momentarily shifts her tone.*

I don't do drugs no more because of you and when you are born
I will tell you drugs are bad and evil and you must not take them
ever but this is a LIE because drugs are so fucking GREAT!
They make you feel –

*The music kicks in hard again and her tone changes back. She
moves to the music.*

Like your skin is prickles with happy and you melt to other
bodies and your blood go fast and slow and normal I don't like
strangers touch me but tonight I like their sweat on me legs
pushes on mine, even hands on my bum I like it, I like strangers
touch me –

I KISS A GIRL! AND I LIKE IT! HA! Only for fun just cos we
are friends, I mean I will never see her fucking again but
tonight, here we are like the best friends and we laugh so hard
and dance and our hairs stick and I turn and there is Babac at the
bar, he smile, he talk to my cousin but he smile at ME and his
teeth are white in his skin, and that is when I realise I have taken
off my top and I dance in just my bra! But not dirty you know,
not to be sexy I was just hot I want Babac to dance too but
Goran keep talking HE IS SO BORING!

And I make a face and Babac laugh his teeth are white he has
nice eyes, Goran still talk the floor is sticky the light is bright
his teeth are white my top is gone – I don't care I buy another! –
I am on a man's shoulders I stretch my arms the beat is strong
my fingers look long he give Goran money Goran stop talking
AT LAST I am high in the air I touch the stars my body is
beauty I close my eyes sweat run down his teeth are white the
light is bright I feel like free.

The music stops. DIJANA *stops moving. Breathless.*

Now I say in my head, when I think of Babac, I say I fell in love
with him teeth-first!

She checks her mouth in the mirror again. Throws it down.

And one week later cousin Goran have to go to business so I move here with Babac. With your daddy.

It was July this month and so hot. And Babac buy me ice cream. He buy me ice cream every day. Not just vanilla flavour. Double Caramel Magnum. Every day.

And this is how I know. That he fall in love with me too. And then there was you.

DIJANA*'s phone rings. She scrambles for it. Looks at it. Puts the phone to her stomach.*

It for you.

Beat. Poker face. Then she grins and answers.

Only joking! Hello yes how can I help you?

Yes this is the right number.

She cradles the phone in her neck and scrabbles through the pages of a large red book. She finds a pen and takes the lid off with her teeth.

Sorry you say again please.

Right good. How long sir?

And what do you look for today sir?

Okay. Yes we can do. Home visit or...

Okay. What time you like please sir? If before five o'clock p.m. it is happy hour you get two for the price of one.

No. Okay she come at nine. May I have address please sir?

Yes... yes... yes okay. Sorry?

I see. Uh-uh. That is no problem. I am...

Sorry. That is

sad.

Beat.

Yeah. Okay. Without is twenty pounds UK extra but if you want is okay.

Yeah she do that. That without is also twenty pounds UK extra.

Yeah she do that. Yeah she do that.

Yeah she do that, okay, her name it will be Vesna, yes, you like her. No worries sir, have a nice day.

She hangs up. Starts finding another number in her phone. Puts the phone to her ear and waits.

He is poor bastard. He is in wheelchair. Life is a shit sometimes, hi Vesna?

The call has been answered. As DIJANA *talks she takes out the mirror, examines her mouth, takes another tissue and scrubs at her lips. Then throws it away.*

Kako ste? Kako je Danijel? [How are you? How's Daniel?]

Nemoj me jebat?! Ozbiljno? Dobro sam ti da je pizda! [You're kidding me? Seriously? This man is taking the piss!]

Okay yes Imam rezervaciju za vas – [I have a reservation for you –]

19 Ainsworth Road. Is Hackney. One hour.

Što? [What?] I don't know postcode. Why you want –

Sat Nav? You have –

Slušati, On je u invalidskim kolicima. Da, u invalidskim kolicima. Što? dobro ići i raditi u dućan onda! Devetnaest. Ne, *devetnaest!* [Listen, he's in a wheelchair. Yes. A wheelchair. What? Well, go and work in a shop then! Nineteen. No, *nineteen!*]

She hangs up.

Sat Nav.

She looks in the mirror. She examines her mouth. She takes a tissue. She rubs at her mouth.

When you are born I get new job. Babac can get someone new to do phones. I work in a office maybe. Or be an actress. I am so good at acting. That would be a cool thing to tell your friends at school yes?!

She throws the tissue away. Feels down the side of the armchair for something: a packet of cigarettes. She takes one out and sticks it in her mouth. Lights it. Opens the window and smokes leaning out of it.

Babac does not like me – (*She motions to the cigarette.*)

When we first are together, when I smoke he make big fucking fuss, like he pretend to cough and choke!

But now I am pregnant, he let me do whatever I want! Is so fucking great being pregnant!

She takes a drag on her cigarette and coughs. She looks at the audience. Guilty. Then she freezes. Overcome by an intense pain. She holds herself. Waiting it out. It goes. She reprimands her stomach, pretending to be angry.

Hey! Stop this please! Is only one. How you like I kick you so hard!

She quickly kisses her hand and puts it on her tummy. She gets up and opens the door. Peers out.

Babac? Baby?

No one is there, she shuts the door again.

Anyway

She takes a series of furious drags, feeling bad about it but wanting to savour it, then throws it out the window. Closes the window.

Is reward.

Today I do so much cleaning!

Hello and welcome to *How Clean is Your House?*

VERY CLEAN! Clean clean clean. I dust, I wash, I hoover. Today all I do is hoover! Hoover... ing?

She picks up a tattered book and flicks through it.

Yes. Gerund. Yes. (*Holds up the book.*) I learn so fast! My mama say to me, Learn English little clown and you will be master of your destiny! She did not say nothing about gerunds though. Hoovering. Yes.

I hoover here and I hoover there. In this room and

Another room. Another room not here. Maybe ten minutes on bus. Shoreditch.

*She takes out the mirror and examines her mouth. Grabs
a tissue and rubs at her lips.*

Sorry. Just

checking.

*She smiles. Plumps a cushion. Picks up a can of air freshener.
Sprays it round the room.*

So this is my crib!

Crib means house!

I think you are gonna really like it. I have made it so nice for you.

We have television made by Hitachi, we have stereo made by
A-iwa, we have (do not forget) hoover made by

She checks.

Hoover! Also many plug sockets. So many plug sockets!

There is like seven fuckin plug sockets in here. So many.

You know we are so lucky. We have so much.

You know I could say, anything I could say, like I want...

I want George Foreman Grilling Machine!

And Babac he would buy me

She clicks her fingers.

like that.

Babac he would buy me. Babac would buy me because he
love me.

Beat.

Maybe we should get George Foreman Grilling Machine.

*She thinks. Then takes out her notebook (her account book from
Part One) and writes this down.*

But I do not take the piss, you know? I am not stupid, uh –
trophy? girl. I did not come here to just like, sit on my ass!
I work! Totally I work I answer phones like all fucking day,
night sometimes too and it is easy but also you must be organise

like to, uh – cordinate? it. So yeah I collect monies, I do accounts and stuff. Your mama she is flat out all day!

Sometime Babac say to me, You have a head for numbers Dijana Polančec.

I never hear this expression before I think it is so funny. I don't know why...

She trails off and takes out the mirror again. Examines her mouth. Scrubs at her lips with a tissue.

Sorry. Sorry just I think I can see...

Something or... I dunno.

Like something.

She shakes her head and laughs. She throws the tissue away. Rubs her tummy.

What I saying? Before?

Oh! Yes, how good is Babac to me! Too good! Like, sometime I say to him Too much! You gotta stop!

And he is like Is okay you will pay me back someday but I know he joking because he kiss me on my head when he says!

He always kiss me on my head when he joking. Or when he has been pissed and shouted. Shouting?

She stops. Picks up her grammar book.

Shout-ing. Is gerund also. Most things with 'ing' are gerunds. Words you do with 'ing' they are gerunds.

Not fucking. I mean sometime gerund. When you do fuck, this gerund.

But when you say like, Oh that dress it is so fucking nice, that is not gerund.

I dunno what that is.

Just a nice fucking dress – (*She interrupts herself seamlessly and quickly takes out the mirror again.*) Sorry please but I worry I really think there is something. On my lip there is... something like a red...

Um... pozlijeda?

Or a… swolling or

I dunno. I just. I freak out a bit.

Shit. This morning you know, I tell you before I go to
Shoreditch to clean the room which is so like NOT my job but
Babac says the maid is sick so someone gotta do it and… What
is, is I was doing the clean

I change sheets and I hoover floor and I tidy. Empty bin and
stuff. And I am about to do bathroom when *she* come out. The
girl who… in the room. And I feel bad about this. Because I had
never met one before you know because, well –

she look like shit. And she go Hi and I go Hi and she go, I never
see you before and I go, Yes I know I am usual on phones.

And she go, Yeah I used to do that.

Pause.

I don't think she understand me cos her English was like even
so fucking worse than mine, so I say it again like the same thing
but more loud so she understand.

NO. I ONLY WORK THE PHONE.

And she is so rude then she go Yeah I hear you stupid bitch. And
that is, you know, that is not cool cos I am like her boss the wife
of her boss – I mean not married, me and Babac we are not
married but soon. After you is born maybe!

And she just stand there. Smile at me. I don't like it. And she go
again. She go, I work the phones too she say.

Beat.

When, I say.

Like, one year ago, she say. When I get here.

From Jamaica, I say?

Fuck off she say. I am not Jamaican. I am African. I come here
from Uganda to work phone for Babac. And after I was maid.
You clean? I say. Yeah. I clean, she say.

Beat.

What, you hoover? I say.

Yeah I hoover she say. And clean the sheets and empty bin and tidy she say

And now, she say, Now I do this.

And she kiss me. On the cheek. She kiss me.

Beat.

I just left. You cannot have a sensible conversation with Jamaicans.

Beat.

When I get home I have bath very hot because I have pain and because this girl kiss me and I am scared to catch something from her.

She looks in the mirror. Examines her mouth. Scrubs her lips with a tissue.

Like AIDS virus.

Or face herpes.

She turns back.

I am being so stupid right? Only cos I think I feel a tingle and that is what the advert say when you feel a tingle buy Zovirax so maybe I should do that. Maybe we have? In kitchen, I check.

She exits, hurriedly. The sound of drawers clattering, off. She comes back in. Worried.

We do not have. I must buy.

Her phone starts to ring. She pulls it out, smiles at the name on the display. She answers it.

Hi baby! What? Yes I am just –

Tonight?

They come here?

What friends?

Okaaaaay. But baby I still don't feel so good.

Yes – same thing.

Yeah I know, is fine, is normal but baby – TAKE THAT BACK. TAKE IT BACK NOW that is shit thing to –

Okay. Sorry. I know, but baby what time is flight tomorrow?

Flight. Plane. Holiday. What time?

You don't know?

Well can you find this out please? Because –

Yeah, okay I am not – yeah I see you soon. Yeah I will. Yeah. Yeah listen –

I love you baby!

Baby I am losing y –

Baby?

Baby?

Babac?

She sighs in exaggerated frustration and hangs up. This is what girlfriends on the TV do.

He has got friends coming round! We go on holiday tomorrow and he has friends coming!

What friends, I said? You hear me say that right?

Just friends he says!

HA!

MEN!

RIGHT?!

Right! They get hairy but they stay little boys. I am so happy you are a girl baby!

But is okay he is scared sometime. My mama say *my* daddy was so scare when I come, he move to Russia! HA! Babac is so different though. He totally love his little spanner in the works! That is what he call you! How fuckin cute is this!

She takes out the ultrasound image from Part One.

Cos look, you do look a bit like spanner. If you do this:

She squints her eyes and stares at it.

A bit. I dunno. Who fuckin care right! Is cute.

She puts the image away, leans over and whispers to her tummy.

When you come I will get your name in a tattoo on my back. So you will be with me always. I pick the spot just here.

She lifts up the back of her top to show the area just above her leggings (where the tattoo is in Part One).

We make you in Brighton. Babac have business there. And I go with him. A day of vacation. Was fabulous! When you come out I will take you there and we will swim in the sea. I promise to you. We will swim and eat chips. The water is cold and delicious! Babac watch from pebble and when I run out he hold towel out for me and rub me dry and we eat chips in the car and we make love on back seat and the home of the seatbelt dig in me but I don't mind and after I just know, I know we had made you. And when the doctor tells me some weeks later by how long I am pregnant I work out the sums and I know I am right.

I told you I have a head for numbers!

So yeah. I think this day in Brighton was the time I was the most happy in my whole long life.

Beat. DIJANA *stares out the window. Enjoying her memory.*

I still think on your name. Maybe Margaret. Or Miquita. And Angela I like too. I cannot decide. You know I am so bad at decisions! It make me so stress! So I ask Babac this morning, he is no help, he say it stupid to name baby before it come out. You will have to stay inside, that way I will not have to choose!

She leans over and talks to her stomach.

How you like that, little clown! You stay there for ever in me!

DIJANA *is hit by another intense pain. She freezes, waiting it out.*

Little clown not like that very much! So.

The pain goes. She takes a breath. Smiles.

So maybe I ask the audience! (*She laughs.*) Hey, you know how cool it would be to go on programme like this? To be the one who sits in the big black chair and all my make-up done and to be the one to say...

THERE IS CASH IN MY ATTIC!

Beat. DIJANA *laughs.*

No, I am joking, joking, is wrong show! Wrong show. I know this!

I WANT TO BE A MILLIONAIRE!

She laughs.

And then we know all the answers and win all the money. That would be so cool yes? Then Babac and me we never have to work we just lie in bed all the day and listen to Capital Radio and do sixty-nines and eat Double Caramel Magnums.

DIJANA *takes the hoover out. Comes back in. Beat. She smiles. Bites her lip.*

This gonna sound weird yes?

But I need to tell you. I have to tell someone. My heart feel like it gonna burst.

She sits. Holds her bump. Speaks softly. Telling a secret.

What I want to say is. I never really like it before, you know

...sex

I mean I like it yeah I guess it was okay I get off and everything but with Babac is so

different is so...

Like I get wet for him!

She clamps her hand over her mouth, enjoyably outraged at herself.

It is so bad to say that right! Special to you!

No but serious I just *think* about him, just THINK and here inside me is, you know, is like wanting like

...fizzy! Like Alka-Seltzer in my pants! And like I love

how heavy he is

on me and I love

how safe I feel

holded on the bed, he is on top of me

and I love

the smell of him. The smell of him drive me crazy!

This is so gross but... when I put his shirts in the machine I put my face in them first, in the armpits!

Beat.

I just. I never felt this before.

I just want him. And I don't know no way to say it but

She speaks rapidly in an Eastern European language, explaining exactly what she means in a way that satisfies her for the first time. Then stops. Relieved to have said it at last.

Beat. DIJANA *laughs.*

I wish I could say it so you understand!

I wish I could.

And I know this sound like I am like, so full of myself, but I love also how much I can be proud of myself.

Cos I *make* this happen. This morning, when I give my passport to Babac, I look at it and I think

WOW!

how much has happen since I last went on the plane! I never done nothing brave in my whole fucking life before and maybe I still be stuck in shit-smell apartment married to fucking coach driver but I save my money so hard and I book the ticket. And I be brave. And I come here. And I am scared but also I hope. And I meet a man. And I fall in love. And I make you! And I learn the language better and better. And now the man who sell Turkish sweet on Kingsland Road know my name. And I work. And I have Oyster card. And I have iPhone! With Apps! And I make my life. And I am so

so

happy.

Beat. A door slams somewhere else in the building.

(*Under her breath.*) Babac! Babac is home. (*Loudly.*) HI BABY!

She gets up. She takes out the mirror. Fusses with her hair. Scrubs at her mouth. Rushes to the door. As she turns away from us, we see there is now a little blood on the back of her dress, where she has been sitting on it. A spreading stain.

She's about to open the door but stops. Smiles. Turns back.

You know. He think I not see but

he put my passport in the safe. With all the monies.

When I see that it almost make me cry.

He put it in the safe to keep me safe.

And then he make me a vacation. Just like that! I don't know you can go on a plane when you are so full of baby as I am. But Babac say is fine. I say, How you know! And he say he call NHS fuckin hotline okay! So you see, he take care of everything.

Another painful twinge. She grits her teeth.

Hey you calm down in there please!

No more talking now.

It is getting late. You must sleep.

Tomorrow we are going on holiday.

Tomorrow we are flying. On a plane.

I tell you, you will love it.

She smiles. She makes gestures like an air hostess.

The exits are here

here

and here!

This last one is the door. She pushes on the door handle. The door will not open. She is surprised.

She tries it again. Leans her weight on it. She bends down. Looks through the keyhole.

Babac?

She moves back and rattles the handle. DIJANA *bangs on the door. Laughs.*

Babac! Stop talking to your friends and come rub my feet!

She bangs again. Then again. Then repeatedly. Feeling that her panic is irrational but feeling it nonetheless.

Then she stops. Listens. Tuts. She takes out her phone. Dials.

After a moment we hear a distant ringtone. But the call is not answered. She frowns. Shrugs. Hangs up.

She takes a fresh tissue. She scrubs at her mouth. Hard, rubbing it raw. Distressed now.

I feel a tingle. I definitely feel a tingle.

DIJANA *throws the tissue down. Walks to the window. Strokes her stomach absent-mindedly.*

You know. If the day is clear, you can see the Canary Wharf from here.

And the light that blink on the top.

This is where the business people work.

I think one day maybe I work there too.

Beat.

I have a head for numbers you know.

A lighting change. The packing is now lit to form the shadow of the London skyline on the wall. There's the Gherkin, the London Eye, the Houses of Parliament, Canary Wharf. Seats of money and power. Places full of tourists and men in suits, with money to burn and wives that don't understand them.

DIJANA *looks out the window and the shadows get longer and longer, eventually not resembling a skyline at all, instead appearing as nothing so much as a spreading, shapeless, enveloping darkness.*

Somewhere, a starling is singing.

The End.

small hours

Ed Hime and Lucy Kirkwood

small hours was first presented in the Michael Frayn Studio Theatre (downstairs) at the Hampstead Theatre, London, on 11 January 2011, with the following cast:

WOMAN   Sandy McDade

Director   Katie Mitchell
Designer   Alex Eales
Lighting Designer   Philip Gladwell
Sound Designer   Gareth Fry
Assistant Director   John Higgins
Casting   Wendy Spon

Characters

WOMAN

STEVEN (*offstage*)
MUM (*offstage*)

A WOMAN *sits on the sofa wearing headphones that stretch to a stereo system.*

There is a plastic bag at her feet, containing her purchases from her trip to the corner shop: a litre of Coca-Cola in a plastic bottle, some bars of chocolate, half of a plastic-wrapped Dundee cake.

She is listening to dance music and her eyes are closed.

The music is turned to a high volume.

Its tinny echoes leak from the headphones.

The WOMAN *opens her eyes.*

She reaches down and takes the bottle of Coke from the plastic bag, unscrews the lid and drinks some.

She screws the lid back on and puts it down again.

She takes her headphones off.

She takes her mobile phone from the pocket of the coat and looks at it to establish what time it is.

On seeing the time she gets up, goes to the radio and turns it on to the BBC World Service.

The end of the 3 a.m. news broadcast.

The news broadcast ends and the weather report plays. It includes a severe weather warning for Scotland.

When the weather report finishes, the radio station carries on into another programme.

The WOMAN *crosses to the landline to make a phone call.*

The call is not answered.

The call goes through to answerphone.

WOMAN. Hi.

    She realises the radio is still on.

    She hangs up. She turns the radio off. She realises she is feeling hot.

She takes off her outdoor coat and hangs it over a chair. She takes her boots off and leaves them by the chair.

She picks up an air freshener and sprays it about the room.

She picks up clothes, moves them to a different part of the room.

Next to the sofa, she finds a pair of man's shoes. Well-used trainers.

She takes one of the shoes off her hand and sniffs her hand.

She goes to her mobile.

She locates the number for her local cinema on the mobile and dials.

The call is connected.

VOICE (*off*). Welcome to Odeon Cineline. Please say the name of the Odeon cinema you would like to visit.

WOMAN. Camden Parkway.

VOICE (*off*). Did you say Muswell Hill?

WOMAN. No.

VOICE (*off*). Please say the name of the cinema you would like to visit.

WOMAN. Camden Parkway.

VOICE (*off*). Did you say Camden Parkway?

WOMAN. Yes.

VOICE (*off*). What film would you like to see at the Odeon Camden Parkway?

WOMAN. *The Social Network*.

VOICE (*off*). Did you say *Tron the Legacy*?

WOMAN. No.

VOICE (*off*). What film would you like to see at the Odeon Camden Parkway?

WOMAN. *The Social Network*.

VOICE (*off*). Did you say *Tron the Legacy*?

WOMAN. No.

VOICE (*off*). We're sorry we are unable to help you today. Please call back between 9 a.m. and 5 p.m. Monday to Sunday.

WOMAN. No.

VOICE (*off*). We're sorry we are unable to help you today. Please call back between 9 a.m. and 5 p.m. Monday to Sunday. Good Bye.

The automated service hangs up.

The landline rings. She looks. She hangs up her mobile, goes to the landline and picks it up. We do not hear Steven's voice.

WOMAN. Hi. Me.

STEVEN (*off*). I called earlier.

WOMAN. When?

STEVEN (*off*). Half an hour ago. Did you go out?

WOMAN. To the shops.

STEVEN (*off*). What about Esme?

WOMAN. Took it with me.

STEVEN (*off*). You just did it again!

WOMAN. No I didn't. I didn't.

STEVEN (*off*). Everything okay?

WOMAN. Yeah fine.

STEVEN (*off*). What does that mean? 'yeah fine'? are you alright?

WOMAN. Yeah fine.

Pause.

STEVEN (*off*). Did you hear the forecast tonight?

WOMAN. Are you off-air now? No I missed it.

STEVEN (*off*). There was a severe weather warning, you should call your mother.

WOMAN. A what? A severe weather warning, for where?

STEVEN (*off*). Your mum.

WOMAN. I can't hear you. You're breaking –

STEVEN (*off*). Hang on, hang on (shit).

She waits.

I'll call you on the landline.

WOMAN. I don't want you to.

STEVEN (*off*). Why not?

WOMAN. Because I don't.

STEVEN (*off*). What's happening, Mag?

WOMAN. I said, I'm fine.

Pause.

STEVEN (*off*). So you're going to call your mum then?

WOMAN. Why would I speak to my mother? It's after midnight.

STEVEN (*off*). It's gone three.

WOMAN. It's after three then.

STEVEN (*off*). But you'll call her in the morning? Dalkeith's right in the middle –

WOMAN. Yeah well my mother can cope with a bit of severe weather. It's severe weather has to cope with my mum.

STEVEN (*off*). What? I lost you there –

WOMAN. I said it's severe weather leather feather forget it, are you knackered?

STEVEN (*off*). Yeah a bit. Yeah, going to bed now.

WOMAN. Yeah me too. What did you have for lunch?

STEVEN (*off*). Cheese and mother-fucking pickle.

WOMAN. That's nice. What did you have for dinner?

STEVEN (*off*). Some pasta thing.

WOMAN. That's nice. What are you going to have for breakfast?

STEVEN (*off*). I don't know, Mag, would you give it a rest? You okay?

WOMAN. I said I'm fine can you leave off now please thank you.

Pause.

STEVEN (*off*). Yeah. Sorry. How you sleeping, my love?

WOMAN. Yeah fine. Got a whole two hours last night.

STEVEN (*off*). Your boyfriend keep you up, did he?

WOMAN. What boyfriend? I haven't got a boyfriend.

STEVEN (*off*). Yeah. I know. It was a joke.

WOMAN. Oh. Funny.

Pause.

STEVEN (*off*). I miss your face.

WOMAN. I miss your face too.

STEVEN (*off*). Not long now. Six weeks and I'll be back at the weekend –

WOMAN. What can you see?

STEVEN (*off*). What can I see?

WOMAN. From the window.

STEVEN (*off*). Manchester.

WOMAN. Manchester, I know 'Manchester', I meant. What bit.

STEVEN (*off*). The bit with all the smog.

WOMAN. That's nice.

STEVEN (*off*). If you like smog.

WOMAN. I like smog.

STEVEN (*off*). I like you.

WOMAN. Do you want to see *The Social Network*?

STEVEN (*off*). When?

WOMAN. At the weekend.

STEVEN (*off*). Yeah. Great. Will we be able to get a babysitter?

WOMAN. What for?

STEVEN (*off*). What do you mean 'what for'?

WOMAN. Why do we need one?

Pause.

STEVEN (*off*). For Esme!

Pause.

WOMAN. We'll just take it with us.

STEVEN (*off*). You're doing it again.

WOMAN. Sorry.

STEVEN (*off*). I'm sorry. I'm just worried about you. It's late. You should be asleep.

WOMAN. I know it's late. I know I should be.

STEVEN (*off*). Then why are you still up?

WOMAN. Because I like to say goodnight to you.

STEVEN (*off*). I love you.

WOMAN. Alright.

STEVEN (*off*). Did you hear me?

WOMAN. Yeah.

STEVEN (*off*). Okay. Sleep well,

WOMAN. Speak in the morning.

Pause.

Love you too.

Steven hangs up.

She hangs up.

She switches on the TV.

She flicks through the channels.

She stops on a shopping channel.

A female presenter is displaying a kitchen gadget that chops, grates, blends and peels all kinds of foodstuffs with ease and convenience.

She watches the shopping channel.

A group of drunk people walking home. Happy, loud noise; hollering and singing.

She turns off the TV and stands still in the middle of the room listening to them.

The people outside laugh harder, calling to each other, and pass by.

She searches the room for her handbag.

It is an oversized, expensive-looking leather bag in a bright colour.

She looks in the bag but does not find what she is looking for.

She pulls the cushions off the sofa.

She finds what she is looking for: a small make-up bag. She finds it under the sofa.

She slowly puts on her make-up with the aid of a small hand mirror.

She closes her compact and puts on her coat and warm comfortable boots.

From off, a baby coughs.

She wonders to herself why she was getting ready to go to work.

The baby coughs again.

She stands still, listening.

A while passes and there is no other noise from the baby.

She goes to the sitting-room door, closes it completely.

Off, the baby starts crying.

Wet suddenly spreads across the chest of her thin top as her breasts express milk.

The baby continues to cry.

She turns the TV on. She flicks through the channels and finally stops on a repeat of a cookery programme presented by a glamorous, beautiful woman. The programme is filmed in the woman's own kitchen, which is well-appointed and well-decorated. This woman cooks a meal, which she tells us is very simple to make. Her children eat this meal with her and enjoy it very much.

Her attention drifts from the programme after about ten seconds, but she leaves the TV on.

She picks up the landline phone and goes to dial but stops.

She listens to the dial tone.

She takes the blanket from the sofa and wraps it round her shoulders.

She sits on the floor.

She dials the phone. We do not hear Mum's voice.

MUM (*off*). Hello?

WOMAN. Hi Mum, it's me.

MUM (*off*). What are you doing calling me, it's three o'clock in the morning.

WOMAN. I'm fine. How're you?

MUM (*off*). I was in bed, is something the matter?

WOMAN. I'm sorry. I just heard on the radio about the severe weather warning.

MUM (*off*). What are you doing calling me at this time of the night?

WOMAN. There's a severe weather warning in Scotland.

MUM (*off*). What you talking about?

WOMAN. A severe weather warning morning in the morning.

MUM (*off*). Is Steve there? Put Steve on!

WOMAN. I just thought it was important.

MUM (*off*). The baby's crying!?

WOMAN. It's fine.

MUM (*off*). I can hear her! Is she alright?

WOMAN. No that's.	MUM (*off*). Is She Okay?
I think it's upstairs.	Are you sick?
I think it's upstairs.	Is she sick?

I've got to go.

She hangs up.

She shrugs off the blanket.

She feels in the pocket of the coat she took off before and takes out a baby monitor, switched off.

She looks at it.

She switches it on.

The crying comes through the baby monitor, as well as directly from the bedroom.

She puts the baby monitor on the floor.

She looks at the hallway hall door.

She goes into the hallway.

She is gone for two minutes.

The landline rings.

We hear her singing to the baby, off.

The baby continues to cry.

It is still crying when she comes out of the room, closing the door behind her.

When she comes out of the room she is holding a nappy sack.

She sits on the sofa. She puts the nappy down on the sofa next to her.

She watches the television.

The landline begins to ring.

She picks up the air freshener and sprays it about from her seat.

The baby continues to cry.

The landline stops ringing.

She gets up, exits and returns with a vacuum cleaner.

She plugs it in and begins to vacuum the floor and the upholstery.

Her mobile starts to ring.

She turns it off.

She is concentrating on vacuuming this room.

She puts down the vacuum cleaner, as if she does not notice it is still running.

It lies on the floor, switched on, as she goes to her CD collection and lays out four or five CDs on the floor.

After examining the artwork, she picks one and puts it into the stereo system's CD player and presses play.

She is confused by the lack of sound coming from the speakers of the stereo system.

She turns it up but there remains no sound.

She does not understand why the speakers aren't working.

She examines one.

She turns and sees the headphones, lying where she left them earlier.

They are still plugged in to the stereo system.

Upon moving closer, she can hear the music playing through them.

The vacuum cleaner continues to run and the baby continues to cry.

She looks at the wire running back into the stereo system for a moment.

She pulls the jack out of the socket.

Loud music suddenly booms out of the speakers.

She mouths the lyrics and moves to the music, but slowly.

The sound of the vacuum cleaner, and the baby crying, continues.

She looks at the vacuum cleaner and turns up the music loud.

The first part of this song is her favourite part, and so when the song has played halfway through, she takes it back to the beginning of the track and listens again from the start at this high volume. She does this at least five times.

There is banging from upstairs.

She does not react to it.

The banging continues.

The landline rings. She does not react.

Presently, a knocking, then a banging on the front door, off.

Eventually, she recognises the sound.

She turns off the music.

She turns off the TV.

She switches off the vacuum cleaner.

She sits and waits to see what the response from the door will be.

The banging stops.

She waits.

There is nothing more from outside the door.

The landline rings.

She unplugs the phone from the wall.

She stares into space. She begins to shake.

The baby continues to cry.

She empties the plastic bag on the floor.

She picks up a bar of chocolate and eats it, still listening.

She gets up and crosses to the hallway door.

She opens the hallway door and goes to the bedroom door.

She enters the bedroom.

Some time after this the crying stops.

She comes out of the bedroom.

She closes the door behind her.

She picks up the air freshener and sprays it at the door.

She sits on the coffee table edge and has another drink of Coca-Cola.

She turns off the lights in the room.

She sits back on the sofa.

Outside, the birds have started to sing.

Presently she gets up and leaves the room by the door to the hallway.

The room is dark and quiet.

NSFW[*]

---

[*]Not Safe For Work

NSFW was first performed at the Royal Court Jerwood Theatre Downstairs, London, on 25 October 2012. The cast was as follows:

RUPERT	Henry Lloyd-Hughes
CHARLOTTE	Esther Smith
SAM	Sacha Dhawan
AIDAN	Julian Barratt
MR BRADSHAW	Kevin Doyle
MIRANDA	Janie Dee

Director	Simon Godwin
Designer	Tom Pye
Lighting Designer	Guy Hoare
Music & Sound Designers	Ben & Max Ringham
Casting Director	Amy Ball
Assistant Director	Rosy Banham
Production Manager	Paul Handley
Stage Manager	Laura Flowers
Deputy Stage Manager	Sarah Hellicar
Assistant Stage Manager	Lou Ballard
Stage Manager Work Placement	Louise Quartermain
Costume Supervisor	Jackie Orton
Vocal Coach	Budgie Salam

Characters

CHARLOTTE, *twenty-five*
RUPERT, *twenty-eight*
SAM, *twenty-four*
AIDAN, *early forties*
MR BRADSHAW, *late forties*
MIRANDA, *late forties/early fifties*

Note on the Text

A forward slash indicates interrupted speech.

A comma on its own line indicates a beat; a silence shorter than a pause, or a shift in thought or rhythm.

Thanks

I would like to thank Simon Godwin, Dominic Cooke, Mel Kenyon and Ed Hime. There are also a number of people who generously gave of their time, knowledge and experience who do not want to be named, but they know who they are and I thank them too.

L.K.

1.

The editor's office of Doghouse *magazine, a weekly publication for young men. The magazine's name appears in neon on the wall. Beyond the door, an open-plan office.*

There is a pool table, a fridge of drinks. A dartboard. The editor's desk has a desktop Apple computer on it. There are framed prints of topless photo shoots on the walls. A cricket bat in the corner. An enormous Liverpool FC flag strung from the ceiling. The pool table is strewn with toys and gadgets and computer games that the magazine has reviewed or is reviewing.

CHARLOTTE, a middle-class girl from outside of London who now lives in Tooting, is sitting on a chair, a folder in her lap, furiously writing notes. She has other files on the floor which she consults from time to time.

RUPERT, an upper-class boy from Berkshire who now lives in Hoxton, watches her. Bored, he yawns, looks about the office. Wanders over to the pool table and gives it a kick.

RUPERT. When I first started here, we used to play on that all the time.

This place has gone to the fucking dogs.

He sits down on the floor at CHARLOTTE's feet.

Scratch my head.

Without looking away from her work, or stopping writing, CHARLOTTE reaches a hand out and scratches RUPERT's head. He groans in pleasure.

SAM, a working-class, university-educated boy from outside of London who now lives in Archway, enters, juggling a cardboard tray of coffees. He's sweaty and frantic.

SAM. Am I late? Is he here?

CHARLOTTE takes one of the coffees. RUPERT takes another.

CHARLOTTE. He's in a meeting with finance. Running late.

SAM. There was this woman in Starbucks, and she couldn't make up her mind, she kept saying 'There's so much *choice*, isn't there!' and *laughing*, / I nearly –

CHARLOTTE. Sam? Calm down.

SAM. No just the thing is, is I was late on Monday too and I can't, / I just can't –

RUPERT. Mate. Last year I was reviewing absinthe for the June issue. I got completely munted, walked in here, Aidan's taking a meeting with Roger fucking Highsmith, yeah? I don't remember a thing but apparently I took out my cock and balls, jiggled them in my hand, said 'How d'you like them apples?' and threw up on his folding bicycle. I'm still here, aren't I? It's media. You're not going to get fired for being late with some coffees.

CHARLOTTE. Yeah well, it's different for you, isn't it.

RUPERT. How is it different for me? I am a member of the workforce.

CHARLOTTE *stares at him*.

CHARLOTTE. D'you know how Rupert got this job, / Sam?

RUPERT. Classy. Really fucking classy, Charlotte.

CHARLOTTE. D'you think he did an interview? D'you think he spent hours checking the font on his CV?

RUPERT. Century Gothic, thank you and actually yes I did an interview and FYI, I didn't conduct it on my knees, like some / people we COULD MENTION –

CHARLOTTE. He got a / THIRD. In ART HISTORY.

RUPERT *sings, in a rather beautiful baritone, to the tune of 'Mandy' by Barry Manilow:*

RUPERT. 'Oh Charlotte, you came, and you gave me chlamydia.'

CHARLOTTE. Shut up! What's wrong with you?

RUPERT. What? I'm just messing with you.

CHARLOTTE. Sam doesn't know that.

RUPERT. Sam, I was messing about. It was jokes.

CHARLOTTE. I did not give him chlamydia.

RUPERT. No. Of course she didn't. Of course.

Of course.

He winks at SAM, *scratches his crotch. Mouths the sentence 'It was crabs' at him, shielding his mouth from* CHARLOTTE*'s view.*

CHARLOTTE. What did you say?

RUPERT. I said IT WAS CRABS.

CHARLOTTE *throws down her files, goes for him, he dodges her, laughing.*

Her Secret Garden's crawling with pests, Sam! Omnem relinquite spem, o vos intrantes!

She catches him, puts him in a headlock, sinks him to his knees.

CHARLOTTE. Where's your copy? Aidan's going to ask, what am I going to tell him?

RUPERT. You'll think of something! / (*Laughs.*) Ow!

CHARLOTTE. Do I look like your mother? Do I look like your / fucking mother, bitch?

RUPERT. Oh, don't let's fight, darling! Not in front of the child!

CHARLOTTE. I'm serious, you fucking waste of space –

RUPERT. Sam, she's flirting with me! You're a witness, she's flirting and it's hurting!

AIDAN *enters. A middle-class, educated, good-looking man. He is carrying a large oblong item, covered in brown paper and protective wrapping.*

He stops, stares at the scene. CHARLOTTE *and* RUPERT *disentangle themselves. Beat.* AIDAN *carries on across the room to his desk, takes his jacket off, dumps his bag.*

AIDAN. Great issue. I really mean that.

SAM *rushes to bring* AIDAN *his coffee.*

(No, I'm alright, Sam, had one upstairs.)

SAM *takes the lid off the coffee, knocks it back in one go.*

The circulation's finally taken a leap, it's early days, but the heart monitor is flickering, it's definitely flickering. Print journalism lives to fight another day.

A half-hearted cheer from the others. He holds up the parcel.

Just arrived from the print shop.

He pulls off the wrapping to reveal a large framed print of a topless girl, kneeling on an unmade bed. It's not a professional-standard image, it's been taken by an amateur. The girl has very large breasts, and is in a pose that emphasises this, arching her back, presenting her arse. A sexy face, lips apart, a finger in her mouth. She is undoubtedly beautiful, but also very natural, her make-up is a little crudely applied, her hair is a little wild, she wears a white-cotton pair of everyday pants, chipped blue nail varnish, plastic bangles on her wrists. AIDAN takes down last year's winner from where it hangs on the wall, and places the new print in its place.

Lady and gentlemen, meet *Doghouse*'s Local Lovely, 2012.

They all look at it.

CHARLOTTE (*reading from the caption*). 'Carrie, eighteen, likes *Twilight* books and theme parks.'

RUPERT. Chestington World of Adventures!

CHARLOTTE. It's retarded. At least last year's had the reading age of a grown-up.

RUPERT. Charlotte was reading Proust when she was eighteen.

CHARLOTTE. Rupert was playing soggy biscuit when he was eighteen.

RUPERT. Still do. Lovely end to an evening, a good round of old SB.

CHARLOTTE. What were you doing when you were eighteen, Sam?

SAM. Revising.

CHARLOTTE. No but for fun.

SAM. Revising. Pretty much from when I was sixteen, to when I came here, I was revising.

AIDAN*'s looking up at the print on the wall.*

AIDAN. I really like this.

RUPERT. Carrie, meet Humbert Humbert.

AIDAN. No, I do, I mean. Aesthetically. I think this is what we should be going for. Much more natural than last year's. Natural's good. There was a sort of, plastic quality to last year's, around her –

CHARLOTTE. Tits.

AIDAN. No, I meant more in her / energy –

CHARLOTTE. Tits.

AIDAN. I mean, there was a quality, an overall quality that I found a bit, intimidating. But this is good, it's very real very next-door very normal. How many entries did we have this year?

SAM. Nine hundred and sixty-nine.

RUPERT *laughs.* CHARLOTTE *gives him a look.*

RUPERT. Sixty-nine.

AIDAN. Not bad. Up on last year.

CHARLOTTE. It was Sam's choice.

AIDAN. Yes, I know. It's an excellent choice, Sam.

SAM. I thought she looked friendly. Sort of, approachable.

They all look at the print.

CHARLOTTE. Yeah, that's the word. Approachable.

'

AIDAN. Once more unto the breach.

AIDAN *sits behind his desk.* RUPERT *and* CHARLOTTE *grab the two other chairs in the office,* SAM *has to make do with a beanbag.*

I just want to start by saying thank you. I know how hard you've all worked, these last few issues, and I want you to know it's been noted, and appreciated. Charlotte, I'll send round an email, but if you could pass on my gratitude to the rest of the staff?

CHARLOTTE *notes this down.*

However, there's a long way to go. The climate is very hostile. As you know, two of the publications in our demographic have gone under in the last three months.

Half-hearted cheer from CHARLOTTE, RUPERT *and* SAM.

We've gained a little from their readership, but not as much as we'd like. And this is an opportunity, I don't think we've fully grasped that yet, I mean we've got the C2DEs, they're with us, but if we're clever we can broaden our appeal, scoop up some of those ABC1s – you don't look excited.

Everyone tries to look excited.

This is exciting. We're not talking about editorial overhaul, but a tactical *repositioning*. There's an existing mission statement, no one's saying touch the statement, Roger's certainly not saying *that*, but I'm giving you licence here to be *bold*, guys, be brave, yeah? There's always room for jokes, there's always room for boobs, that's a given, but what else is there room for?

RUPERT *puts his hand up.*

Rupert?

RUPERT. Bums?

AIDAN. Bums don't sell, what I'm saying is, is let's really *live* in the spaces *between* the boobs, yeah? Let's not let them outgrow us, I want you all to keep putting yourselves in the head of that eighteen- to thirty-five-year-old man. Thinking about who he is and what he wants to spend his disposable income on, what does he talk about with his mates, what makes him laugh, what *Doghouse* magazine can give him that he can't get anywhere else.

So, on that note.

Our next Man Challenge.

The others groan.

Who wants to go to the Arctic for a week? Charlotte?

CHARLOTTE. Survey says uh-uh.

AIDAN. Rupes?

RUPERT. Already been.

AIDAN. When?

RUPERT. School trip.

SAM. What's it like?

RUPERT. Pretty cold.

AIDAN. We'll get you some mittens.

RUPERT. No. I'm sorry but no, I did the diet. You said, if I did the diet I didn't have to do any more Man Challenges for at least six months, you said.

AIDAN. But this one will be fun.

RUPERT. I ate nothing but meat for six weeks, Aidan.

AIDAN. The readers loved it.

RUPERT. I had to go to the hospital to get my bowel medically dis-impacted.

AIDAN. The message boards went crazy.

RUPERT. And before that I did the sleep deprivation, I was hallucinating for five days. I saw pixies in my soup. Do you know what that's like? To be eating a bowl of minestrone and see evil pixies frolicking on your spoon?

CHARLOTTE. Is that a Nigella?

RUPERT. You promised. No more Man Challenges.

AIDAN. Okay. Sam?

SAM. Yes?

AIDAN. Do you want to go to the Arctic?

SAM. When?

AIDAN. Next week.

SAM. It's my girlfriend's birthday.

AIDAN. Take her! See how many times you can have sex in sub-zero temperatures.

RUPERT. Before it goes black and falls off.

AIDAN. We'll call it 'Love in a Cold Climate'.

CHARLOTTE. It's what Nancy Mitford would have wanted, Sam.

SAM. No, I'd, really like that, it's just – I've booked a thing. For
   my girlfriend's birthday, it's her thirtieth / and –

RUPERT. Harold and Maude.

SAM. And I want to make it special so I booked this thing, I've
   been saving up my holiday time – I did clear it with Sarah.

AIDAN. What is it?

SAM. It's just, a thing.

CHARLOTTE. A thing.

SAM. A thing, a treat a, surprise.

,

CHARLOTTE. Yeah?

SAM. No I'm just. It's a bit.

,

Well, she's called Rona. My girlfriend. Her parents named her
after this island, in Scotland, which was where, well, they always
said that's where they fell in love, and they always promised to
take her, but they never did and now, well, they both died, her
mum last year, her dad like, five years ago.

And I've booked a sleeper train to Glasgow. And I've hired
a car and, we're going to drive out there, you have to go on
a ferry and I found this, tiny little house on the beach that used
to be a shepherd's hut only someone did it up, it's in the middle
of a bird sanctuary and – she's got this thing about puffins, she
just –

Well, she really loves puffins, like if you ever need to get her a
present, you just get her something with a puffin on it, like a
mug or a T-shirt and she just, that just makes her day, and you
can see them, the puffins, from this house and we both, we
really like swimming in the sea, especially when it's cold, that's
one of our things. And. And.

And I bought a ring.

So when we get to the island, and we've seen the birds, and
we've swum in the sea –

I'm going to ask her.

,

So if it's alright, I'd rather not go to the Arctic.

,

RUPERT. I think I'm in love.

CHARLOTTE. That's very… that's, / very lovely, Sam.

RUPERT *rubs at his eyes, tearful.*

RUPERT. I've gone. I've actually gone.

AIDAN. Write it. Write about that for us.

SAM. You want me to –

AIDAN. You want to be a writer or not?

CHARLOTTE. No, he wants to spend another nine months fetching your cappuccinos and judging tit shots. That's why you did your MA, isn't it, Sam?

AIDAN *stands, excited.*

AIDAN. No see this is what I'm talking about. We have an opportunity here, to move the readership on. The boys who started reading us ten years ago, they're grown-ups now, they're not out on the pull every Friday, they're settling down, they've got mortgages, girlfriends they love. The climate is changing. They're not just reading us for the tits any more.

RUPERT. Uh, I think the tits are quite a big part of it.

AIDAN. Okay, but they want to find a pair of tits to grow old with.

RUPERT. Again, I think they want to get old, while the tits stay the same age.

AIDAN. 'How I Proposed to My Girlfriend.' Seven hundred and fifty words. What do you think, Sam?

,

SAM. Wow.

AIDAN. Great.

SAM. Yeah, but –

AIDAN. What?

SAM. Just not sure –

AIDAN. You're nervous, don't be –

SAM. I'm not but –

AIDAN. I've read your samples.

SAM. I just / don't think I want to.

AIDAN. You're a good writer, what?

SAM. I don't want to write about it.

AIDAN. Why?

SAM. Because it's private.

AIDAN. The proposal?

SAM. Yeah.

AIDAN. But you just told us about it.

SAM. Yeah / but –

RUPERT. You did just tell us about it, mate.

SAM. But you're my friends.

AIDAN. I'm not your friend.

SAM. No, sure but –

AIDAN. We're your colleagues, I'm your boss. That's why I'm asking you to – anyway, you don't have to write the reality, you write the *Doghouse* version. When Rupert wrote the piece on being dumped by Pippa Middleton, that wasn't you know that wasn't gospel that wasn't, you know, vérité, was it?

RUPERT. No. For a start, okay, it was *me* that dumped *her* –

The others groan, they've heard this grievance rehearsed before.

CHARLOTTE. Yeah yeah, we know, you're too good for her –

RUPERT. For the party planner? Yes, / as a matter of fact –

AIDAN. What I'm saying is, this isn't, I'm not asking for gonzo journalism here. I mean, hopefully the real thing won't go wrong but it would be good, wouldn't it, Charlotte, if when Sam writes about it, it goes wrong? A little / bit –

SAM. Wrong?

AIDAN. You know, awry.

RUPERT. Tits up.

CHARLOTTE. Just, structurally, if there were some obstacles –

AIDAN. You might forget the ring.

RUPERT. Or you might get cold feet.

CHARLOTTE. The island might've been used for chemical-weapons testing and the beach might be littered with the bodies of dead puffins.

AIDAN. Keep it light.

RUPERT. Get pictures.

AIDAN. Yes, get pictures, Charlotte, can we loan Sam a decent camera?

CHARLOTTE *nods, writes a note.* RUPERT *looks to* AIDAN.

RUPERT. Although. I mean. What's your girlfriend look like?

SAM *laughs.*

SAM. Well, this is really funny actually because I always say she reminds / me of –

RUPERT. You got a picture?

SAM. Oh. Yeah.

SAM *whips out his phone, finds a picture on it, gives the phone to* RUPERT. *Turns back to* AIDAN *as* RUPERT *examines the picture.*

It's not that I'm not very grateful for the opportunity.

RUPERT *makes a face and behind* SAM's *back mimes the words 'big girl' to* AIDAN. SAM *turns,* RUPERT *cuts the mime and hands the phone back to him.*

RUPERT. Beautiful. Bet you wouldn't like her when she's angry though.

SAM. What?

AIDAN. You came to me, Sam, you sat in that chair during interview and claimed you wanted to be a journalist, on this publication –

SAM. I did, I do –

AIDAN. And I was very clear about / what that entailed, we're –

SAM. I know –

AIDAN. – interested in your life, we need to know, / about your life –

SAM. Yeah, no I will, just –

AIDAN. What?

SAM. Just not about this one thing.

AIDAN. Why not?

SAM. Because –

AIDAN. I'm not trying to bully you, I just don't / understand the problem here –

SAM. Because it doesn't just belong to me, it belongs to her as well.

RUPERT. Stop talking about your herpes, Sam!

CHARLOTTE. Have you actually got an STD?

RUPERT. Fuck off.

CHARLOTTE. Just you go on about them all the time.

RUPERT. Actually, Charlotte, yeah, I think I've got like, AIDS, really really badly, cos I feel really tired and it stings when I wee. Actually I did get thrush in my mouth once from this girl so God knows what else she was harbouring. It worked in a Budgens.

CHARLOTTE. So not Pippa then.

RUPERT. No, not Pippa, God, I think her name was… I want to say Francesca? I mean, fuck, I hope not Pippa because I was hacking bareback that summer, if you catch my –

AIDAN *sharply shushes* RUPERT.

Rude.

AIDAN. Sam?

SAM. No I just feel. This is a, it's a private thing. For me and her. And it's, I mean I hope it's something that will only ever happen once to us. Which is. You can't say that about a lot of things. Can you, so I don't want anyone else to...

I mean, it's none of their business.

The public.

,

AIDAN *regards* SAM *for some moments.*

I'm really sorry. I could write a sort of general piece on –

AIDAN. I was really looking for a personal angle. Just that's our house style.

SAM. Okay, well... thank you, anyway. / For asking –

AIDAN *stands behind his desk, starts glancing through the layouts left there for his approval.*

AIDAN. No, I mean. I think it's a shame for you, cos it's an opportunity, isn't it, but if you don't want it then. Can I get some coffee please?

SAM *hesitates,* AIDAN *looks up at him.*

Sam?

SAM. Yeah.

SAM, *uncertain, grabs his jacket, leaves the room.*

AIDAN. Where are the gaming reviews?

CHARLOTTE *looks at* RUPERT.

RUPERT. I'm just polishing.

AIDAN. Well, go and polish then.

RUPERT *starts to leave.*

Actually, one minute.

RUPERT *turns back.*

RUPERT. Yes, boss?

AIDAN. Do you own such a thing as a pair of snow shoes?

RUPERT *gradually realises what he is implying.*

RUPERT. No. No. You can fuck off. You can fuck right off. I'm not going.

AIDAN. Pack a few books. Kendal Mint Cake. You may be some time.

RUPERT. This is discrimination!

AIDAN. Against what?

RUPERT. Against privilege! You only make me do this stuff because of my dad!

AIDAN. No, I do it because it's funny.

RUPERT. I'm not doing it. I'm just not. There is absolutely no way I'm freezing my bollocks off in the Arctic for your sadistic pleasure, no, I'm just not, you can fire me, I don't care, that's what a trust fund means, not having to take this sort of shit from people like you. There is no way, Aidan, I'm serious. Absolutely no way.

AIDAN. I'll let you do the Louise Mensch interview.

RUPERT (*panicked*). You have to let me do that anyway, that's my contact, Aidan, mate, don't fuck about, / I set that *up* – !

AIDAN. Charlotte, would you like to interview Louise Mensch?

CHARLOTTE. Wow, / thank you, I'd love to.

RUPERT. That's my contact – alright! All-fucking-right I'll go to the Arctic! Fuck's sake.

RUPERT *goes.* CHARLOTTE *smiles at* AIDAN, *gets up to follow* RUPERT.

AIDAN. Charlotte, wait a moment.

He crosses to her, shuts the door, they are standing very close, he looks at her.

You alright?

CHARLOTTE. Yeah.

She smiles.

You alright?

AIDAN *nods. Smiles.*

AIDAN. Bit tired.

CHARLOTTE. Yeah?

AIDAN. Didn't get much sleep last night.

CHARLOTTE. No?

AIDAN. What about you?

CHARLOTTE. What?

AIDAN. Did you get much?

CHARLOTTE. Sleep?

AIDAN. Yeah.

CHARLOTTE. No. But I'm that much younger than you though, aren't I? You don't need it the same way. Not when you're my age.

CHARLOTTE *smiles.* AIDAN, *amused. They look at each other… but this is not the time or place.* AIDAN *smiles. Gestures to a chair.*

AIDAN. Have a seat.

She sits. He sits in his desk chair.

I hope you don't think I'm interfering.

,

CHARLOTTE. Okay?

AIDAN. I've got you an interview.

CHARLOTTE. Who's it with this time? The naked yoga teacher?

AIDAN. No, *for* you. At the Indie.

,

CHARLOTTE. Are you – am I being fired?

AIDAN. No, no it's not – it's on the arts desk. I thought you might want a crack at it.

CHARLOTTE. Well. Yeah. But –

AIDAN. If you don't get it, there's still a job for you here. But I think you will get it.

CHARLOTTE. Okay. Thanks. I think. Sorry, just it does feel a bit like I'm getting fired –

AIDAN. I think you're very talented. I think you should succeed, on your own terms.

CHARLOTTE. But is my work not –

AIDAN. Your work is fine. Excellent even, within the parameters of – but do you actually want to be working here? In this environment?

,

CHARLOTTE. Can I be honest?

AIDAN. Please.

CHARLOTTE. I just like working. Getting paid. I got a First, you know.

AIDAN. I do.

CHARLOTTE. When I first came down to London I couldn't get arrested. I did three years of unpaid work placements and internships before I came here and that's fucking shit. Slave labour. And then I spent three months getting screamed at by Trinny and Susannah because I didn't know what a gilet was, and then I came here, which, yeah, it's not like my *dream* or anything but it's on my CV and I can pay my rent and yeah. I mean I actually – I haven't actually told you this but I am actually part of a group, a women's group and I sort of. Lie to them. About what I do. But the way things are, right now. All my mates are on benefits and I don't. I don't want that. So if it means I'm working, for money then –

Then I can deal with a few tits here and there.

RUPERT *runs in.*

RUPERT. Aidan.

AIDAN. I've told you, knock.

RUPERT. Carrie.

AIDAN. Who?

RUPERT *gestures to the photo of the Local Lovely on the wall.*

What about her?

RUPERT. I've got her father on the line.

AIDAN *and* CHARLOTTE *look at each other, smile.*

AIDAN. Uh-oh. Daddy's had a wake-up call.

They laugh.

RUPERT. Yeah. He says she didn't send the picture in.

AIDAN. No, of course – that's not how it works. The boyfriend takes the picture, the boyfriend sends it in.

RUPERT. Yeah but she doesn't know anything about it.

AIDAN. Right. But the consent forms would have been –

RUPERT. Yeah but her dad's saying that she's saying that she didn't sign any form –

AIDAN. Who dealt with this? Sam!

SAM *comes running in, in his jacket.*

SAM. I was just going, I forgot / my wallet –

AIDAN. Forget the coffee.

SAM. No, it won't take / a minute –

AIDAN. Do we have consent forms on file for the Local Lovely shots of Carrie?

SAM. Yeah. I think – yeah, do you want me to get them?

AIDAN. Who sent them in?

SAM. Her boyfriend. Think his name was Mark… something. I can get you the forms.

RUPERT. Yeah well, they're not together any more, and she didn't know he sent it in, and her dad's on the phone having a fucking aneurysm.

SAM. What? But the form – there's a photocopy of her passport –

RUPERT. The boyfriend must have forged it.

AIDAN. Or she's lying.

CHARLOTTE. Yeah but how did her dad find out? You wouldn't tell your dad.

RUPERT. He bought the magazine. She didn't even know she was in it till he saw it. He's pretty fucking raw about it. He's really, you know, really like…

AIDAN. What?

RUPERT. Northern. I tried to change my accent to make him like me more but I think he thought I was Jamaican.

AIDAN. Charlotte, go and field this, will you? Calm him down, use your – soft skills or / whatever they call –

CHARLOTTE *gets up but* RUPERT *pulls her back.*

RUPERT. No, wait, before you – there's something else.

,

AIDAN. What is it?

RUPERT. You're going to pop a bollock.

AIDAN. Rupert.

RUPERT *gestures to the print on the wall.*

RUPERT. She's fourteen.

,

SAM. What? What?

SAM *grasps for a chair.*

RUPERT. She is. She's fucking fourteen.

AIDAN. No. No, no, this is not –

RUPERT. The boyfriend's only fifteen.

AIDAN. What's a fifteen-year-old boy doing taking pictures like that of a young girl?

RUPERT. He thought she could win the competition.

AIDAN. It's disgusting.

RUPERT. She did win the competition.

AIDAN. Fuck. Fuck. No, it's alright.

,

RUPERT. Aidan?

AIDAN. Thinking, I'm thinking. What does he want?

RUPERT. Well, he probably wants his fourteen-year-old daughter to keep her bra on, but it's a bit late for that.

AIDAN. Charlotte? What do you think he wants?

CHARLOTTE. Your head on a stick?

AIDAN. Call the distributors. We need to pull this from the shelves.

CHARLOTTE. It's already been out three days.

AIDAN. Put a plaster on it. Get on to Online Content, get them to remove it from the site – no wait, first go and talk to him, do what you can to calm him down, then put him through. Fuck. I need to speak to a lawyer, get legal on the phone too.

   CHARLOTTE *goes*. SAM *is curled up on the floor, trying to breathe*.

SAM. I didn't know.

AIDAN. Come on, Sam, mate, get up, it's alright, it's okay.

SAM. I'm not – I feel so – am I a...

AIDAN. *No*.

SAM. No because she's – I mean I picked her – I found her the most – I spent hours looking at those – choosing which one to – like, if I close my eyes, I can still see her, that's in my brain now, that's actually stored in my – I can't erase that – I think I might. I think I might be a paedophile.

AIDAN. We can contain this. This can be contained.

   RUPERT *is looking at the print in wonder.*

RUPERT. I just can't believe it.

AIDAN. I know.

RUPERT. No but I mean, fourteen?

AIDAN. I know. I know.

RUPERT. Cos I'm not being funny but –

AIDAN. What?

RUPERT. Well, sorry, but have you seen the balcony on it?

,

AIDAN *stares at him.*

AIDAN. Get out.

RUPERT. What?

AIDAN. Seriously. I won't have that. What's wrong with you? She's a child, go and slam your head in a door.

RUPERT. Sorry. Sorry but why am I / getting the –

AIDAN. You were supposed to be watching Sam, mentoring his, you have to protect people, if you don't protect them this is what happens!

RUPERT. This is my fault? Mate, ten minutes ago you were basically rubbing yourself off to her, suddenly her tits are out of bounds? Talking to me / like that, what's your damage?

SAM *begins to groan loudly and continually.*

AIDAN. Of course they are, can you hear your – she's fourteen, my 'damage'? My damage is we're all about to get fired. My *damage* is you're a stuck-up little prick who thinks he's somehow / above what is happening here –

RUPERT *pulls out a Dictaphone from his pocket, switches it on, holds it in* AIDAN'*s face.*

RUPERT. Go on. Go on. Come on, mate, bring it on –

AIDAN. Get that out of my, what is that?

RUPERT. That's my fucking *dossier*, mate, you pushed me to this, I've worked here three fucking years, you take every chance you can to *shit* on me, from a *height*, just cos you think being born in a *coal hole* somehow gives you / the right to –

AIDAN *grabs the Dictaphone from* RUPERT, *throws it down.*

AIDAN. Get the fuck out of my office, you fucking Eton mess!

RUPERT *runs out as* CHARLOTTE *looks in.*

CHARLOTTE. Aidan, her father's on line two.

AIDAN. What's his name?

CHARLOTTE. Mr Bradshaw.

AIDAN. Mr Bradshaw. Where do they live?

CHARLOTTE. Manchester.

AIDAN. Will he come to London?

CHARLOTTE. I'll ask.

AIDAN. Great just just just (Sam, be quiet) just keep him talking, give me a, give me a moment to think, Sam, mate, please!

> CHARLOTTE *runs out.* SAM *stops groaning and starts to cry.*

Wait, Charlotte?

She runs in again.

I'm going to need you to book a, a hotel (shut up, Sam) somewhere really, a suite, just, blow the hospitality budget, do you mind?

CHARLOTTE. On it.

He gestures to the Liverpool FC flag on the wall.

AIDAN. Take the Liverpool flag down. And I need a photograph of a girl.

CHARLOTTE. Topless?

AIDAN. No, not – fucking hell, Charlotte, a fourteen-, a fifteen-year-old girl, with all her clothes on, in a garden or something, you know, bucolic. Call the picture library.

CHARLOTTE. Right.

AIDAN. Print it. Frame it. Put it on my desk.

CHARLOTTE. Okay.

AIDAN. Charlotte? I'm really sorry about this.

CHARLOTTE. I don't care.

AIDAN. No but. I'd hate for you to feel like I think this is okay.

CHARLOTTE. I don't.

AIDAN. It's not okay. This is not okay.

CHARLOTTE. I know. She's fucking fourteen.

AIDAN. This is not that sort of publication. We have nothing but the deepest respect for the women, the legally adult women, that we feature on our pages. I don't want you to feel uncomfortable working here.

CHARLOTTE. I don't feel uncomfortable.

AIDAN. Good. That's good.

CHARLOTTE. I just feel really sad.

They look at each other. CHARLOTTE *goes.* SAM *is still on the floor.*

AIDAN. Sam, get up.

SAM. I can't.

AIDAN. We didn't know.

SAM. I chose the photo.

AIDAN. These things happen. It's not your fault.

SAM. No but I think it, I think maybe it is, because, because…
,

AIDAN. Because what, Sam?

SAM. No I just. I did, I had a feeling, I had this, quite, a deep feeling of deep, unease, or

AIDAN. A feeling is not, there was no / reason for you to –

SAM. Dread. Actually, but I get that quite a lot, feelings of dread.

AIDAN. I'm sorry, but your feelings are not my priority / right now –

SAM. No but when I rang him up, the boyfriend, to tell him, she'd won, I had to, talk him through the consent form and his voice was a bit, croaky a bit sort of –

AIDAN. Shit. Okay. Shit.

SAM. Yeah, like breaking, but he said he had a cold, and after, he made a request. To be friends with me. On Facebook / and I –

AIDAN. You didn't, please tell me / you did not –

SAM. No, I thought it'd be, crossing a line and also, also I'd talked to him, on the phone and to be honest, I honestly thought –

AIDAN. Yes?

SAM. I thought he was a bit of a twat, sorry, so I didn't, accept his
– but I did have a look at his photos, and there was, this one
folder called 'Year 8 go to the Somme', and there were pictures
of him, with her, with Carrie or it looked like her standing in a
field of white gravestones, you know the ones like teeth with
poppies growing, and she was doing that 'V' sign, that peace
sign girls always do and, he was behind her sort of laughing,
sort of grabbing her, like –

He grabs, with two hands, where his breasts would be.

They were in uniform. School uniform, not.

And, and I had quite a big wave of it then, the dread, but. But then
I always get that when I think about the Somme because.

AIDAN. Sam. This isn't.

SAM. Because it's the Somme and what else can you think.

SAM leans over, hands on his knees, hyperventilating. AIDAN
rubs his back.

AIDAN. Because there's no way they can know this, is there? /
They don't know you saw those photographs.

SAM. When I was sixteen, me and my girlfriend Michelle Berry, we
watched a documentary about men who'd had their faces blown
off in Ypres. After the plastic surgery they looked worse, all these
boys deformed like little slitty mouths and trunks for noses and
I said to Michelle, would you love me if I looked like that?

AIDAN. Can we just focus / please?

SAM. And she said no. She said no, that fucking turns my stomach,
you'd rather be dead, wouldn't you?

AIDAN. Carrie was, she was in school uniform, and you didn't
think to –

SAM. No I just thought, it's old, it's just, people have their whole
lives on there, don't they?

AIDAN. No that's. Understandable. And there is a consent form.

SAM. There are photos of me from when I was thirteen on there,
I look like a foetus, I didn't think – it never crossed my mind
that she might not be –

AIDAN. The consent form has been signed.

SAM. Except now I can remember very clearly. There was, I did have –

AIDAN. What we are talking about is forgery –

SAM. There was this feeling of dread.

AIDAN. – that's what we're talking about.

SAM. Which eventually passed.

But she's a little girl. I picked a little girl. Out of nearly a thousand a little girl I picked a little girl –

AIDAN. You didn't know.

SAM. She likes *Twilight* and going to theme parks!

AIDAN. Don't mention this to anyone. It's alright, but don't.

SAM. Rona's going to kill me.

AIDAN. Are you listening to me?

CHARLOTTE (*off*). Aidan! He wants to talk to you, line two!

AIDAN. Here. Go and have a cigarette, get some air, wash your face.

AIDAN *takes out his cigarettes, offers them to* SAM.

SAM. I don't smoke.

AIDAN. It'll make you feel better, just – Rupert!

SAM. Cigarettes give you cancer. Heart disease.

AIDAN *shows him the packet*.

AIDAN. Not these ones, these just harm your unborn child, Rupert, get in here!

RUPERT *enters*. AIDAN *gestures to* SAM, *who is rocking back and forth*.

Take him to the pub, sort him out.

RUPERT. Say please.

AIDAN. Rupert, *please* stop being a fucking prick and help me out here.

RUPERT *pulls down his trousers and pants, drags his bare arse across* AIDAN's *desk and walks out again.*

You're – that is not – that's strike one!

RUPERT (*off*). Stick it up your arse, you fucking prole.

CHARLOTTE (*off*). Aidan! Line two!

AIDAN. Thank you, yes!

AIDAN *races round to the phone.*

SAM. Aidan?

AIDAN. What.

SAM. I'm having another one.

AIDAN. Right.

SAM. A feeling of dread.

AIDAN. I'm sorry, Sam. I have to take this.

SAM *nods. He stumbles out of the room.* AIDAN *takes a deep breath. Picks up the phone. Pushes a button.*

Mr Bradshaw.

Sudden black.

2.

The next day. MR BRADSHAW *in* AIDAN*'s office. He is holding a blue plastic bag with his book, reading glasses and some papers in it.* AIDAN *shakes his hand.*

AIDAN. You found it okay?

BRADSHAW. The taxi brought me right to the door.

AIDAN. You didn't have any problems?

BRADSHAW. No.

   CHARLOTTE *enters.*

AIDAN. This is Charlotte.

BRADSHAW. Hello, Charlotte.

CHARLOTTE. Great to meet you, Mr Bradshaw.

   She shakes his hand.

AIDAN. Can we get you anything, Mr Bradshaw? Tea? Coffee? Beer?

BRADSHAW. Bit early for that.

AIDAN. We can send out for anything you like. Have you eaten?

BRADSHAW. I had breakfast at the hotel.

AIDAN. Full English?

BRADSHAW. Continental.

AIDAN. It's on us, you know. Go for your life.

BRADSHAW. I have angina.

AIDAN. I'm sorry to hear that.

BRADSHAW. Have to watch my diet.

AIDAN. Lots of exercise.

BRADSHAW. I play golf sometimes.

AIDAN. A man after my own heart! What's your handicap, can
I ask?

BRADSHAW. Three.

AIDAN. Three! Mine's – mine's – much higher than that, okay.
Okay. Please. Take a seat.

MR BRADSHAW *sits. Looks round. His eyes land on the
dartboard.*

You like darts?

BRADSHAW. No.

AIDAN. Okay. We'll reimburse your travel costs, of course.
You've come from Manchester, yes?

AIDAN *sits behind his desk.*

BRADSHAW. That's right.

AIDAN. Great city. Great city. I'm a Man U fan myself actually.

BRADSHAW. I don't follow football.

AIDAN. No. Waste of time. Just talk to Charlotte, she'll take it
from petty cash. The train fare. And the taxis. Anything you
like. Wouldn't want you out of pocket.

BRADSHAW. That's very generous.

AIDAN. The hotel is alright?

BRADSHAW. It's very nice.

AIDAN. Good. No, I'm glad about that. I looked it up myself, of
course, but five stars, what does that even mean nowadays?

BRADSHAW. It's a very generous gesture.

AIDAN. Not at all, not at all. Least we could do. You sure you don't
want a tea, coffee? We can send out for / anything you like –

BRADSHAW. Can I have a glass of water?

AIDAN. Water sure. Still, sparkling?

BRADSHAW. Just tap is fine.

AIDAN. Charlotte, a water for Mr Bradshaw. Tap. You want ice?
Lemon?

BRADSHAW. No thank you.

AIDAN. No ice, no lemon.

CHARLOTTE *goes. Beat.*

She'll just be a moment.

A long pause.

BRADSHAW. I'd like to start by –

CHARLOTTE *returns with the water. She remains, standing, throughout.*

AIDAN. Here she is! One water. No ice, no lemon!

BRADSHAW. Thank you.

AIDAN. Cold enough?

MR BRADSHAW *nods.*

Because the tap runs a bit warm sometimes and it's a hot, I mean, this climate.

BRADSHAW. Yes.

AIDAN. This heat. In March. Bloody mental, isn't it? Is it like this up north?

BRADSHAW. No it's more. Cloudy.

AIDAN. It's a different world, isn't it?

CHARLOTTE. Can I get you anything else?

AIDAN. Would you like anything else, Mr Bradshaw?

BRADSHAW. The water is fine, thank you.

AIDAN. Charlotte's my lifeline. I wouldn't make it through the day without Charlotte. She went to Oxford, you know.

BRADSHAW. Congratulations.

AIDAN. Very clever girl, Charlotte. Sorry, Char, is that a bit patronising?

CHARLOTTE. No.

AIDAN. No, cos I'd hate to make you feel – Charlotte should be patronising me, Mr Bradshaw, / she's that –

BRADSHAW. Can we get down to it?

AIDAN. Sure. Sure.

   ,

   Shall I start or –

BRADSHAW. I'd like to –

AIDAN. No, right, fire away.

BRADSHAW. Okay. Well, obviously I'll be taking this to court.

   ,

AIDAN. Right.

BRADSHAW. That can't be a surprise to you.

AIDAN. No, well, obviously, you're angry. And –

BRADSHAW. I think what you've done is disgusting.

AIDAN. Uh-huh.

BRADSHAW. And I think that should be recognised, and someone
   should be called to account for that.

AIDAN. Absolutely, but –

BRADSHAW. You agree.

AIDAN. Oh I do. One hundred per cent. I've already fired the
   employee who was responsible for signing off on the picture.

BRADSHAW. Well, I'll have to take that on trust.

AIDAN. You can see his P45 if you like? Charlotte, can you show
   Mr Bradshaw a copy of Sam's P45?

   CHARLOTTE *goes to a filing cabinet, takes out a sheet of
   paper, shows* MR BRADSHAW. *He scans the paper.*

BRADSHAW. Good. Well. Good.

   ,

   That's a start.

AIDAN. We're taking this very seriously, Mr Bradshaw.

BRADSHAW. Should hope so.

AIDAN. But I have to tell you.

BRADSHAW. Should hope you were, taking it seriously, but what
   does that mean from people like you?

AIDAN. I have to tell you, you don't have a case.

BRADSHAW. I'm speaking with a solicitor.

AIDAN. You're wasting your money.

BRADSHAW. That's my business, isn't it, my money, my business, he's quietly confident.

AIDAN. Is he.

BRADSHAW. Yes, it's early days but he's quietly confident.

AIDAN. I'm sorry to. But we have good lawyers. Expensive lawyers, we have to. You're not special, I'm afraid. This sort of thing happens all the time. I've run this by our legal team, they're very clear on this, the legality of this, we are not liable. They laughed, actually – but I said to them, hold on, guys, come on, let's just have some human bloody compassion here, let's think about this man, this innocent man who's had to deal with the fact that his fourteen-year-old daughter has got herself in a situation whereby her body has been put on show for all to see I mean come on. Let's be sensitive to that. So we put our heads together, we crunched the numbers and what we want to do for you, for the worry, for the inconvenience, for the shock, is we want to offer you twenty-five thousand pounds.

'

BRADSHAW. I don't want any money.

AIDAN. I'm offering you twenty-five thousand pounds. You can take that now, we have the cheque already – show him the cheque, Charlotte.

CHARLOTTE *shows him the cheque.*

That's yours, that's signed off, you can bank it today.

BRADSHAW. I want it to be recognised that your magazine broke the law.

AIDAN. Tax-free.

BRADSHAW. It's not the money.

AIDAN. This is done. The magazine is in the shops, it's being bought as we speak, we can't change that. What we can change is the life of that girl, your daughter. We can give you enough money to see her through university. Enough money to get her on the property ladder. What we're talking about here is her future.

BRADSHAW. Her future is fine, thank you, she doesn't need you to finance her future.

AIDAN. Then what do you want? Because this won't even make it to trial. This is an open-and-shut case of forgery, a forgery perpetrated *against* us. You have no recourse here.

BRADSHAW. Yes but he said you'd say that.

'

AIDAN. I'm sorry, who?

BRADSHAW. Your employee, the black chappy.

AIDAN. I beg your pardon?

BRADSHAW. No, I'm not like that. It was just to distinguish, because I spoke to him, on the phone.

AIDAN. There's no one of that description working here.

BRADSHAW. He was West Indian or, Jamaican, he had a funny accent, I'm not an expert.

AIDAN *and* CHARLOTTE *look at each other.*

He rang me back, last night. He said if it didn't stand up in court I should go to the press. He said I could sell the story, that the papers would print this –

AIDAN. I'm afraid you've been the victim of a disgruntled employee.

BRADSHAW. And they'd print your photo, next to it, and your name, and that this would destroy you, and this magazine, and everyone would know what a grubby, diseased, perverted man you are. He said I could cut you out like a cancer.

'

AIDAN. He said that.

BRADSHAW. He did. He did say that and he has given me the, contact details, of a number of big editors at big newspapers, who he says would be very interested in this story.

AIDAN. And you intend to –

BRADSHAW. Yes.

AIDAN. And there's nothing I can –

BRADSHAW. No. I'm sorry but there it is.

,

AIDAN. Can I ask, I'm sorry, I know this is a very difficult thing to, but can I just ask how you became aware of the –

BRADSHAW. Indecent photographs of my child?

AIDAN. Exactly, because your daughter didn't tell you about this incident, did she? No, I don't blame her, it's an awkward conversation.

BRADSHAW. She's absolutely beside herself.

AIDAN. Is she? That's awful, but what I'm getting at is, this came to light because well, you saw it, didn't you?

BRADSHAW. I don't follow.

AIDAN. You saw it yourself. In the magazine. In the magazine which you bought.

BRADSHAW. Not a crime. Buying a magazine.

AIDAN. Of course it's not. You're entitled.

BRADSHAW. Just a magazine.

AIDAN. Just a magazine, absolutely, just a men's magazine that you, as a consumer, are completely entitled to buy. I mean, we're not living in bloody Abu Dhabi, are we!

BRADSHAW. I don't usually look at the pictures, if that's what you're getting at.

AIDAN. Sorry!

BRADSHAW. What?

AIDAN. No. Nothing.

AIDAN *picks up an old copy of* Doghouse, *leafs through it.*

BRADSHAW. I like the articles.

AIDAN. You like the – no, sorry, I'm just wondering which ones in – is it 'How to Upgrade Your Girlfriend'? Or 'Travels with my Erection'?

BRADSHAW. It's the articles, all of the, I read them on the bus or sometimes in the pub –

AIDAN. The articles are shit. No offence, Charlotte. But no one buys our publication principally for the literature. I think it's important to acknowledge that.

BRADSHAW. If you're suggesting –

AIDAN. I'm not suggesting anything except that you, like all of us here, appreciate certain types of images, that happen to be of beautiful girls in a state of undress.

BRADSHAW. Not young girls.

AIDAN. That's simply human. That's just aesthetics.

BRADSHAW. Not young girls.

AIDAN. No. But eighteen, nineteen, twenty. Young compared to us old codgers, eh, Mr Bradshaw!

BRADSHAW. Not fucking fourteen. Sorry.

AIDAN. No, of course. Four years older than fourteen.

BRADSHAW. Eighteen's different to fourteen.

AIDAN. But you can see our dilemma? Your daughter *looks* like an eighteen-year-old.

BRADSHAW. But she's not eighteen, is she, she's –

AIDAN. And she's got a boyfriend, with whom, I'm sorry to, but with whom I think we can take it as read she is having a, well, a sexual relationship?

BRADSHAW....

AIDAN. Okay, and that boyfriend has taken photographs of her, and sent them to us, on the premise, the deceptive premise that she is eighteen. That those breasts were the breasts of a legal adult.

BRADSHAW....

AIDAN. And to be honest, there was probably a moment, wasn't there, when your eyes went over this photograph and for a minute –

BRADSHAW. No.

AIDAN. No, come on, let's, in the spirit of – there would have been a moment, before you saw the face, before you, recognised the face and the feelings became more complicated, there would have been a moment where your feelings about this picture were in fact, very simple, because you're looking at this picture and what you're experiencing is –

BRADSHAW. No.

AIDAN. Very simply, very purely, an aesthetic experience of, what?

BRADSHAW. I didn't look.

AIDAN. Of very simply, very purely, a beautiful pair of firm, young breasts.

BRADSHAW. I didn't see.

AIDAN. I'm sorry, Mr Bradshaw, but that's a bit, I find that quite confusing because if you didn't look at the picture, in the magazine that you bought, how did you come to make the phone call and be sitting here?

BRADSHAW. A friend.

AIDAN. A friend.

BRADSHAW. That's right.

AIDAN. A friend recognised her.

BRADSHAW. Yes.

AIDAN. Good friend?

BRADSHAW. Yes.

AIDAN. Old friend?

BRADSHAW. Yes.

AIDAN. Recognised her… face, did he?

,

BRADSHAW. I'm not being funny, son, but you want to watch your fucking mouth.

,

AIDAN. I'm so sorry, Mr Bradshaw. That was callous of me. I was only trying to prove a point, I went too far, I should have known. I'm a father. I've got a daughter. Like you, Isobel, she's fifteen. See. She plays the flute.

He shows MR BRADSHAW *the framed photo on his desk. It's of a teenage girl in a garden. Looks at it himself, fondly.*

God knows how I'd feel if I was in your position right now. If…
Isobel was, doing that sort of – doesn't bear thinking about. The
idea that I just hadn't noticed that my fourteen-year-old child
was having a sexual relationship under my nose.

BRADSHAW. You can't watch them the whole time, can you?

AIDAN. I'll be honest with you, it would break me. It would
actually break me. Is that how you feel?

BRADSHAW. Yes.

AIDAN. Of course you do. You feel broken. At the idea that these
pictures even existed. If I'm honest, I think that's what's really
upset you here. The idea of another man's hands all over your
little girl's body. Right under your nose. Am I right?

BRADSHAW. This isn't the issue.

AIDAN. No. No. But actually it is, isn't it? It isn't and it is. A man's
hands on her body. And other men, men like you, looking at her.

BRADSHAW. The issue is that she is underage, and you published
without her consent.

AIDAN. But we didn't. We have the form. The form is signed.

BRADSHAW. Not by her.

AIDAN. But how were we to know that?

BRADSHAW. By checking, you have to check these –

AIDAN. But her lover forged the information. Her passport –

BRADSHAW. He's not her lover.

AIDAN. And the fact remains that she allowed herself to be
photographed, in this manner.

BRADSHAW. In private, she allowed it, / not –

AIDAN. Kids today, right! When I was fourteen, I was still
climbing trees! Going camping with my mates, hanging round
the shopping centre. Not covering myself with baby oil and
reclining on a waterbed so my lover could photograph me!

BRADSHAW. Don't use that – he's not her – he's taken advantage,
you've all, taken advantage of a young, of my – it's criminal.
You should be in prison, all of you –

AIDAN. Her lover is who should be in prison. He's the liable party here.

BRADSHAW. He is, he's already in – he stole a car, he was drunk, he's a fucking simpleton.

AIDAN. He's not good enough for her.

BRADSHAW. No he's bloody not, she's well shot.

AIDAN. But then who would be! I know there's not a man in the world good enough for my Isobel! A man laid a finger on her I'd, I'm talking about any sort of man here, he laid a finger on her, I'd set fire to him! You just want to wrap them in cotton wool, don't you? Wrap them up in cotton wool and keep them safe from harm.

BRADSHAW. Yes. Yes. Exactly.

,

AIDAN. Yes. Exactly. And twenty-five thousand pounds. Buys a lot of cotton wool.

MR BRADSHAW *stands*.

BRADSHAW. I don't want the money. Making me sick, going on about the bloody money! I didn't come for that, that's / not why I –

AIDAN. Then why did you come?

AIDAN *picks up a sheet of paper from his desk, scans it*.

BRADSHAW. Well, for one I came to, I came to, come here, and see, I wanted to see who, would, the face of the man who has ruined my girl's, dragged her through the, I wanted to see his, see your face and smash it in, smash it into the –

BRADSHAW *advances on* AIDAN.

AIDAN. Smash it into the what, Mr Bradshaw?

BRADSHAW. Just – smash it in, smash your bloody face in.

AIDAN. You're unemployed, is that correct?

BRADSHAW. What?

AIDAN. You're unemployed, is that correct?

,

BRADSHAW. I'm a jobseeker.

AIDAN. Without a job, is that correct?

BRADSHAW....

AIDAN. Yes, that's correct. You live off a jobseeker's allowance and your daughter permanently resides with your ex-wife?

BRADSHAW *sits*.

BRADSHAW. How do you know this?

AIDAN. Oh, we're very resourceful here. How many times do you see her in a month, your daughter, sorry, Carrie?

BRADSHAW. Depends, doesn't it?

AIDAN. But not on a daily basis?

BRADSHAW. No, because –

AIDAN. So we can say, largely speaking, on a week-by-week basis, you are largely absent from Carrie's life?

BRADSHAW. We speak, on the phone and we go to the cinema or for a walk.

AIDAN. Every week? Twice a month?

BRADSHAW. Yes. But we speak on the –

AIDAN. You see your daughter for a few hours, twice a month?

BRADSHAW. This is none of your business.

AIDAN. But it's not surprising then, is it?

BRADSHAW. What isn't?

,

AIDAN. Do you know what magazine I subscribe to? *New Scientist*. I love it! I am such a geek at heart, aren't I, Charlotte?

CHARLOTTE. Yeah.

AIDAN. Charlotte will tell you. I'm a total nerd. My idea of fun is sitting on my roof terrace, with a beer, reading *New Scientist* magazine.

I like this magazine because I never fail to find something of interest in it. Every time I read an issue of *New Scientist*, I understand the world that I am living in a little better.

He gets up, looks for a particular copy of the magazine in a pile, flicks through it.

Blows your mind, some of this stuff. Completely blows your –

He finds the article he is looking for, shows it to MR BRADSHAW.

– for example, look at this.

He waits while MR BRADSHAW *reads the article. After a moment,* AIDAN *turns to* CHARLOTTE.

What this particular article says, Charlotte, is that girls who grow up with absent fathers begin menstruating years earlier than girls whose fathers are present, as primary-care givers. That's just a scientific fact. Puberty starts at a young age when the father is not around.

I suppose this must be something very primal, very hard-wired, to do with abandoned young girls needing to be able to attract a mate at an earlier age, in order for that mate to provide the protection, the male influence that she should, by rights, be receiving from her father.

When the father is absent, she is endocrinally forced to become sexually available.

,

My Isobel's flat as a board, thank God!

MR BRADSHAW *offers the magazine back.*

You can keep that if you like. I subscribe electronically now –

MR BRADSHAW *drops the magazine on the floor.*

BRADSHAW. I'm sorry. I'm sorry, but what are you trying to –

AIDAN. Your daughter is very developed for a fourteen-year-old. I'm sorry to speak so bluntly, but the point is, those two facts, your… absence, as a father, and her, accelerated development, biologically speaking (which of course has led to this unfortunate mix-up in the first place), those two things are, well, they're linked, aren't they?

BRADSHAW. No, I don't accept that.

AIDAN. It's in the *New Scientist*, Mr Bradshaw. It's not up for debate. So you can understand, can't you? I mean, obviously the anger, the hurt you feel clouds any rational – but you can see how the mistake was made?

BRADSHAW. I don't accept this, what you're –

AIDAN. How we ourselves were deceived? And that you, as a father, your actions, your – I'm so sorry – your failures as a parent have biologically impacted on your daughter, to the extent that at fourteen years old, her body has given her commands, hormonal commands, that she had no choice but to obey.

BRADSHAW. We're very close, we speak on the phone, we read vampire stories.

AIDAN. This is a, it's a mistake, it's unfortunate, but it's done. It can't be undone.

BRADSHAW. We go to Alton Towers. She's my girl. She's my girl –

AIDAN. Shh. It's okay.

BRADSHAW. She was my little, you've taken that away, my little funny wriggly creature, you've stolen her, scabs on her knees and the brace on her teeth – I used to do metal-detecting, and she'd get me to run the metal detector over the brace and she'd just, scream with laughter when it beeped and make me do it again.

AIDAN. And she's got lovely teeth to show for it.

BRADSHAW. She had a special brush. To get in the, because when she ate, specially cabbage or, crisps, it would get stuck in the brace, and she'd do it on purpose, grin at me and this grin, it would, it would just cripple me, this grin, the food stuck in it, and you've taken it you've, spoilt it, the sound of her breathing, when she fell asleep on me on the sofa, we used to watch *Only Fools and Horses* videos, that was what we liked, and I wouldn't move all night just listen to her breath whistle through the metal till it was morning and her mum came to take her away again.

He breathes through his teeth so it whistles.

It was that sort of sound.

AIDAN. Was it?

BRADSHAW. Yes. It was like that.

,

AIDAN *looks at* CHARLOTTE. AIDAN *looks back at*
MR BRADSHAW.

AIDAN (*gentle*). And when you go home later? Will you tell
Carrie what happened here today?

,

Will you tell her you were offered twenty-five thousand pounds,
and that you turned it down because of what a decent bloke you
are?

,

And when you tell her, will she put her arms around you, her
thin, white arms covered in plastic bracelets, chipped blue nail
varnish, will she kiss you on that shining bald spot and say
'Well done, Daddy. You're my hero'? Is that what you think
she'll do?

,

MR BRADSHAW *stares at him*.

Or will she smile at you sadly, pity you, hate you even. And go
back to getting them out for the lads because what else has she
got to offer the world?

A pause. Then MR BRADSHAW *suddenly laughs*.

BRADSHAW. Bloody hell, what's it like being you? Do you even
like girls? Or is it water water everywhere and not a drop to
drink? (*To* CHARLOTTE.) Bet he's a right laugh, is he,
sweetheart, when he's not busy soliciting children?

AIDAN. WE DID NOT COERCE YOUR DAUGHTER. We did
not go round to her house, with a gun, threatening violence, we
don't go *out* with a *net* to find girls like Carrie. We don't have
to. Why? Because they queue up. They come to us.

He glances at CHARLOTTE. *She is standing very still, staring
straight ahead.*

That's what girls like Charlotte here don't like because it
doesn't fit, you see, it doesn't fit. It's not her idea of freedom,
I'm sorry, Charlotte, but that's what it is, it's a choice. It is a
freedom. So you see, don't you, Mr Bradshaw? The truth of it
is, we're only leading your daughter around the town square
because –

Well –

– in one way or another –

– she wants to be led.

CHARLOTTE *quietly steps out of the room.* BRADSHAW *registers this. Looks back at* AIDAN. *Beat.*

BRADSHAW. She seems a nice girl.

AIDAN. She's a very nice girl.

BRADSHAW. Yeah?

AIDAN. Yes.

BRADSHAW *stands, picks up the framed photograph from the desk, examines it.*

BRADSHAW. Must be nice working in an environment with girls like that about. I used to work in pest control, all I saw was wasps' nests and molehills all day.

MR BRADSHAW *replaces the framed photograph on the desk, takes his phone out, takes a picture of* AIDAN. AIDAN, *disquieted by this.*

AIDAN. Mr Bradshaw –

BRADSHAW. You think I just stepped off the boat, you can't tell me anything about my Carrie I don't already know. I would die for that girl, cos she's mine, but she's a pain in the arse. She's had more opportunity than anyone ever gave me. Teachers offering to coach her, books, trips, computers. Her mother's got her own business, killed herself so she could have French lessons, ballet, all that. She doesn't want for nothing except the things we won't give her. Took her to see Father Christmas at the Arndale Centre three years ago, he takes her on his knee, says 'And what do you want for Christmas?' She says 'I want a Labradoodle and a boob job,' I just about died of shame cos I drink with Graham sometimes, and he looked up at me, over his white beard and I could see him thinking 'What the bloody hell have I got on my lap?' Her friends are bright young women, don't give a toss about anything but shopping. But she's a nice-looking girl and she's worked out how to get on with it, that's not stupid, to my mind, that's canny. Her cousin's got four A levels, works in a Greggs. Speaks fluent German, all she gets for it is a discount on sausage plaits. I'm well aware that all you've done is give her the rope to hang herself with, but I don't want any part of it.

AIDAN. Then what do you want, Mr Bradshaw?

BRADSHAW. I want to destroy you. Not this magazine, but you, personally. I want every man or woman who ever thinks about doing your job to know there are men like me who will see to it that they are exterminated.

,

CHARLOTTE *steps back in quietly, closes the door.*

Did anyone ever tell you your daughter looks exactly like the girl in the orange-squash adverts?

He takes AIDAN*'s picture again.* AIDAN *looks at* CHARLOTTE.

AIDAN. No.

BRADSHAW. Well, she's the spit.

AIDAN. Mr Bradshaw –

BRADSHAW. I think we're done here, don't you?

AIDAN. Your bravado is embarrassing. You've already accepted free travel, accommodation, perks, spoils, whatever you / want to call it –

BRADSHAW. The least you could do.

AIDAN. The least we could do and we did it, but truth of it is your daughter is, sorry but there it is. She's fourteen. And this is what she wants.

BRADSHAW. I'm going to the papers, / I'm going to the BBC, my MP, I'm going to tell them, because this is, a man stands up, a man has to stand up, someone has to stop this because is this normal? Because it makes me feel like we're, the world is mentally ill, oi, I'm talking – I'M TALKING don't and – financial! Did you think I'd? Stuff your bloody cheque, keep it, you'll need it cos I'm going to put you on the streets, d'you hear me, I'm going to put you on the bloody streets! Oh, for –

AIDAN. We are the victims here. We have gone out of our way to take care of you, even in the knowledge that should this go to court you haven't got a chance in hell, we have considered your feelings, we have offered you financial, very generous financial restoration, for what? For your moral outrage? To compensate you for your failing to educate your child how / not to be an exhibitionist little tramp?

MR BRADSHAW *fumbles for his bag, knocks over his water.*

BRADSHAW. I'm going now.

AIDAN. Don't forget your plastic bag.

BRADSHAW. This is not finished.

AIDAN. Charlotte, show Mr Bradshaw out.

CHARLOTTE *starts to guide* MR BRADSHAW *to the door.*

CHARLOTTE. This way, Mr Bradshaw. That's it.

BRADSHAW. I am not finished.

AIDAN. I am. Goodbye.

AIDAN *sits down at his desk, busies himself with papers. Does not look up.*

BRADSHAW. You'll hear from my solicitor.

AIDAN. Looking forward to it, goodbye.

BRADSHAW. Don't – dismissing me, I won't be, / dismissed –

AIDAN. I said goodbye.

BRADSHAW. You can't throw me out.

AIDAN. I'm not. I mean I could, but I'm not.

AIDAN *finds the cheque on his desk, casually tears it up.*

BRADSHAW. I know what you're doing. I know what this is.

MR BRADSHAW *shakes* CHARLOTTE *off.*

AIDAN. This is nothing. This is simply the end of our meeting, and I have a busy morning ahead. If you want a car, we'll call you a car –

BRADSHAW. I don't want a car, I want –

AIDAN. Or the bus stop's over the road. Outside the chip shop, Charlotte will show you. Charlotte, show Mr Bradshaw to the chip shop. Don't let him go in though! He's got angina.

CHARLOTTE *tries to guide him out again, he shakes her off roughly.*

BRADSHAW. Wait.

Wait.

,

Forty.

CHARLOTTE. No.

AIDAN *looks up. Laughs.*

BRADSHAW. I won't beg, forty.

AIDAN. I'm offering you twenty-five.

BRADSHAW. Forty thousand pounds.

CHARLOTTE. Mr Bradshaw, please.

AIDAN. I'm offering you twenty-five.

BRADSHAW. Fifty.

AIDAN. I don't think you understand how this works.

BRADSHAW. Okay, forty.

AIDAN. Twenty.

BRADSHAW. You said twenty-five.

AIDAN. Fine.

BRADSHAW. You tore up the cheque.

AIDAN. We'll issue a new one. We'll post it today.

BRADSHAW. I can't trust that.

AIDAN. I have the papers already drawn up. I have the contract right here.

He goes to a desk drawer, takes out the contract. Puts it on the desk. MR BRADSHAW *cautiously flicks through it. Looks up.*

BRADSHAW. Can I think about it?

AIDAN. Take your time.

,

I mean, we do have to resolve this today but. Take as long as you want.

A long pause. As long as possible. MR BRADSHAW *makes a low, animal sound.*

BRADSHAW. Okay.

AIDAN. Okay?

BRADSHAW. Okay.

AIDAN. Okay! No, that's wonderful, that's really – that was tough, wasn't it? But we got there! I feel like Churchill at Versailles –

MR BRADSHAW *stares at* AIDAN. *His fist twitches.*

– you're doing the right thing. Isn't he, Charlotte?

CHARLOTTE....

AIDAN. You are, Charlotte agrees, you are doing the right thing. Charlotte belongs to a group, Mr Bradshaw, a women's group so you see she knows about these things, she cares about them, so you can take it from her, can't you?

AIDAN *offers him a pen. He takes it.* MR BRADSHAW *stares at the pen.*

BRADSHAW. This is, this is, filth. I feel, you're, you're a, I feel mucky.

AIDAN. Go back to the hotel. Your five-star hotel. Run yourself a bath. Wash it off.

BRADSHAW. Fuck you.

AIDAN. The papers, Charlotte.

    ,

Show Mr Bradshaw the papers please.

CHARLOTTE *shows* MR BRADSHAW *to the papers. He leans on the desk to sign them. As he does:*

Did they give you the room with the view over Regent's Park, like I asked?

BRADSHAW. Yes.

AIDAN. You can see the zoo from there, can't you? I like the bird enclosure. Do you like the bird enclosure, Charlotte?

,

Charlotte, I said do you like the bird enclosure?

,

CHARLOTTE. I like the monkeys.

AIDAN. Charlotte likes the monkeys. I like the bird enclosure. There's something for everyone at the zoo.

,

MR BRADSHAW *gives* AIDAN *his pen back.*

Thank you. Charlotte, give him the cheque.

CHARLOTTE *doesn't move.* AIDAN *fetches the cheque himself, hands it over.*

There you are. We'll call you a car.

BRADSHAW. I'll get the bus.

AIDAN. You don't want to be on public transport on a day like today. Not in this heat. Not in this climate.

BRADSHAW. I want to get the bus.

AIDAN. Okay. But before you. I just want to tell you. I don't expect you to believe me but.

My heart is breaking for you. Really. Honestly truly.

AIDAN *puts out a hand.* MR BRADSHAW *looks at it. Takes the hand, pulls* AIDAN *towards him, squeezing hard, he backs* AIDAN *towards the desk. He is surprisingly strong.*

BRADSHAW. I hope you rot in hell.

He spits in AIDAN'*s face.* AIDAN *manages to pull himself free, wipes his face. Retreats behind his desk.*

AIDAN. Okay.

MR BRADSHAW *goes to exit.* CHARLOTTE *catches him by the arm.*

CHARLOTTE. Mr Bradshaw?

Listen.

When she reaches eighteen.

When she's old enough to access that money.

Tell her.

Tell her to call us.

And if they still look like that.

We'll put her on the cover.

He stares at her for a moment. Nods at AIDAN.

BRADSHAW. He's too old for you.

BRADSHAW *goes.* CHARLOTTE *shuts the door.*

AIDAN. That was unnecessary.

CHARLOTTE. You can talk.

AIDAN. That was, necessary force, that was, the ends justify the means, I have to protect jobs. He could have damaged us, you do know that? I'm just doing my best, Char, this is, we're on the ropes as it is. Lawsuit like that, in this climate –

CHARLOTTE. I know. But I couldn't help it.

AIDAN. You don't think I'd actually talk to a man like that if I had any choice in the matter, do you? When he started on about the metal detector, I nearly broke then. I nearly actually broke.

CHARLOTTE. Embarrassing.

AIDAN. You didn't have to say that.

CHARLOTTE. I'm sorry.

AIDAN. It's okay just –

CHARLOTTE. I just felt like I had to.

AIDAN. I need a shower.

CHARLOTTE. It's just he reminded me of my dad.

AIDAN. Did he?

CHARLOTTE. Yeah.

,

AIDAN. No harm done.

CHARLOTTE. I fucking hate my dad.

AIDAN. I know.

He touches her arm. She pulls away, goes to exit.

Sweetheart?

,

She looks back at him from the doorway.

CHARLOTTE. What?

AIDAN. Nothing. What do you tell them?

CHARLOTTE. What?

AIDAN. Your group. Your women. What do you tell them you do?

CHARLOTTE. I say I'm an estate agent.

Sudden black.

3.

Nine months later. The editor's office of Electra *magazine, a weekly publication for young women. As before, the magazine's name in neon on the wall. Framed past covers. Healthy-looking women Photoshopped to perfection. There is a massage table to one side, strewn with products that the magazine is road-testing. Products are very important here.*

MIRANDA, *trendily but classically dressed in black. She sits on the edge of her desk, which holds papers, magazines, and a desktop Apple computer.* SAM *sits in a chair in front of her. In the background, the sound of heightened office chatter, female laughter, voices. They've knocked off early, the sounds of socialising rather than work. Maybe some faint strains of music.*

MIRANDA. It's a fun office.

SAM. Great.

MIRANDA. Bit crazy.

SAM. Yeah?

MIRANDA. Yeah. You don't have to be mad to work here – but actually you do a bit!

They laugh. MIRANDA *picks up a tube of moisturiser, moisturises her hands.*

We often go for drinks after work.

SAM. Uh-huh.

MIRANDA. Do you like going for drinks after work?

SAM. Sure.

MIRANDA. Then you'll fit right in.

An eruption of female voices, laughter, screams, off.

You can hear, can't you? Lot of fun. Lot of laughs. Lots of work too of course.

SAM. No, of course.

MIRANDA. We don't always start drinking at three o' clock on a Friday afternoon.

SAM. I did wonder about the champagne!

MIRANDA. Yeah, it's not funny actually. Meredith, our Beauty Ed. She's having a really rotten time of it.

SAM. I'm sorry to hear that.

MIRANDA. Yeah, it's very upsetting. We're all very upset. She's been in chemo four weeks now. And she had this gorgeous hair, I mean advert hair, and I don't want you to think she's a vain woman, because she's not, but losing the hair has definitely hit her hard. But so what we were going to do tonight, was we were all going to shave our heads, bit of a you know little act of sort of solidarity.

SAM. Wow, that's. That's so nice, what a lovely –

MIRANDA. Yeah well, that's just sort of the atmosphere here.

SAM. So it's Dutch courage is it?

MIRANDA. What?

SAM. The champagne. For the big… shave.

MIRANDA. Yeah well, actually, in the end what happened was, was factors came in to play so what we're doing instead is throwing her a little party instead, just for her, and we're all dressing up as our personal heroines, because that's what Meri is, to us.

SAM. So you're – sorry, you're dressing up as her?

MIRANDA. No, different women, like Beyoncé or Catwoman. Or Isabella and Angela both wanted to come as Marilyn Monroe so we've got two of them and Fabienne's being a sexy Joan of Arc!

SAM. She's French is she?

MIRANDA. Well, French-Canadian. We do talk very freely here, about female issues. If that bothers you –

SAM. It doesn't bother me.

MIRANDA. Great. The pay's quite minimal at first, I'm sorry about that.

SAM. That's fine.

MIRANDA. No but I do feel really bad about that. I feel so sorry for you guys, coming out of uni now. I mean the climate.

SAM. Yeah.

MIRANDA. You really just have to take what you can get, don't you? And the perks are good. We often have free samples of products. A lot of what we do here is about product. Shampoo, moisturiser, low-calorie salad dressing. Bags. Anti-wrinkle bras, that sort of thing. You can take them home and use them.

SAM. Brilliant.

MIRANDA. Or give them to your girlfriend probably.

SAM. Oh. No.

MIRANDA. Boyfriend, even.

SAM. No, I'm – I did have a girlfriend but. We're not together any more.

MIRANDA. What happened? You don't have to tell me.

SAM. Okay.

MIRANDA. I'm not allowed to ask actually.

SAM. Right.

MIRANDA (*Nazi accent*). 'But we have ways of making you talk!'

They laugh.

No, what's important is you mustn't feel pressurised.

A long pause.

SAM. No, it's just –

MIRANDA. Yeah?

SAM. It was just a combination of things that had, built up for a while and sort of, came to a head recently.

MIRANDA. Because of the fourteen-year-old girl?

,

SAM. Aidan told you.

MIRANDA. It's the industry, isn't it? Word gets about. He feels very bad apparently.

SAM. I know.

MIRANDA. But you did sign it off. And there had to be some accountability, didn't there? Don't worry, I completely understand. My heart goes out to you, it really does. Specially in this climate.

SAM. Yeah.

MIRANDA. Yeah. Yeah. Yeah. Her or you?

SAM. Sorry?

MIRANDA. Who broke it off?

SAM. Uh, it was a mutual, a mutual sort of, both of us –

MIRANDA. Well, that's what people always say, isn't it?

SAM. No but it actually was –

MIRANDA. But who said the words?

SAM. Both of us.

MIRANDA. Both of you said the words! At exactly the same time?

SAM. No but –

MIRANDA. So who said the words?

SAM. She did, it was her, but that / was after –

MIRANDA. That's all I wanted to know. Simple question, lovely!

SAM. No but I pushed her to, I basically forced her to, I've not been myself, I, I've found it quite difficult, the last nine months, I've found it quite difficult to process what, what – happened. And what that means.

,

MIRANDA. I don't think it means anything, does it?

SAM. Well, that was her opinion, but –

MIRANDA *moisturises her hands*.

MIRANDA. It makes me laugh, your generation, you always want to find the meaning! Thought we'd got past all that! Shit happens! What does shit mean? Nothing, it's just shit!

SAM. Well, it did mean something actually, it meant I lost my job, it meant I spent some time thinking I might be arrested, it meant I sort of changed, as a person which made her sort of, change around me, it meant that she's moved out and the furniture was all hers so I'm sleeping on the floor, in a bag and eating dinner off an inflatable stool. Shit. Sorry I'm sorry, I didn't mean to say shit, that's just. Inappropriate, can I start again?

,

MIRANDA. And that's it, is it? You and her?

SAM. The interview. Can I start again?

MIRANDA. Definitely dead in the water?

SAM. I'm still hopeful.

MIRANDA. Course you are. You'll sort it out. You're brilliant. You're a catch. I'd love to have you as my boyfriend!

SAM. Okay well. Thanks.

MIRANDA. I am seeing other people for the position.

,

SAM. I. Well, that's –

MIRANDA. For the job, I mean.

SAM. Oh! Of course. Yes.

MIRANDA. You thought I meant!

SAM. No, no I just –

MIRANDA. What, d'you think you're out of my league!

SAM. No of course not, I just –

MIRANDA. Menopausal old hag's coming on to me, argh!

SAM. No, no you're, you're very, I mean you're an attractive, / a very –

MIRANDA. So Friday night? You want to get a drink?

,

No, I was joking anyway, that's how we roll in this office, you'll get used to it. But I am seeing other people. I just want to make sure you understand that. It's not fair otherwise.

SAM. No I appreciate your honesty.

MIRANDA. And I hope you don't mind me saying but you're overqualified for the job.

SAM. Really?

MIRANDA. On paper. That surprises you? Aidan's given you an excellent reference. What do you think of Aidan?

SAM. He's been an inspiration to me. It's been a, privilege, an honour, to work with someone with such a, such a visionary attitude towards print journalism.

MIRANDA. He's a troglodyte.

SAM. Right.

MIRANDA. Don't you think?

SAM. Yes.

MIRANDA. You agree that he is a troglodyte?

SAM. A bit.

MIRANDA. I'm not completely naive, I do understand that C2DEs make different demands to ABC1s, I do understand that while he might belong in the latter he has to cater for the former so there's maybe some degree of, whatever, conflict for him there, and of course the market dictates content so I do understand, yeah, that that's just his job, that's the climate but still.

She takes a sip of water.

He's a piece-of-shit troglodyte.

,

MIRANDA *moisturises her hands.*

SAM. Well. I wouldn't be sitting here if it wasn't for Aidan, so.

MIRANDA. He didn't get you this interview.

SAM. But. When you called. You said I'd been recommended, I assumed he –

MIRANDA. Aidan wouldn't piss on you if you were on fire, lovely, one of our present employees recommended you.

She picks up SAM*'s CV, scans it.*

SAM. Who?

MIRANDA. What?

SAM. Who recommended me?

MIRANDA. You've got a very good degree.

SAM. One of your employees –

MIRANDA. From a good university.

SAM. Doesn't mean anything though, does it? These days.

MIRANDA. No. *Electra* is a largely female-run publication. That's just how it is. You won't mind being at the bottom of the ladder in an office full of women?

SAM. Of course not.

MIRANDA. This is just a question I ask all of our male applicants.

SAM. I won't mind.

MIRANDA. You might. Over time.

SAM. I won't.

MIRANDA. Others have.

SAM. I need this job. I really really need it.

MIRANDA. The climate.

SAM. I've been out of work nine months. I'm about to lose my flat.

A knock at the door.

MIRANDA. We're all about to lose our flats, lovely.
Metaphorically speaking, come in!

RUPERT *enters with a tray; a cafetière, two mugs, milk. His face is expressionless, but his eyes are very wide open, his forehead is stretched taut, plastic-looking. His eyebrows plucked into neat arches.* SAM *stands, surprised.*

It's Miss Havisham!

SAM. What?

MIRANDA. Your mysterious benefactor! When Rupert heard how Aidan treated you, he said, you've got to get this guy in, kept nagging and nagging us! He's your biggest fan!

SAM. Oh right. No it's just, sorry, I got – because Magwitch is the – in *Great Expectations*, Miss Havisham isn't Pip's benefactor, it's Abel Magwitch.

,

I mean he thinks it's her, but it's not.

,

It's Abel Magwitch.

,

The convict.

,

MIRANDA. Say thank you then!

SAM. Sorry, yes, thanks, Rupert. This was – really decent of you.

He shakes RUPERT's *hand.* RUPERT *makes a small sound. Tries to smile.*

MIRANDA. Poor sausage, he's been having a time of it. His dad cut him off. Just like that. Said it would be character-building, didn't he? You know who his dad is, yeah?

SAM. Um. Yeah.

MIRANDA. Yeah see, to me, that's child abuse. To bring a child up in a certain way then pull the rug like that. Anyway, what would I know, he's alright, aren't you, babe?

A small sound from RUPERT.

Yeah. Rupert's been with us five months now. The girls love him. Embarrassing, the way Aidan treated him, but that's Aidan. He's a stranger to human dignity.

RUPERT *makes a small sound.* MIRANDA *holds his face, examines it.*

Bloody hell, babe, how much did they give you?

Rupert had Botox injections this morning, Sam. It's this new feature we're doing, 'What it Feels Like for a Girl'. Each week we get a man, well, Rupert, to investigate a different aspect of normal female experience. He walked down Oxford Street in a miniskirt, he's had his eyebrows threaded, / he's –

SAM. Threaded.

MIRANDA. Threaded, exactly, he's been on the Atkins since October! Nothing but meat for two months, his breath stinks! It's just part of our feminist agenda.

SAM. Right. It's like 'Man Challenges'.

MIRANDA. No, it's nothing like that. He's off to Brazil next week, aren't you?

RUPERT *makes a small sound.*

SAM. Oh, wow. That sounds, is it Rio? I've always wanted to see Mardis Gras.

MIRANDA *laughs.*

MIRANDA. Different kind of Brazil, lovely. Rupes, your eyes are watering. Shazia's got some hankies, off you pop, babe.

RUPERT *makes a small sound, nods, exits.* MIRANDA *smiles at* SAM.

Black?

SAM. Sorry?

MIRANDA. Coffee?

MIRANDA *plunges the cafetière, pours two mugs out.*

SAM. Oh. Yes. Thanks.

MIRANDA. Milky one for me, naughty! No, it's skimmed, it's alright, do you mind if I just give you a trial exercise?

SAM. No. Of course.

MIRANDA. Lovely. Okay. I'm going to pop you down here.

She steers him up from his chair, seats him in her chair, behind the desk, leans over him to operate the mouse on her computer.

This is something we do with everyone, just open this up...

She clicks on a file.

Three JPEGs of three women.

SAM. Famous or normal?

The file is opened. She leans back.

MIRANDA. Famous, obviously. Beach shots. You know how to use Photoshop I take it?

SAM. Yeah.

MIRANDA. You know how to draw a red circle using Photoshop?

SAM. Well. Yeah.

MIRANDA. Good. Show me.

SAM. Sorry?

MIRANDA. This one. Show me on this one.

SAM. Show you what?

MIRANDA. Show me how you can put red circles around the flaws on this woman's body, and then caption them.

SAM. This woman?

MIRANDA. Yes.

SAM. Her?

MIRANDA. Yes.

SAM. Is this a trick?

MIRANDA. That would be a waste of my time.

SAM. No of course but –

MIRANDA. It's just a simple exercise we ask / everyone to –

SAM. She was number three in our 'Hottest Hollywood Honeys' last year.

MIRANDA. Our?

SAM. Sorry. *Doghouse*. She was number three.

MIRANDA. Okay well, we're not small boys drooling over girls that wouldn't look twice at us now, are we?

SAM. No.

MIRANDA. We're confident, modern, media-literate women between the ages of twenty-five and forty-five who earn upwards of twenty thousand pounds a year, aren't we?

SAM. Yes.

MIRANDA. We're leaders, thinkers, dreamers, shoppers, upscale ABC1 women with upscale ABC1 purchasing habits (we're not cold-calling Ginsters pasties for a problem-page sponsorship here). We care about achieving a two-state solution in the Middle East and we think female genital mutilation is totally out of order but actually you know that's not all we want to think about when we've had a long day and that's not a crime, is it?

SAM. No. Of course not.

MIRANDA. We love shoes! LOVE LOVE LOVE!

SAM. Who doesn't?

MIRANDA. You understand I'm speaking synecdochally here, don't you? That's what our readership is so that's what we are, yes?

SAM. Yes. But –

MIRANDA *moisturises her hands.*

MIRANDA. So that's how we have to think now, lovely. With our brains, not our genitalia. So, just have a little look at the picture and show me where her flaws are.

SAM. But she's perfect.

She sighs.

No, I don't mean – for normal women, for normal women she's a, a –

He thinks he is saying what she wants to hear.

She's an unhealthy role model – projecting, well, damaging standards of unnatural physical, you know. Perfection.

MIRANDA *laughs.*

MIRANDA. Sorry, lovely, does this look like the *Guardian*?

SAM. Sorry?

MIRANDA. She's not perfect.

SAM. No but. I mean, she's an actress. She's a film star. It's her job to be perfect.

MIRANDA. She's not perfect. Nobody is perfect. I'm not perfect. Our readers aren't perfect. I need you to point out the ways in which this woman is not perfect.

SAM. But she is.

MIRANDA. Have you got a girlfriend?

SAM. No. I told you –

MIRANDA. I'm sorry, you did, I was listening, I just, right now I'm a bit all over the place, I've got the painters in.

SAM. Sure.

'

MIRANDA. That wasn't a metaphor for my menstrual cycle, I do actually have people in, painting my flat and it means everything is covered in dust sheets and I can't find anything, it's a fucking nightmare, so I'm a bit distracted.

So you said, I'm sorry, you did, you did have a girlfriend but you don't any more.

SAM. Yes.

MIRANDA. And did you love her, this girlfriend?

'

Did you love her?

SAM. Yes.

MIRANDA. But properly. Properly love her. Not just because you're – what, twenty-one, twenty-two?

SAM. Twenty-four.

MIRANDA. Twenty-four, right, and even though she wasn't actually The One, as in you couldn't see her as a long-term life partner, the mother of your children, et cetera, for the time being she would do, you liked her enough so that when she said 'I love you' it was easier just to say it back than open up a whole hornet's nest of hurt feelings and recrimination, so you allowed her to think that you loved her, that this was actually going somewhere, and you allowed her to think this for, say, five-and-a-half years, even though during that time you were, well, not actively on the look-out for other, but certainly, entertaining other, certainly open to, certainly keeping, you know, one eye on the market, you don't mean you loved her in that way?

SAM. No.

MIRANDA. No!

She laughs.

Just me then!

MIRANDA *moisturises her hands.*

So you loved her? Properly loved her?

SAM. Yes.

MIRANDA. You found her sexually attractive?

SAM. Well, yeah. Of course. Very.

MIRANDA. But sometimes I expect, you noticed something, a little thing perhaps and that thing brought you up short, perhaps you noticed it when she was in the shower, washing herself, or maybe after sex, when you were lying in bed together naked.

SAM. I don't – I'm not sure what you're –

MIRANDA. A small thing. A mole that made you feel sick to look at it. Or a fungal infection in the toenails.

SAM. No. No I don't –

MIRANDA. Not even something as noticeable as that even, just maybe, a sagging, somewhere. Or a texture.

SAM. A texture?

MIRANDA. To the skin, a roughness or a dimpling.

SAM. Yeah well, that's just – skin, isn't it?

MIRANDA. And once you'd noticed it, you couldn't stop noticing it.

SAM. That's just what skin does.

MIRANDA. In effect I'm asking you to think about the moment when you realised that the girl you were in love with was not perfect. What the physical detail was that prompted that moment.

SAM. There wasn't. There wasn't a moment.

MIRANDA. For example. Have you noticed that one of my breasts is significantly larger than the other?

SAM. No.

MIRANDA. Don't kiss my arse.

SAM. I'm not.

MIRANDA. Sorry, but if you kiss my arse I don't want you in this
office. I'm sharing my physical flaw with you in the spirit of trust,
of understanding. I know it sounds a bit bloody Greenham
Common but that's what I've brought to this publication, as
editor. The idea that any dream, any desire, any anxiety is valid,
and chances are there's a woman out there who shares those
dreams. Those desires. Those anxieties. And they should be able
to read about those dreams, desires and anxieties in a magazine.
Electra is that magazine.

SAM. Miranda. Can I just?

MIRANDA. For example, sometimes I'll come in and Yolanthe
will be there, at her desk, and I'll just fire at her, straight away,
I'll just throw a thought at her, like 'I'm worried about ovarian
cancer,' or 'I'm really scared I'm boring in bed.' Or whatever,
and she'll catch that thought and run with it and three hours
later, I've got a thousand words of insightful, gently humorous
copy on my desk, and I publish that copy, and do you know
what happens? We get letters. We get emails. From women.
From the women who read our magazine and they say 'Thank
you. Thank you, *Electra*. I thought I was alone and then I read
an article in your magazine and I realised that I wasn't.'

SAM. All the letters at *Doghouse* were written by us.

MIRANDA. Yes well, that'll be part of your job here too. But
sometimes, we get actual letters, genuine letters from the
genuine public who are genuinely affected by what they read in
our pages.

SAM. How many?

MIRANDA. Well, it's a dying form of communication, the letter,
so. That's something we're working on too. Social media,
making it easier for real women to connect with us on their
terms. Because we want to give them what they want. If they
don't like something, we can change it. We can be anything they
want us to be.

But that starts with the honesty between us, here in this office. So what I'm doing, is I'm asking you to be honest, I'm asking you to share something personal with me, not for the sake of it, not because I'm especially interested, or because I'm a creepy old cow!

She laughs.

But because this office runs on healthy discourse, on a back-and-forth of shared vulnerabilities. Your ability to share your personal life with us is a litmus test of your commitment to the larger mission statement here. We want to connect. We want to provoke. We want to know what it was about your girlfriend that made you pause for a moment and wish she'd just get it together and sort it out. What was that thing?

SAM. I can't think of anything.

MIRANDA. You can.

SAM. Honestly I can't.

MIRANDA. One thing.

SAM. There wasn't.

MIRANDA. One thing about your girlfriend that physically repulsed you.

SAM. If there was something, I'd tell you but –

MIRANDA. Was your girlfriend a supermodel?

SAM. What?

MIRANDA. Was your girlfriend a supermodel?

SAM. No.

MIRANDA. Your girlfriend was not a supermodel.

SAM. No she was a. She was a chef, a / sous chef, she preps the veg –

MIRANDA. The only way she could have been physically flawless is if she was a supermodel, and you're saying to me she was not a supermodel, so a priori, there must be something.

And frankly, I've met Naomi Campbell, and even there, you wouldn't believe the crow's feet on it so.

She laughs.

Sorry. I'm being silly now, that's me, you'll get to know my sense of humour.

SAM. I can't think of anything. I'm sorry.

'

I'd like to be able to but. I loved her. I do love her. I actually can't right now deal with the idea that she's gone, that I might not ever wake up with her again, or go on holiday, because I think, sorry if this is a bit, but I think she's my soulmate. Stupid things like I love watching her eat, the way she eats is so... and she's funny and beautiful and. Brave and – like, we were on the Tube once, it was really crushed and there was this man, he wasn't like a tramp, he was in a suit, he had a briefcase, and she realised this man had taken his, you know – his... penis, out, through his flies, and he was sort of, rubbing it on her but the Tube was so packed you know, so people didn't notice, but when she saw it, she started shouting really loud, 'Look at his chipolata!', till everyone was looking at them – and you'd think that would be really embarrassing, wouldn't you? But I just loved that, she's just, fearless and what happened is the whole Tube, together, starting chanting at him, we're all chanting together at this man, 'Chipolata! Chipolata!' and I thought: I actually feel like part of something, you know? For the first time in my life I feel like I'm part of something, like we, people, together, can change things. People can stand up and stop shit things happening. Because that's what it was like when I was with her, I felt... connected to the world, and all the things the world could be if we were just, better versions of ourselves, so it's like that better world was sort of a shared space that existed in both our heads, so there was like a world, that we lived in together, that we'd helped to make and it was just for us, it was our secret. We had a secret and we lived in it together and –

– and that's it, really.

I just really –

– love her.

'

MIRANDA. Do you know what the irony of that story is, Sam?

SAM. Yes.

MIRANDA. No you don't. The irony of that story is that one day your ex-girlfriend will no longer be twenty-two and slim and smooth. There will come a day when builders don't whistle. When schoolboys at bus stops no longer whisper as she passes. When men on Tube trains no longer want to rub their genitalia on her.

And when that day comes, do you know how she'll feel?

SAM. She's not twenty-two. She's thirty.

MIRANDA. She'll feel like a fucking ghost.

A pause. MIRANDA *takes a sip of water.*

Thank you so much for coming in. We'll be in touch.

,

SAM. That's, is that it? Are we –

MIRANDA. That's it, lovely. Shazia will show you out.

MIRANDA *moisturises her hands.*

SAM. I've got lots of ideas.

SAM *picks up the portfolio case resting against his chair.*

I made a mood board, I don't know if you want to –

MIRANDA. We'll let you know.

SAM. Okay, when do you / think that'll –

MIRANDA. Like I said, I'm seeing other people.

MIRANDA *takes an electronic cigarette out of her bag, draws on it.* SAM *is on the verge of tears.*

SAM. But sort of, / ballpark –

MIRANDA. There's a process here, we have to / process you all –

SAM. Yeah I get that, I know, I'm just asking I'm just because I can't spend another weekend like that if I'm just going to get a phone call on Monday then just, you could just, couldn't you, because it would save us all, it would save us all –

SAM *starts to cry. He battles it fiercely.* MIRANDA *offers him her electronic cigarette.*

MIRANDA. It's just vapour.

SAM *takes it, gathers himself.* MIRANDA *withdraws to her desk, starts typing.*

You should do some more internships. Work experience, pad your CV out a bit.

SAM. I can't afford to work for free any more.

MIRANDA. Then you're not hungry enough.

MIRANDA *keeps typing.* SAM *watches her work.*

SAM. How do you do that?

MIRANDA. What?

SAM. Type and talk at the same time.

,

MIRANDA *keeps typing.*

MIRANDA. It took me a very long time to learn.

She glances at him, keeps typing.

You take care now, lovely.

SAM *leaves, closes the door behind him.* MIRANDA *stops typing. She stares at the screen, her fingers hovering over the keys. She breathes. A long time. Then brisk, she picks up her phone, presses an extension. Waits.*

Shazia, I'm just finishing up here. Yeah he's just come out, poor love. Meri alright? Yeah, is she yeah? Tell her I'll be out in a sec – yeah, that's right, 'Tonight Matthew...!' Okay. Okay, cheers, babe.

RUPERT *enters. He has changed into his costume, is dressed as Margaret Thatcher.* RUPERT *clears the coffee things and goes. As the door opens, we hear that the party beyond is getting going. Loud synthetic R&B/pop comes through the door.* MIRANDA *makes a face, shuts the door.*

She puts on some music through her computer. As she gets ready for the party she sings along to music, dances a little. She strips down to bra, knickers and tights. She applies a line of hair-removal cream to her top lip. She pulls on a tight pair of Spanx over her existing underwear. She runs a straightener through her hair. She reapplies her make-up. She pulls on a pair of exfoliating gloves and rubs at her upper arms. She moisturises

*her upper arms. She soaks some cotton wool in orange juice
and eats it. She unzips a garment bag hanging on the back of
her door, takes her costume out and puts it on: a neat-waisted
jacket with some corsetry and leg-of-mutton sleeves, but low-cut
in the front, a straight high-waisted Edwardian skirt. She slips
two chicken fillets into her bra. She pulls from under her desk a
plastic Waitrose bag. Takes out a pair of stilettos from it, puts
them on. She opens a drawer. Takes out a hammer. A knock on
the door.* MIRANDA *sighs. She goes to get the door,
remembers, quickly wipes the hair-removal cream off her lip
with a tissue. Another knock at the door.*

Come in!

SAM *is standing there. He doesn't speak or move.*

Oh. Hi, Sam.

*He doesn't move. As if the will to return to this room is a
delicate thing, and might be punctured by sudden movement.*

Can I help you?

,

You look a bit peaky, d'you want to… sit down, would you like
a glass of water?

,

Sam?

,

She turns off the music. SAM *stares straight ahead.*

Lovely?

,

Can I –

SAM. She had very large nipples.

,

MIRANDA. Did she?

SAM. Yes.

,

Yes they were very large.

,

MIRANDA. I've only got a minute.

SAM. Please.

> MIRANDA *nods. Guides* SAM *to her desk.*

MIRANDA. Sit down, lovely.

> *She pulls out her chair. He sits down in her chair behind the desk.*

You were saying.

> SAM *breathes. Looks down.*

SAM. Yes they were very large they were completely disproportionate to her actual breasts.

MIRANDA. And you didn't like that?

SAM. Well, I loved her so.

MIRANDA. But it repulsed you a little bit.

SAM. No, not repulsed, not –

MIRANDA. But if you could have changed that, that detail about her, you would?

> '

Lovely? If you could, you / probably –

SAM. I spose. Maybe. Yes. If I had to.

MIRANDA. I don't blame you. That sort of thing, if I saw her, your girlfriend, if I used the same gym as her and I saw her in the showers I would notice that too and, can I be honest with you, something like that would probably make me a bit queasy.

SAM. It wasn't a thing, / I liked her breasts, it wasn't like a –

MIRANDA. You know and of course she was probably crippled internally by the knowledge of her deformity.

SAM. She never mentioned it.

MIRANDA. Well, she wouldn't, lovely. Not to you. Seriously, you wouldn't believe the letters / we get on this topic.

SAM. She's quite confident.

MIRANDA. The emails. You know, the whole time you were making love, she was probably consumed by this. By the desperate hope that you hadn't noticed.

SAM. It really didn't affect her. Us.

MIRANDA. But it did affect you, lovely. You broke up. Because
you had noticed, hadn't you? You had / noticed.

SAM. Yes. But that's not why we –

MIRANDA. Yes?

SAM. Yes. / I noticed.

MIRANDA. Yes, men do. Men do notice these things because,
frankly, publications like the one you used to work for create a
climate. They create a climate, and she would have known that
– you said she was clever so trust me, she would've known that.

SAM. I hope not.

MIRANDA. No, lovely, she would.

,

She leans over him, clicks up the JPEGs on the screen again.

Look at the pictures. Examine the pictures. And do the same
thing you did to your girlfriend. Just notice.

SAM. Notice what. In particular?

MIRANDA. Anything. Wrinkles. Acne. Crow's feet. Orange-peel
skin. Thigh bulge. Sagging breasts. Flat chests. Double chins.
Facial hair. Bad boob jobs. Misaligned toes. Caesarean scars.
Visible pubic hair. Bingo wings. Varicose veins. Yellow teeth.
Tan lines. Muffin tops. Veined hands. Erect nipples. Bitten nails.
Black roots. It's there if you look for it. I'm just asking you to
look for it.

SAM. Erect nipples aren't really a flaw, as such, are they?

MIRANDA. Anything disgusting.

SAM. I mean, in cold water, in the sea, that's quite a natural –

MIRANDA. Anything unsightly.

SAM. We used to seek out erect nipples at *Doghouse*!

He laughs. She doesn't.

MIRANDA. Put a red circle around it. Caption it. Go on to the
next one.

Can you do that?

,

Lovely?

,

Do you think you can do that?

,

Sam? I'm sorry, but the girls are waiting, do you think you / can
–

SAM. Yes. I can do that.

,

MIRANDA. Go on then.

,

SAM *puts his hand on the mouse. He starts to work on the images. She stands behind him, scrutinising his work over his shoulder. She moisturises her hands.*

Good.

,

Very good.

,

This is great, Sam.

She keeps her eyes focused on the screen and his work as she reaches into her handbag, takes out a green, purple and white sash and slips it on.

This is wonderful.

,

This is exactly what I asked for.

Sudden black.

End.

CHIMERICA

Chimerica was first performed at the Almeida Theatre, London, on 20 May 2013 and transferred to the Harold Pinter Theatre, London, on 6 August 2013. The cast was as follows:

TESSA KENDRICK	Claudie Blakley
JOE SCHOFIELD	Stephen Campbell Moore
LIULI/JENNIFER	Elizabeth Chan
MICHELLE/MARY CHANG/ DENG	Vera Chok
DAVID BARKER/PETER ROURKE/PAUL KRAMER/ OFFICER HYTE	Karl Collins
FRANK HADLEY/HERB/ DRUG DEALER	Trevor Cooper
BARB/DOREEN/MARIA DUBIECKI/KATE/JUDY	Nancy Crane
MEL STANWYCK	Sean Gilder
FENG MEIHUI/MING XIAOLI	Sarah Lam
YOUNG ZHANG LIN/BENNY	Andrew Leung
ZHANG WEI/WANG PENGSI	David K.S. Tse
ZHANG LIN	Benedict Wong

Other parts were played by the company

Director	Lyndsey Turner
Set Design	Es Devlin
Lighting	Tim Lutkin
Sound	Carolyn Downing
Video	Finn Ross
Costume Design	Christina Cunningham
Movement Director	Georgina Lamb
Casting	Julia Horan CDG
Associate Director	James Yeatman
Assistant Director	Ng Choon Ping
Dialect Coach	Michaela Kennen
Mandarin Coach	Bobby Xinyue
Fight Director	Bret Yount

From 2nd September 2013, the following cast changes took place: Wendy Kweh replaced Vera Chok, Liz Sutherland replaced Sarah Lam.

Author's Note

It is a fact there was a Tank Man. It is a fact that photographs were taken of him. Beyond that, everything that transpires in the play is an imaginative leap.

This is especially the case with the journalist at the centre of the story, who is not based in any way upon a real person, alive or dead. Nor is he an amalgam of many of them. Joe is purely a fictional construct.

One of the reasons I felt able to take this liberty was that the image of the Tank Man we are familiar with in fact exists in a number of forms in common currency. There are at least six recognised versions, the play takes place in an imagined universe in which there are seven. In reality, Jeff Widener's is the most famous, and I'm very grateful to him for allowing us to use his version in the publicity for the play. Versions of the shot were also taken by Stuart Franklin, Charlie Cole, Arthur Tsang Hin Wah and Terril Jones. Again, Joe is not a cipher for any of these men.

The sources the play draws on are too vast to list here, but special mention must be made of both Don McCullin's book *Unreasonable Behaviour*, and *When China Rules the World* by Martin Jacques, works I found myself returning to again and again over the years, along with two of Susan Sontag's works, *On Photography* and *Regarding the Pain of Others*, and the PBS documentary on the Tank Man. Niall Ferguson coined the term 'Chimerica', I read it in his book *The Ascent of Money*. In writing Ming Xiaoli I found Anchee Min's recollections in both the Taschen book of Chinese Propaganda posters and her own book, *Red Azalea*, very useful.

The play took six years to write, and accrued debts to many people in that time. I would like to thank:

Jack Bradley for commissioning me to write the play, and both he and Dawn Walton for their guidance and support in its early incarnations. Ben Power for rescuing the play when it became homeless, and for his dramaturgy and encouragement. Rupert Goold and Robert Icke whose long-term faith in the play is the

reason it made it to the stage. Michael Attenborough and Lucy
Morrison for embracing the play with such passion, giving it a
home at the Almeida, and moving heaven and earth to ensure it had
the best possible production. Es Devlin and Chiara Stephenson,
whose wonderful designs greatly influenced the ideas and rhythms
of the final drafts. Robin Pharaoh, whose crash course in doing
business in China was invaluable. Choon Ping and Bobby Xinyue,
for their insights into Chinese language and culture, and their work
on the Mandarin translations. Stuart Glassborow. Ruru Li. John
Bashford and the students of LAMDA. Mel Kenyon, for her
tenacious support and incisive notes.

Most of all, Lyndsey Turner, for her rigorous dramaturgy,
dedication, hard graft and theatrical imagination. The debt the play
and I owe to her cannot be overestimated.

And always, Ed Hime.

L.K.

'Images transfix. Images anaesthetise.'

Susan Sontag

Characters

JOE SCHOFIELD
FRANK HADLEY
MEL STANWYCK
TESSA KENDRICK
ZHANG LIN
HERB
BARB
ZHANG WEI
DOREEN
PAUL KRAMER
WAITRESS
YOUNG ZHANG LIN
LIULI
MARIA DUBIECKI
DAVID BARKER
MARY CHANG
WOMAN IN STRIP CLUB
MICHELLE
OFFICER HYTE
DRUG DEALER
JENNIFER LEE
FENG MEIHUI
PENGSI
PENGSI'S WIFE
MING XIAOLI
KATE
DENG
PETER ROURKE
DAWN
JUDY
GUARD
BENNY
NURSE

Also CROWDS, WAITRESS, AIR HOSTESS, SOLDIERS,
COUPLE IN RESTAURANT, BARMAID, GIRL IN STRIP
CLUB, CAMERAMAN, GUARDS, GALLERY ASSISTANT

Note on Text

A forward slash (/) indicates an overlap in speech.

A dash (–) indicates an abrupt interruption.

Starred dialogue indicates two or more characters speaking
simultaneously.

Words in brackets are spoken aloud but given incidental status in
the line.

A comma on its own line indicates a beat.

A beat doesn't always mean a pause but can also denote a shift in
thought or energy. When lines are broken by a comma or a line
break, it's generally to convey a breath, a hesitation, a grasping for
words. Actors are welcome to ignore this.

Chinese Names

For those who do not know, it's worth noting that in Chinese names
the family or surname comes first, the given name second.
Traditionally a generation name, shared by family members of the
same generation, prefixes the given name.

So in Wang Pengfei, Wang is his surname, Peng his generation
name, which he shares with his brother, and Fei his given name.

Married women do not take their husband's surname but retain
their own.

ACT ONE

Scene One

*An image of a man with two shopping bags in a white shirt,
standing in front of a line of tanks. It is important he is Chinese…
but we cannot see this from the photograph. It is important it was
taken by an American… but we cannot know this simply by looking
at it. It is a photograph of heroism. It is a photograph of protest.
It is a photograph of one country by another country.*

Scene Two

*5th June, 1989. A hotel room overlooking Tiananmen Square.
Split scene,* JOE SCHOFIELD *(twenty) is speaking on the landline
phone with his editor,* FRANK *(forty-five), in the newsroom of
a New York newspaper.* JOE *has his camera slung round his neck,
watching the square below. It's around ten a.m. for* JOE, *eleven
p.m. for* FRANK.

FRANK. We're trying to get you on the ten fifteen out of Beijing
   tomorrow morning, but the airport's in chaos, the BBC might
   have a spot on their charter, did you meet Kate Adie yet?

JOE. No, I don't think so.

FRANK. She's a doll. Underneath, you sure you're not hurt?

JOE. I told you, I'm fine.

FRANK. I should've never sent you overseas, not so soon, not on
   your own, a situation like this, you need experience –

JOE. It was a student protest, didn't know it was gonna turn into a
   massacre, / did we?

FRANK. You're not even old enough to drink, chrissakes, what
   was I – don't go out again, okay? You stay there, in the hotel,
   just focus on getting those films back to us.

JOE. You gonna give me a front page, Frank?

FRANK. Yes, Joey, I think three hundred Chinese people being gunned down by their own government warrants a little more than a hundred words on page six, don't you?

JOE. It was more than that. I was down there, Frank, it was – three hundred, is that what they're saying? I don't know, but it was a lot more than –

JOE freezes, looking out of the window.

Oh fuck.

JOE moves to the window, crouches down, watching the man who has walked out.

FRANK. Joe?

JOE. Oh fuck, what is he doing? What is he – Jesus, get out of the road, you stupid –

JOE realises the man's actions are entirely intentional.

Oh my God.

FRANK. What's going on there? Joey, talk to me, what are you –

JOE. This guy. He has these… bags, like grocery bags and he… he just walked out in front of the tanks, and he's just standing there like – I mean, they could just run him right over. But he won't move, he *won't move*, he's, he's incredible, I wish you could…

JOE stares, transfixed, breathless. Unconsciously copies the Tank Man's movements, as if he were holding two shopping bags.

FRANK. Okay, Joe, don't worry, we're going to get you / out of –

JOE. Will you just shut up a second?

Frank, this guy, he's my age.

I think I'm about to watch him get shot.

Silence. JOE picks up his camera. Starts taking pictures.

FRANK. Well, did they do it yet?

JOE. No. Not yet. I'm gonna put down the phone for a second.

JOE lays the receiver down. Takes pictures. Suddenly, banging on the door.

(*Sotto.*) Shit.

He gently hangs up the phone.

FRANK. Joe? What's happening –

Lights down on FRANK. JOE *quickly winds his camera film to the end. Takes the film out, grabs more used films from his bag, empties dirty underwear out of a plastic bag, puts the films in, ties a tight knot. The phone rings.* JOE *makes a silent gesture at it, runs off, to the bathroom. The phone stops ringing. The banging ceases.* JOE *returns without the films. Listening. He goes to the door, puts his ear to it. Puts a new film in his camera, takes shot after shot of the carpet. Shaking with adrenaline. Gathers his camera bag, film. Pulls on his jacket. The phone rings, he dives for it, whispers:*

JOE. Frank?

Lights up on FRANK.

FRANK. Jesus, Joey, what are you trying to do to me!

JOE. There were fucking guards outside the door!

FRANK. Well, are they gone? Are you okay?

JOE. Yeah! My heart's fucking, like, you know?

FRANK. Yeah, what about your films?

JOE. I put them in the toilet tank –

FRANK. Good boy. You get a good frame of that guy?

JOE. I don't know, I was just spraying and praying, listen, Frank, I'll call you back –

FRANK. You will not call me back, you stay on this line, / you hear me!

JOE. Frank, I lost him, I / have to –

FRANK. What d'you mean, you lost him?

JOE. I mean I can't see him any more, I have to go down there, see if I can –

The door smashes open. A swarm of CHINESE SOLDIERS *enter.* JOE *drops the phone, stands, puts his hands up, backs away.*

FRANK. Joe? JOEY!

Lights down on FRANK *as the* SOLDIERS *shout at* JOE *in Mandarin.* JOE *remains frozen with his hands up as one* SOLDIER *steadily aims at him while another grabs his camera, takes the film out, throws the camera against the wall. Punches* JOE *in the stomach,* JOE *sinks to the floor. Chaos, violence, shouts in Chinese dialects as we travel forward twenty-three years to…*

Scene Three

A plane. JOE *is forty-two years old.* MEL STANWYCK (*forty-five*) *to his right,* TESSA KENDRICK (*English*) *to his left, reading a magazine, knocking back a cocktail.* JOE *and* MEL *have beers.*

MEL. It's a seven-star hotel, Joe. Why wouldn't you want to stay in a seven-star hotel?

JOE. I told you –

MEL. The website says it has an 'auspicious garden'.

JOE. Yeah but I haven't seen Zhang Lin / for –

MEL. Sure, right, your friend.

An AIR HOSTESS *enters.* TESS *speaks quietly to her, she takes* TESS*'s empty glass and goes.*

JOE. First time I went back to Beijing, Mel, I was so green you wouldn't believe it, Zhang Lin asks to meet me, offers to teach me Mandarin, he bought me a *suit* – I ever tell you that, he bought me a fucking Armani suit! We only have two days, I just want to hang out with him a little. And Frank won't sign off on your expenses, staying in a place like that.

JOE *shows* MEL *some photographs on his phone.*

MEL. Ah, I'm gonna haggle them down. I gotta spend two days in a Chinese plastics factory, I want a seven-star mini-bar to fall asleep with. (*Re: the photos.*) What's this?

JOE. Somalia.

MEL. You see Greg out there?

JOE. You didn't hear?

MEL. Dead?

JOE. Only from the waist down. Thirteen-year-old sniper.

MEL. Man, that sucks.

PILOT (*voice-over*). Welcome to Flight 9012 from New York JFK to Beijing, approximate landing time in fifteen hours.

> MEL *hands the phone back. The* HOSTESS *brings* TESS *a fresh drink.*

MEL (*sotto*). You know, that's her third since we sat down?

JOE (*looks, shrugs*). Complimentary, isn't it?

MEL. I'm just saying, fifteen hours next to Zelda Fitzgerald, could be a bumpy ride.

> TESS *looks at them.* MEL *immediately grins, friendly, raises his beer.*

Cheers!

> TESS *looks back down at her magazine.*

TESS. A pansy with hair on his chest.

JOE. Excuse me?

TESS (*turns a page*). That's how Zelda Fitzgerald described Hemingway.

> *Pause.* JOE *and* MEL *look at each other.*

MEL. Switch seats with me.

JOE. No. (*To* TESS.) So is this your first time in Beijing?

> *She looks up from the magazine. Smiles.*

TESS. Yes.

> *She looks back down at the magazine.* MEL *leans across* JOE.

MEL. Business? Pleasure?

TESS (*still reading*). Are you asking or offering?

MEL. Oh, honey, I'm no good for either, hey listen, I got a tip for you: *don't eat the chicken.*

JOE. Don't listen to – you can eat the chicken, the chicken / is fine –

MEL. The average piece of Chinese chicken, if you were an athlete, and you ate this chicken, I tell you the steroids they pump into that shit, you would fail a doping test.

JOE. Don't freak her out.

MEL. True story.

JOE. You speak Mandarin?

MEL. And don't eat the beef either, 'less you're sure that's what it is.

TESS *sighs, closes her magazine.*

TESS. I can read it a bit.

MEL. They have this *paint*, okay, they paint the chicken, so it looks like beef, but it ain't beef. It's the Lance Armstrong of the poultry world.

JOE. Mel, tell her about the place.

MEL. What place?

JOE. The place, our place, with the *bāozi* and the asshole waiter.

MEL. Oh my God, yeah, okay, you have to go to this restaurant –

JOE. Write it down for her.

MEL. I'll write it down for you, you like spicy food?

TESS. I have an asbestos mouth.

'

JOE. So what are you working on out there?

TESSA. I can't really say.

JOE. No, sure but?

'

JOE *and* MEL *look at her, expectant.*

TESS. I categorise people. By, well, anything, purchasing habits, political affiliations, sexual politics. I'm refining the profiling system that… this company uses, we have a Western model but it has to be adapted to the Chinese market.

MEL. Man, I hate this shit.

TESS. Excuse me?

MEL. This 'if you picked mostly As, you're a summer-wedding kind of girl!' *scheisse*, this insistence people are some… bovine breed, self-selecting themselves into bullshit constellations, tell me what my *future* is off the back of whether I take sugar or sweetener in my coffee. I know Democrats who play golf with Donald Trump, I've met dirt-poor Polish guys who can recite the works of Walt Whitman by heart, millionaires who don't know how to hold a fucking fish knife, you're going to a country of one *billion* people to make some nice boxes to put them in?

TESS *stares at him. Drains her drink.*

TESS. Okay, I've had, like, four of these now, but I'd say, let's see, I'd say you're probably a… Group O, with Group B characteristics.

MEL. Group O, Group O, I mean, what a *sad*, what a really *prosaic* way to view / your fellow humans!

TESS. Within that, I'd place you as an Anti-Materialist. At some point you were probably Urban Cool with a bit of Bright Young Thing, but I think that ship has sailed, don't you? You see your work as a career rather than a job, you identify yourself as international rather than national, you have no brand loyalty, your favourite movie is *Goodfellas*, you believe cannabis should be legalised, that contraception is a woman's responsibility, that little can be done to change life, that children should eat what they're given, and that real men don't cry.

'

I'm sorry, that's quite a limited, I'd need to ask a few more questions.

JOE. She's a witch.

MEL. No, okay, because okay a) that thing about the contraception is just plain wrong, because *I* had a vasectomy, b) *Goodfellas* isn't even in my top ten.

TESS. *Singin' in the Rain*?

MEL (*takes out his book*). I want to read now.

TESS. I know, it's awful, isn't it? No one likes to know to they're unremarkable. (*To the* HOSTESS, *her glass*.) 'Scuse me? When you get a sec? Cheers.

JOE. You gonna do me now?

TESS. I'm not a machine.

PILOT (*voice-over*). Ladies and gentlemen, we are now approaching take-off. The time is eight fifty-two p.m. local time and the skies are clear.

The plane starts take-off. TESS *shuts her eyes.*

TESS (*sotto*). Oh, shit. Oh, shit.

JOE (*grins*). What's the matter? It's only China, coming towards you at five hundred miles an hour.

TESS. Stop it!

JOE. Are you okay?

TESS. No. No, I'm scared we're going to crash and die.

JOE. Take-off's the worst. You'll be okay once we get in the air.

MEL. You know why they tell you to adopt the brace position? So your teeth don't smash and they can identify your body by your dental records.

JOE. Mel! Leave her alone, she's scared.

MEL. Aren't we all, sweetheart. Aren't we all, listen to this: '"I like to kiss very much," she said. "But I do not do it well."'

JOE *takes* TESS*'s hand.*

JOE. Hi. I'm Joe Schofield.

TESS. Tessa Kendrick.

MEL (*looking at the book cover*). This guy. This fucking guy.

JOE *and* TESS *look at each other as the plane soars into the sky.*

Scene Four

Tiananmen Square. A huge image of Mao. JOE *shakes* ZHANG LIN's *hand.*

JOE. So you haven't changed one bit.

ZHANG LIN. No, I have two more inches here – (*His stomach.*) It's rude of you not to notice.

JOE. That's the hotel I was staying in, over there. I can see my window –

ZHANG LIN. Yes, yes, I know, you told me. Fifteen up, four across, it's strange they haven't renamed it after you yet. Have you eaten?

JOE (*makes a face*). Factory cafeteria food.

ZHANG LIN. Right, your trip. Did it go well?

JOE. Terrifying. You ever been to one of those places?

ZHANG LIN. My brother's a foreman in a factory, just outside Beijing.

JOE. Mel spoke with these women, they were earning like fifty dollars a month, working fifteen-hour days, sleeping on the floor –

ZHANG LIN. Zhang Wei started like that. The one he works in now, it's much better. He earns a thousand dollars a month. His son's been studying at Harvard.

JOE. I just, I felt so guilty –

ZHANG LIN. Yes, you're right, we all blame you too. I think I read a book once, about the *Mayflower*, crossing the Atlantic. Apparently this was quite terrifying also. You've heard o this ship?

JOE. Yes, Zhang Lin, I have heard of the *Mayflower*. But they're not travelling to a whole new country –

ZHANG LIN. Of course they are. It just occupies the same part of the atlas as the old one.

'

JOE. You should've been a lawyer, you know that?

ZHANG LIN. I like teaching. I teach Crazy English now, did I tell you?

JOE. Yeah, you said, I thought it was like a metaphor or –

ZHANG LIN. No! I take my students to the roof, we yell English into the sky. You shout, you learn. Conquer English to make China stronger! It's got a sort of fascist aspect but it helps with conjugation. You look tired, Joe.

JOE. Thanks.

HERB, *an American tourist from Boston, approaches* JOE, *spying a white face.*

HERB. 'Scuse me, you're American, right?

JOE. *Désolé, monsieur, je ne peux pas vous aider.*

ZHANG LIN. Joe, behave yourself. My friend is having a joke with you, sir.

HERB. Huh. So I was wondering if you could take picture of me and my wife?

BARBARA *comes over.* HERB *puts his arm round her. Passes his camera to* JOE.

ZHANG LIN. You're honoured. This man is one of the world's finest photographers.

HERB. Barb, you hear that? You famous?

JOE. No, / Zhang Lin, don't –

HERB. No, I mean you in galleries?

JOE. You ever heard of the Museum of Modern Art?

HERB. Sure. Sure I have –

JOE. Well, sir, they never heard of me. You want to shuffle in a little bit?

HERB *and* BARBARA *shuffle closer to each other.*

HERB. Barb's a history nut. She wanted to see Tiananmen Square. Right, hon?

BARBARA. I like to expand my horizons. Pull in your gut Herb.

HERB *sucks in as* JOE *takes the picture.* JOE *grins. Hands the camera back.*

JOE. You guys have a good trip now.

The tourists go. JOE *takes up his camera, turns back towards the hotel, taking pictures.* ZHANG LIN *looks, nervous, at a casually dressed* MAN *holding an umbrella as he wanders closer.*

ZHANG LIN. Joe.

JOE. Can't believe they haven't pulled it down yet. Every time I come back, I get surprised it's still here.

ZHANG LIN. Joe, put your camera away.

JOE *goes to take a picture. The* MAN *opens his umbrella in front of* JOE, *obscuring his shot.* JOE *looks at* ZHANG LIN. *Understands. He puts his camera down.*

You want to drop your bag at the apartment, get a beer?

JOE. Sure.

ZHANG LIN. My brother is coming round. He wants to buy us dinner.

Lights up on ZHANG LIN's *apartment.* ZHANG LIN *and* JOE *with beers. They've been drinking a while, and are muffled against the cold. Every time* ZHANG LIN *takes a sip of his beer, he clinks his bottle with* JOE's. JOE *stands, acting out the scenario he describes.*

JOE. So okay I'm standing there, my editor's on the phone having a fucking conniption, and the Tank Man just walks out, he just walks right out, and my heart is / just –

ZHANG LIN. I know, you said, then the guards come, and you put the films in the toilet / cistern –

JOE. Right, and then he's just... gone, he's just. This guy. Zhang Lin, this fucking guy, I can't, I still can't... because how does a guy like that just disappear? To come out of a massacre, to have the fucking wherewithal to, to, to stand up, to say this is wrong. This is wrong and, and someone has to say so.

He is lost in thought, captivated by his memory for a moment.

ZHANG LIN. Didn't you meet Nelson Mandela?

JOE. People always say that but, it's a politician's job to stick his head over the parapet, they have a whole fucking machine around them, what did the Tank Man have? Nothing. Plastic grocery bags, is all.

ZHANG LIN. And you only have a camera.

JOE. Sure, and in twenty-three years I never did a thing that came close to half a minute of that man's life. Ah, shut up, Joe.

,

You know, you should come to the States.

ZHANG LIN *laughs*.

I'm serious.

ZHANG LIN. It's not possible.

JOE. Sure it is. Cos of the green card you mean? Listen, you know how many Upper East Side assholes want their spawn speaking Mandarin? You could clean up.

ZHANG LIN. Clean up what? Public bathrooms?

JOE. Very funny. I mean it, you should come to New York.

ZHANG LIN. What for? Starbucks? Cockroaches? I can get both of those here.

JOE. Sure, and Walmart and McDonald's, / I know, it's turning into America, but –

ZHANG LIN. You have Walmart. Why are we not allowed Walmart?

JOE. Sure, but seriously, this country –

ZHANG LIN. This country owns you. You don't get to lecture us any more. I subscribe to this website, for my teaching, it sends me new American slangs and phrases each week. You know what phrase I learnt this week? Fiscal cliff.

JOE. I just, I remember being here in 1989 and there was hope, on the streets, in the square, people, like… imagining a, a, a future or whatever / and where has that –

ZHANG LIN. I don't want to talk about this.

JOE. Yeah I know, only I saw it too –

ZHANG LIN. Yes, up in your hotel room, taking pictures. Behind your camera, plane ticket in your pocket, I was there. Down there, in the square, bullets the size of your thumb, yes? Dumdums, they open up inside you. They turned the lights out on us –

JOE. Zhang Lin –

ZHANG LIN. They turned the lights out to scare us and then… I don't know. Maybe they did not come back on again for me.

ZHANG LIN *holds up his empty bottle.*

Shall we have another?

ZHANG LIN *takes another beer from the fridge. Searches for the opener.*

JOE. I'm sorry. It's just. I don't know, you type Tiananmen Square into a search engine here, you get three pages from the Tourist Board, the Tank Man is dead in more ways than one, and what for?

ZHANG LIN. The Tank Man? What are you – you want to reduce this to one man? There were a hundred-thousand of us, Joe, we're not dead! We just made some choices you don't approve of! Have you seen the opener? I can't – anyway, who told you that?

JOE. What?

ZHANG LIN. Who told you the Tank Man was dead?

JOE. I don't know. I just assumed… sorry, what are you – ?

ZHANG LIN (*searching*). Things have feet in this apartment.

JOE. So where is he?

ZHANG LIN. I don't know.

JOE. No but what are you saying?

ZHANG LIN. Nothing. I've been drinking all afternoon, I shouldn't have.

ZHANG LIN *gives up searching. Tries to take the cap off with his teeth.*

JOE. Shouldn't have what?

Don't do that – you'll break a tooth.

ZHANG LIN (*laughs*). You can't handle the tooth!

JOE. Are you saying he's / still alive?

ZHANG LIN. You know this movie?

JOE. But, but is that what you're saying?

ZHANG LIN. Jack Nicholson, / it's pretty good –

JOE. Oh my God. Oh my God, is he alive? Zhang Lin, please, you have to –

ZHANG LIN. It was twenty-three years ago.

JOE. Yes or no?

ZHANG LIN. Joe.

JOE. Yes or no?

,

ZHANG LIN. He went to America, I believe. New York, probably. Many of the organisers went to New York. After. By August, most of my friends were gone.

JOE. You never mentioned this before.

ZHANG LIN. You never asked.

JOE. Did you know him?

ZHANG LIN. No. Not well.

JOE. But – so you know his name?

ZHANG LIN. What does it matter? You know he probably *is* dead, he probably went to America and got hit by a Cadillac on Route 66.

JOE. Do you know his name?

ZHANG LIN. Or his heart exploded, from all the beef.

JOE. What is his name?

ZHANG LIN. He'll have changed it. He'll be called Brian Simpson / or –

JOE. So just tell me. Please.

,

ZHANG LIN. I think it was Wang Pengfei.

JOE. Wang Pengfei?

,

ZHANG LIN. Anyway, don't you have other things to worry about? Your country, it's – what's the word? Fucked?

,

JOE. Okay: you can have my vote. Seeing as how you don't care about getting your own. You pick my candidate and I'll vote for them.

ZHANG LIN. Okay. I like Clinton.

JOE. Okay, well you're four years late for that. Or four years early, I don't know, she just resigned. You got two choices, Obama or Romney.

ZHANG LIN. Romney hates the Chinese. I like Clinton.

JOE. Why?

ZHANG WEI (*off, Mandarin*). Is he here? Is he here?

ZHANG LIN. Women hold up half the sky.

ZHANG WEI *enters, with two shopping bags. He wears neon Nikes, is delighted to see* JOE.

ZHANG WEI (*Mandarin*). He's here!

ZHANG WEI *dumps his bags. Shakes* JOE*'s hand enthusiastically.*

ZHANG LIN. This is my brother, Zhang Wei. (*Mandarin.*) This is Joe. He just gave me his vote.

ZHANG WEI (*Mandarin*). An election every four years. No wonder they can't get anything done.

ZHANG LIN. He speaks Mandarin.

JOE (*halting Mandarin*). Not very well.

ZHANG WEI (*English*). My boy. My boy Benny. Harvard University.

He gestures to ZHANG LIN, *'tell him'.*

ZHANG LIN. My nephew, he just graduated from Harvard. Very smart kid. He's about to move to New York, we'd appreciate it if you looked him up.

JOE. Sure, I'll do that.

ZHANG WEI. My shoes, tell him about my shoes, Dog-face.

ZHANG LIN. He bought Zhang Wei those ugly shoes.

JOE. Very nice, what did he call you? Just then, he called you dog... something –

ZHANG LIN. Oh. Dog-face, yes. It's a family name. When babies are small, we give them a milk name, words that make them sound disgusting. To stop the King of Hell stealing them away. Mine got stuck to me. Let's eat.

JOE. Where are we going?

ZHANG LIN. Somewhere very special, I've been saving up, it's called 'the Pizza Hut'.

JOE. Oh. Sure. Great. I just need to make a call.

Beat. Then ZHANG LIN *cracks up. To* ZHANG WEI, *in Mandarin.*

ZHANG LIN. Did you see his face!

ZHANG WEI. What did you say?

ZHANG LIN. I told him we were going to Pizza Hut!

ZHANG WEI *laughs. Gestures to one of his bags, which contains a spare pair of shoes.*

ZHANG WEI. Just let me change my shoes.

Scene Five

Lights up on FRANK *in his Manhattan corner office, with* JOE *and* MEL. *He is the editor of a major American newspaper. In his late fifties, beautifully dressed. A large, impressive desk.*

FRANK. The Tank Man is dead, you don't think your friend is, let's be civil about this, you don't think he's maybe you know feeding you a crock / of –

JOE. No, but look at how it actually happened:

> DOREEN, FRANK*'s PA enters.* JOE *positions two chairs and a pot plant to represent the tanks.*

> Okay so here, these are the tanks, and this… (*Looks around, sees* DOREEN.) Doreen, can I grab you for a second? Thanks, okay, so – yeah, hold those, that's great, so Doreen is the Tank Man. And she's, he's holding his ground…

> JOE *hands her* FRANK's *briefcase and a backpack to represent the Tank Man's shopping bags.*

> Then this guy on a bicycle comes gliding out. Mel, you wanna –

> MEL *acts the man on the bicycle. He does a jerky circling motion with his right leg.*

> What the hell are you doing?

MEL. I'm on a bicycle!

JOE. Then there's a couple other guys – (*Points to himself.*) They motion him, they guide him… into the crowd… and he disappears.

> JOE *guides* DOREEN *behind a drape. She disappears. Beat.* JOE *looks to* FRANK. *Ta-dah.*

FRANK. Into the arms of the Public Security Bureau where he's shot at point-blank range in the head and thrown in an unmarked mass grave.

JOE. No, but the PSB, they're violent, you know? They bend your arm back, they rough you up. I don't know. The bicycle, the way they… guided him. It was gentle.

DOREEN (*from behind drape*). Are we done here?

JOE. Sure. Thanks, Doreen.

DOREEN *comes out from behind the drape. Puts the file on* FRANK*'s desk.*

DOREEN. I need you to sign off on these.

FRANK. Can it wait? I'm kind of in the middle of... (*To* JOE.) just, give me a minute, okay?

FRANK *quickly opens the file, zips through the couple of contact sheets within.*

No... no... definitely not... maybe this one if you crop it, give me a pen –

DOREEN *hands him a pen, he circles the shot.* JOE*'s eye is caught, he moves closer to the desk.*

JOE. What's this? Are these mine?

FRANK. We can't use this. / (*To* DOREEN.) See if Dina got anything we can go with.

JOE. Frank, this is two weeks' work, why can't you –

FRANK *picks up his cup of coffee and takes a gulp.*

FRANK. Don't play the ingénue with me, you know why, this is not the first time we have had this conversation, they are, without exception, ghoulish. / (This is cold. Doreen? This is cold.)

He hands DOREEN *the cup. She exits.* MEL *rests his feet against* FRANK*'s desk.*

JOE. If it bleeds, it leads, what about this one?

FRANK. No faces. (*To* MEL.) Feet.

MEL *takes his feet off the woodwork.*

JOE. It's a corpse you can hardly see / his –

FRANK. *No faces.* (*Hollering off.*) / Doreen? Coffee? Thank you!

MEL. Leave it, Joe. Butter him up, you said, not / nail his balls to the wall.

FRANK. And my pill, I forgot to take my pill! Why am I being buttered?

DOREEN *comes in with a cup of coffee and a pill.* FRANK *takes the pill. As* DOREEN *leaves:*

DOREEN. You have a meeting with the lawyers at ten.

JOE. So, okay. We were thinking, we do a special. On China. Its history, its future. The centrepiece is a shot of the Tank Man, sitting in Central Park. Alive and well.

FRANK. And where do I put this special?

JOE. In the magazine.

FRANK. That's not really the kind of story sits well / in the –

JOE. It used to be.

FRANK. And I used to have a prostate, shit happens. Lifestyle and leisure, that's the magazine's remit, and this is hypothetical anyway. It's a great idea, boys, I can see why you're excited, but I don't have the money for this.

JOE. You don't have money for one of the great heroes in twentieth-century history?

FRANK. I don't even have the money for our food critic to review anywhere you don't BYOB. Our revenues are down eleven per cent, what am I supposed to do, keep you on payroll, file your expenses, while the pair of you gallivant round the / city –

MEL. 'Gallivant'?

FRANK. Gallivant, jaunt, roam the fucking city in the middle of an election, looking for a man who may or may not still be alive who most likely isn't too excited about having years of anonymity blown by two self-serving newsmen looking to make a scoop.

JOE. You're not interested in China?

FRANK. You know, this dime-store rhetoric is not flattering to you. I *am* interested in China, because I am not a fucking idiot. I just *sent* you to China, didn't I?

JOE. Okay, so why can't we –

FRANK. Because that's not a story about China, that's about America; American jobs, American money, and right now, unless you can give me an angle like that on the Tank Man, I can't let you pursue it, not in the middle of campaign season.

MEL. Okay, so what about this: we take a whole 'God Bless America', 'land of the free home of the et cetera' angle on this, just a balls-out good news story. Cos they're opening their newspapers every day, and it's real wrist-slitting stuff, our national industry getting screwed over by China undercutting them at every turn –

FRANK (*guarded*). Okay, so this is interesting.

MEL. Right, because, because, okay this is what it is, because this man, strike that, this *hero*, brave, noble, persecuted, he escapes from this supposedly superior country, and where does he go? Not London, not Mumbai, not Moscow. He comes to New York. To the States. Because so what if our economy's stalling, our power is ebbing, one thing won't change: America means freedom, it means rights, set down in a constitution, to speak, to protest, to be an *individual*, it is, and will always be, the homeland of heroes.

,

FRANK. See, that wasn't so hard, was it?

MEL. Is that a yes?

DOREEN *enters with a computer printout. Hands it to* FRANK, *he doesn't look at it.*

FRANK. Don't get too excited. I still want you guys in Denver for the first debate, and you still have to find one Chinese guy in a city of – how many Chinese guys, Doreen?

DOREEN. Three hundred thousand. Give or take.

MEL. We got a name, right, Joe?

JOE. Wang Pengfei.

DOREEN. And he's dead.

,

I searched the archive. This is by Paul Kramer, he was our Beijing correspondent at the time, the headline is quite unequivocal.

FRANK. It can't be *quite* unequivocal, Doreen, it is or it isn't unequivocal, there is no scale.

DOREEN. I accessed the New York and the London *Times* too. They're all in agreement.

,

FRANK. Well. Okay. Thanks, Doreen, that… simplifies things a little.

DOREEN (*shrugs*). I mean it was right there, you only have to type it in…

DOREEN *leaves, grumbling, sotto. A pause.*

FRANK. Go to Colorado. There will be other Tank Men.

MEL. But –

FRANK. Mel, don't you have a deadline?

MEL *goes.* JOE *turns to follow him.* FRANK *rubs his eyes.*

Just a minute – Joe? You never think… you're what, like forty? You never think it might be / time to –

JOE. This? Again?

FRANK. – settle down. Put down some roots. I mean, you don't even have a car!

JOE. I live in New York, why do I need a / car –

FRANK. I don't know. So you'll have somewhere to sleep when I fire you, why does anyone have a car? It's freedom.

JOE (*smiles*). You know, there are these three new phrases they just started using in China: *Fang nu. Che nu. Hai nu.* Car slave. House slave. Child slave.

Pause. DOREEN *enters.*

FRANK. You are a very bleak man, anyone ever tell you that? Look, I'm not saying, but there's something to be said for – starting something. Raising a family, some nurse hands you a bundle of, whatever, right there that's, that's *growth*, that's hope in your hands. Watching your kids sleep, wiping the shit from their mouths, taking care of something that's a, it is, it's a… it's a wonderful thing. Y'know?

JOE. Yeah. You're right. Your au pair was a very lucky woman.

,

FRANK. The Tank Man. It's probably for the best. I once spent two months chasing Bob Dylan round Europe for an interview. Closest I got was a flash of sheepskin in Kraków airport. Hippies and heroes, slippery fuckers.

JOE. Never knew you were a Dylan fan, Frank.

FRANK. Only the electric stuff.

JOE goes. FRANK turns to DOREEN.

I'm sorry about before. It was impolite of me to correct you like that.

DOREEN surveys him, inscrutable. FRANK looks at his coffee.

You spat in this, didn't you?

DOREEN. You have Senator Collins on line four.

Scene Six

JOE sits with PAUL KRAMER in Prospect Park, Brooklyn. A pram, a baby crying inside. PAUL softly rocks the pram.

PAUL. The *Herald*? I haven't worked there for twenty years – (*To the baby.*) Good girl.

JOE. I know. But you were their Beijing correspondent in 1989, right? I found this in the archive, / 'Tank Man Executed' –

As JOE shows him a printout, PAUL picks up a soft toy, dances it at the child in the pram.

PAUL. Shhh… sweetie… look at Mr Biggins! Look at him! Look at him! Look at him! Look at him! Look at him! Look at him!

,

Look / at him --

JOE. How about I get us a coffee?

PAUL. We don't have much time. We have a play date at twelve. Let me see that.

He puts his hand out of the pram. Pulls it back. Wipes his hand on his trousers. Grins at JOE.

'I measure my life in baby puke.'

PAUL *takes the article and scans it. The baby gurgles contentedly.*

Yeah, I didn't write this.

JOE. That's your name right there. Paul Kramer.

PAUL. I know. I can read. I didn't write this.

JOE. And you can be sure of that?

PAUL. There are two split infinitives here.

JOE. So someone else wrote it and put your name on it? Was that common?

PAUL. Sure. I was their man out in Beijing. You have a story like this, it looks better if it's written by the correspondent.

JOE. So who was it written by?

PAUL. Some news monkey. Happens all the time. Used to, anyway, you take a trip out of town, go to the dentist or whatever, doesn't matter who's covering you, the sub will stick your name on what they wrote. Looks better that way.

JOE. You never thought about this before?

PAUL. I never saw it before. I was out there. I didn't read the thing, I just wrote for it.

JOE. So if you didn't write this…

PAUL. Do I think it's true?

,

I don't know. After Tiananmen, that whole summer – they were arresting people all over the place. There were public executions on the TV every day, people who'd embarrassed the government a hell of a lot less than this guy.

JOE. So he had to have been executed, right?

PAUL. No, that's not what I'm – hey hey hey no. No! Emily don't chew that, come on –

He reaches into the pram, pulls something free of baby teeth.

(*Proud.*) She's a biter. She already has three teeth. You got any?

JOE. Teeth?

PAUL. Kids.

JOE. No.

PAUL. I'm sorry.

JOE. That's okay.

PAUL. Look, you have to think about the psychology of the thing. It's a gibbet society. They like to make examples. You don't roll a load of tanks into a public square and start firing just for the hell of it, you know? You do it to scare the hell out of people, scare them out of ever trying anything like that again. But you don't make an example if no one's watching. If the PSB had him they'd make damn sure every TV viewer in China *saw* when that bullet went into his skull. And I watched a lot of TV. And I never saw that.

But that's just my opinion.

JOE. No, thank you.

PAUL. No problem. This is for a story?

JOE. I'm trying to find him.

PAUL. Who?

JOE. The Tank Man.

PAUL (*laughs*). Right.

He sees JOE *is serious.*

Oh, okay, well. Good luck with that. I'm gonna have to go change this one.

JOE. No problem. Thanks for your time.

PAUL *exits, pushing the pram.* JOE *takes out his cellphone, dials.*

It's me. Put down the burrito, Mel.

,

Lucky guess, brush your teeth. I'm coming over.

Scene Seven

A Chinese restaurant in Manhattan. TESS and JOE at a table in the dining area. A Chinese couple sit behind them, waiting for carry-out. Young and in love.

TESS. So he's not dead?

JOE. Not according to Paul Kramer.

TESS. So that place you told me about, the restaurant in Beijing? It's gone.

JOE. What? No way, I love that place. Maybe you just got / lost or –

TESS. They built a car park on it. I was starving, I ended up in a KFC, there were all these people taking business dinners in there.

JOE. God, tell me about it, it's so depressing. Beijing's so Westernised.

TESS. I don't think so.

JOE. You kidding me? You flew seven thousand miles, had fried chicken for dinner.

TESS. No I didn't. I had a tree fungus salad and shrimp rice.

A WAITRESS brings their food. TESS looks over it.

(*Mandarin.*) Excuse me, we ordered some lotus root? *Xie xie.*
,

I totally did that to show off to you, so you better be impressed.

JOE. I am. I mean, your accent's terrible, but – no, that's. You're a fast learner huh?

TESS. I've been studying every night since I got back from Beijing. I've been taking a lot of caffeine pills. My piss is orange. I have to admit something terrible.

JOE. Worse than your piss being orange?

TESS. I googled you.

JOE. I googled you too.

TESS. Why?

JOE. Why d'you think? What's 'netball', and why do they make you wear such short skirts to play it?

,

TESS. Joe, this isn't a date. This is really just a, it's a professional thing – I was just looking at your work to, the company I'm working for, it's a credit card and we want an image, to print on it and I, I thought you might be our man and.

JOE. No, sure, don't worry about it.

TESS. It's really awkward now, isn't it?

JOE. No, not at all.

TESS. I don't think it helps to pretend it's not. Why did you think it was a date?

JOE. Why d'you *think* I thought it was a date?

,

TESS. The plane?

JOE. Yes the plane.

TESS. Oh, wow. I mean, no, but it's not exactly. I mean what would we tell our kids?

JOE. Well, I don't want kids so there's no universe in which that'd be a problem.

TESS. No, I wasn't, they're rhetorical kids, I was just. I'm sorry, I should've –

JOE. Like I said, don't worry about it.

Pause. TESS *takes out a folder. A printout from the folder. Slides it over to* JOE.

TESS. So this is the image we'd like to use. And this is the offer we're prepared to make:

She writes a number on a napkin, slides it over. JOE *doesn't look at it.*

JOE. What the hell are you doing, I feel like I'm in a high-school play or something.

TESS. This would be a good thing for you.

JOE. Well thanks, but you can't have it.

TESS. Why not?

JOE. For a fucking credit card? Why d'you think?

TESS. Don't you want to know how many zeroes there are?

JOE. That river, those kids are fishing in? It's one of the most polluted rivers in the world, the rate of childhood mortality in that village is –

TESS. It's a great image.

JOE. Sure, only there's a fucking ceiling on how much money I want to make from a bunch of kids dying in a developing country, okay?

A beat. Trying to lighten the mood:

TESS. So you'd be okay with giving it to us for free, then?

JOE *stares at her. The* WAITRESS *brings the lotus root, goes.* JOE *dishes out food. They eat in silence. Presently:*

Can I ask about your Tiananmen pictures?

JOE. You have to be fucking kidding me.

,

TESS. Oh God no, I *wouldn't* – bloody hell, it was a massacre, Joe. I'm not going to put it on a fucking credit card, nobody would – I just, I can't believe you took that.

JOE. There's like six other guys got that same shot. I was just lucky I had a hotel room window in the right place.

TESS. God, you must've been a baby, I had it on my wall when I was a student. Next to Che Guevara and The Stone Roses.

JOE. Uh-uh.

They eat in silence. Until:

TESS. Do you really not know what netball is? / I mean –

JOE. No, I know what it is. It's a very slow, boring version of basketball.

TESS. Well, I think you'll find actually, when it's played at a high level –

JOE. Can you pass the soy?

    ,

TESS. You're really angry, aren't you?

JOE. Not at all.

TESS. Because I slept with you once and came here without
    intending to do it again?

JOE. No, because I missed a chance to do my laundry to have
    dinner with Ayn Rand. And because actually, bull*shit* you didn't
    have that intention –

    JOE *takes his iPhone out, scrolls through it. Finds the email he
    is looking for.*

TESS. I think I was pretty clear in my –

JOE. 'Dear Joe, can I buy you dinner? I promise not to have sex
    with you.'

TESS. I'm not sure how I could have been more explicit.

JOE. Are you fucking kidding me? That's the least subtle email
    I ever got in my whole life!

TESS. Oh God, yes! Grant me the privilege of being the next
    woman Joe Schofield resents having to go home to!

JOE. Sweetheart, I've resented far better women than you.

TESS. Well, you seemed quite fond of me when your arse was
    banging against the hand dryer of a 747.

JOE. Hey, listen, that was an act of charity, I've been cavity-
    searched on the border of Russia, it was more fun.

TESS. You are so full of shit.

JOE. I don't have to like someone to have sex with them. You were
    scared, I just met you, what am I gonna do, assassinate your
    character at thirty-thousand feet?

TESS. Mel gave it his best shot.

JOE. Yeah well, Mel's an asshole.

TESS. Yeah well, at least he's honest about that –

JOE. You know, I have better things to do / than –

TESS. Oh yes, like what? Hunting the human thimble?

JOE *stands, pulls on his coat, his scarf.*

Yes, please, do just walk away in the middle of a – no, that's, that's really mature. We should do this again some time.

JOE *tosses down money, leaves. The* WAITRESS *comes, takes the money. Stares at* TESS.

He started it.

WAITRESS. We need this table. More people.

Scene Eight

ZHANG LIN*'s apartment.* ZHANG LIN *drinks beer. The TV on.* ZHANG WEI *gestures to the TV.*

ZHANG WEI (*Mandarin*). Turn it off.

ZHANG LIN (*Mandarin*). What do you want?

ZHANG WEI (*Mandarin*). I want to talk to you.

ZHANG LIN (*Mandarin*). Just let me finish this.

ZHANG WEI. Turn it off.

ZHANG LIN. I'm relaxing.

ZHANG WEI. You couldn't let me pay for dinner? You couldn't let me have that?

ZHANG LIN. He wanted to. I was too tired for an argument.

ZHANG WEI. I invited *him*. Doesn't he know anything? Anyway that's it, isn't it? That's a big opportunity wasted, completely wasted –

ZHANG LIN. You don't need to do all that with Joe, he'll look after Benny anyway.

ZHANG WEI. Makes me look presumptuous, though, doesn't it? A man like that, why should he bother with Benny?

ZHANG LIN. Because I asked him to. I've done enough for him over the years. He knows that.

ZHANG WEI. It's alright for you, you've got connections –

ZHANG LIN. What connections?

ZHANG WEI. Teaching officials and their fat-arsed kids how to speak American! But I / don't –

ZHANG LIN. I taught your fat-arsed kid too –

ZHANG WEI. I told you, you don't talk about Benny like that, okay!

ZHANG LIN. What? It's good to be fat, he's strong.

ZHANG WEI. Anyway, he's got some trainer now he's in the States, makes him run round the park with weights tied to his ankles, look at this, he looks like Huang Xiaoming –

> ZHANG WEI *takes out a picture from his wallet, shows* ZHANG LIN, *proud. On the other side of the wall,* MING XIAOLI *starts to cough.*

ZHANG LIN. Maybe if Huang Xiaoming was playing someone who'd been in a terrible car accident.

ZHANG WEI. No need for that. You've got a spiteful tongue, you know that? No wonder I'm the only person you talk to.

ZHANG LIN. I speak to Ming Da Ma all the time.

ZHANG WEI. That nosy Party cat from next door! That's who you talk to?

ZHANG LIN. And my students.

ZHANG WEI. Standing on rooftops! Shouting into the wind, 'I am crazy! I succeed!', or chatting about TV shows with a dying old woman, is that a life?

ZHANG LIN. She's not dying.

ZHANG WEI. Is that / success?

ZHANG LIN. She's not dying, / why would you –

ZHANG WEI. Are you stupid? Can you hear that?

> ZHANG LIN *turns off the TV. Listens to* MING XIAOLI *cough. Beat.*

ZHANG LIN. She has a chest infection.

ZHANG WEI. *You* have a chest infection, the infection is here – (*Points at his heart.*) Look at this place. You make good money, you can't buy some new curtains, a lamp? You could at least get a new TV, you spend enough time sitting in front of it, watching – what is this shit?

ZHANG LIN. I believe it's called *I Want To Become a Stewardess*.

ZHANG WEI. Turn it off.

ZHANG WEI *reaches for the remote*, ZHANG LIN *bats him away. Beat.*

If she was alive, she'd be so ashamed of you.

,

If you're not sleeping again, / then –

ZHANG LIN. I sleep fine.

,

ZHANG WEI. I'll call you this week. Don't ignore me.

ZHANG WEI *exits*. ZHANG LIN *turns the TV to the AV channel. The opening music and narration of* Casablanca. *Pause. Then he opens his laptop, plugs a microphone into it. Mutes the TV. Drains his beer. Hits a control on the laptop, picks up the microphone, speaks into it.*

ZHANG LIN. The 1st of May. 1989. It was hot. I think it was hot. I was eighteen years old. We were both eighteen years old.

We find ourselves in Tiananmen Square in 1989. YOUNG ZHANG LIN *is sitting on the floor, backpack next to him. He is very hot.* LIULI *enters, in a white dress.*

YOUNG ZHANG LIN. Are you okay?

LIULI. I'm fine. Fussing like an old woman.

He goes to kiss her. She covers her mouth.

My breath.

YOUNG ZHANG LIN. How can you throw up, you've barely eaten all week? Here. Have a peach.

YOUNG ZHANG LIN *takes out a bag of peaches.*

LIULI. We're supposed to be on hunger strike, you can't wait till we leave the square? If the cameras see you –

YOUNG ZHANG LIN. My mother always said it's important to eat fruit every day.

LIULI. Your mother called you Dog-face. Your whole family still call you Dog-face, you know why? Because you're still a little baby. A little boy –

Lights up on ZHANG LIN, *in front of the laptop, as he becomes aware of* MING XIAOLI *coughing through the wall.*

ZHANG LIN. A little boy. A little boy, a little –

1989 disappears as in 2012, the coughing grows louder, and ZHANG LIN *slams the laptop shut. Pause. He turns the TV up loud. Opens the fridge.* LIULI *is inside. She wears a red version of the white dress she wears in 1989, and shivers.* ZHANG LIN *closes the door.*

ACT TWO

Scene One

Denver, Colorado. October 3rd, 2012. The night of the first presidential debate. A dive bar. Some drunk Republicans. Some drunk Democrats. JOE *and* MEL *at the bar, nursing beers.*

MEL. No but I mean you really have to, you know, look at yourself, don't you, if you can't hold your own against a man named after a fucking *glove*.

JOE. It's just the first debate. Listen, if we do this. If we find him –

MEL. Okay, Hildy Johnson, cool your boots.

JOE. What's the first question you'd ask?

MEL. Okay, good, number one: what did he say to the soldier in the tank? Number two: what was in his shopping bags, number three: what does he eat for breakfast?

JOE. You'd ask the Unknown Hero whether he has toast or cereal?

MEL. See, this is what you don't understand about writing, it's the detail, it's the human interest, the small intimacies of great souls. You sure we can trust this guy, Zhang Lin?

JOE. Oh, for sure. He's pretty straight, serious, kind of sad, he lost his wife, before I knew him, they were like teenage sweethearts –

MEL. Okay don't look now but Sarah Palin is eating the biggest plate of ribs you ever –

JOE. *Hey.*

MEL. What? I'm listening.

JOE. So we start by combing Chinatown. Every shop, every bar, every nail salon.

MEL. Uh-uh. You got a strategy?

JOE. Well, I guess we just start off by asking people.

MEL. That's it?

JOE. Yeah. I mean, no. I had another idea.

MEL. Yeah? Is it as good as 'we ask people'?

JOE. Shut up, okay, we don't know shit, but what do we know? We know his name. And we know that he has a political conscience. So you check the electoral roll, you get his address, right?

MEL. No.

JOE. What d'you mean 'no', don't just / say 'no' like –

MEL. If he's in New York, he's probably illegal. He won't be registered to vote – Maria! Hey, over here!

MEL *has spotted* MARIA DUBIECKI, *a Democrat senator in her fifties, accompanied by* DAVID BARKER (*twenties*). MEL *waves to her.* MARIA *comes over, followed by* DAVID.

MARIA. Hi, boys. Little late for you to be out on a school night, isn't it?

MEL. Yeah, but I borrowed my dad's ID, what are you drinking?

MARIA. I'll have a spritzer, thank you, dear.

MEL. So, you been raiding Hillary Clinton's closet again?

MARIA. Oh I know, I know, it's awful, isn't it? It's just Wednesdays I always let my daughter pick my outfit, she's nine, she has terrible taste. Are they wasabi peas?

MEL. Knock yourself out, Senator.

MARIA *moves to the table, hungrily eats the wasabi peas.*

JOE. You look radiant, really.

MARIA. Well, thank you, Joe, I'm running on about four hours sleep a night these days, but I sleep in a Tupperware box, and eat nothing but steamed kale, so.

JOE. Well, it's working for you. (*To* DAVID.) Hi, I'm Joe, how you doing?

MARIA. Oh, where are my manners, this is my legislative assistant, Dave, this is Joe.

DAVID. David. David Barker. Hey.

JOE *and* MEL *shake hands with* DAVID. *The* BARMAID *hands* MARIA *her spritzer.*

MEL. So listen, I hear Obama's lining you up for Education.

MARIA. Well, I don't know who could've given you that idea, it's almost like you plucked it from the blue sky to test my poker face, isn't it? How am I doing?

MEL. Oh my God, you could teach a Sphinx how to Sphinx.

JOE. So, Maria, how's morale in the spin room? I hear Barack's back on the Marlboros again...

MARIA. Shhh, don't tell Michelle –

DAVID. Senator, you have a conference call.

MARIA. No I don't, Dave. I need the bathroom. These Spanx are cutting me in half, would you hold this for me? Thanks, look at this place, you could get roofied just by breathing – nice seeing you, boys. Vote, vote, vote.

MARIA *thrusts her drink at* DAVID *and goes. An awkward beat, then* DAVID *follows her.*

MEL. You seen her husband lately? Quit his job, full-time hausfrau, man looks like someone ran him over with a panzer.

JOE (*shrugs*). Don't have kids.

MEL. That's what I'm saying.

JOE. You have two.

MEL. That's what I'm saying. Don't have 'em.

JOE*'s cellphone rings. He checks it.* MEL *gestures.*

Go ahead. You got a smoke?

JOE *hands* MEL *his rollie,* MEL *takes it, exits,* JOE *takes the call. Split scene, lights up on* FRANK, *he's getting a massage from a Chinese woman in his office. Cellphone in his hand.*

FRANK. You want to hear a story?

JOE. Ah, we're kind of in the middle of / something here –

FRANK. Trust me, you want to hear this story: four months ago, in June this year, a woman places a long-distance call to China from Manhattan. She places two adverts in the *Beijing Evening News*. One reads: 'In memory of the mothers who lost on 64'.

'

Joey? Are you listening?

JOE. 64, that's June 4th right? That's the massacre, that's Tiananmen?

FRANK. Correct. You want to know what the second ad said? The second ad said: 'To Wang Pengfei. The Unknown Hero of the square.'

JOE. The Unknown Hero, that's the Tank Man, and Wang Pengfei, that's – are you serious?

FRANK. The girl on the desk takes down the copy, the woman pays in yuan by credit card. And upstairs in his office, some middle-aged Chinese guy yells 'go to print'.

JOE. It was *published*? No. It would have been censored, right?

FRANK. The girl on the advertising desk is nineteen years old. She wasn't born when Tiananmen happened, most of her generation don't *know* it happened, it's been erased from the history books, so when some lady calls up with a bunch of coded messages about one of the worst fucking atrocities in her country's *history*, the girl doesn't think anything but 'how long till lunch?' That's the beauty of censorship.

JOE. So it just gets published? And the Party saw it?

FRANK. Sure the Party saw it. The editor gets fired. The girl gets fired, obviously, can't get a reference, doesn't even know what she's done wrong. Her family are paupers, think a cup of coffee is luxury goods, they cook their food over *dung*, Joe, over *dung*, you get the picture, this is not a girl for whom there is no place like home, so when a friend of a friend of a friend says 'I can get you to New York' /she –

JOE. She thinks she's on a one-way ticket to a Woody Allen movie.

FRANK. Right.

JOE. Except?

FRANK. Sure, except she's got no qualifications, basic English, no work permit and a bunch of fucking Triads breathing down her neck, she winds up in the Garment District, sleeping on the dressing-room floor of a fucking strip club.

,

JOE. Oh, right. So how did you meet her, Frank?

FRANK. None of your fucking business.

JOE. During your missionary work, I guess?

,

FRANK. Her name's Mary Chang. Get back to me when you've climbed off your high horse and I'll give you her number. She's expecting your call.

FRANK *hangs up*. JOE *looks around as* MEL *returns*.

MEL. What happened?

JOE. We got a lead.

Scene Two

A strip club in the Garment District. MARY CHANG *is dancing to a dance remix of David Bowie's 'China Girl'.*

We join her backstage having finished her dance, she wears a towelling robe over her costume. MEL *and* JOE *sit with her. A* GIRL *in the background, similarly dressed in robe and heels, oblivious of them, smoking a cigarette and reading the* National Enquirer.

MARY. They always make me dance to that same shit song.

MARY *takes out her earplugs*.

I only have like five minute. They don't like you have guest back here.

MEL. We only want a minute of your time, ma'am.

MARY (*to* MEL). You are friend of Frank too?

MEL. Friend is kind of a strong word.

MARY. I only met him one or two times, but he is so nice to me.

JOE. Yeah, he's a real do-gooder.

MARY. I google him. He works in a newspaper, right? You think he will give me a job?

JOE. Uh, I don't know.

MARY. Cos I use to work on newspaper in China, you know this?

JOE. Yeah, I'm sorry to hear about what happened with that.

MARY. Not my fault, you know? You know what they did to my people?

JOE. Yeah. It was pretty famous here.

MARY. They shot them! I don't know this!

MEL. Listen, Mary, we know it's kind of a long shot but – you don't remember the name of the woman who placed the advertisements, do you?

MARY. The woman who ruin my life? Yeah, I remember. Feng Meihui. I have my notebook still, you can check?

JOE. No, that's – Feng Meihui? You think that was her real name?

MARY (*shrugs*). Unless she had fake credit card. You look for her? Yeah? You find her – you tell her: 'thank you for nothing', right? 'Mary Chang say "fuck you".'

JOE takes two hundred dollars out of his wallet.

JOE. Here. That's for you.

Gives it to her. MARY *counts it. Looks up.*

MARY. You want me to dance?

JOE. No – no I don't, please, it's for your time. For your help.

A WOMAN looks in.

WOMAN. Mary. Ellie-May. Two minutes.

MARY glances at her, nods. The GIRL in the background tosses her magazine, takes off her robe. She's wearing a sequined stars-and-stripes bikini. She blasts some hairspray at her hair. MARY takes a piece of A4 paper folded five times from the gap between her shoe and her instep. She smoothes it out, gives it to JOE.

MARY. My résumé. You give to Frank? I don't know when he will come here again. I sent him email but he don't reply.

JOE. Sure. I'll make sure he gets that.

WOMAN (*off*). Mary! Move your ass!

MARY. I have to go. Some guy booked us for United Nations.

MARY takes off her robe and goes. JOE looks at MEL.

JOE. What does that even mean?

MEL. I'll tell you when you're older.

Scene Three

ZHANG LIN's apartment. ZHANG LIN sits. Laptop open. The microphone plugged in. A beer bottle, nearly empty, ZHANG LIN drains it. Looks at the refrigerator. Hesitates. Then picks up the microphone, hits a control on the laptop, begins recording. Lights down on ZHANG LIN as we find ourselves in 1989. YOUNG ZHANG LIN on the floor, as before, backpack next to him. LIULI enters, in her white dress.

LIULI. Tell me again about how we met.

YOUNG ZHANG LIN. No. It'll make me think about food.

LIULI. Why?

YOUNG ZHANG LIN. Because of the refrigerator!

LIULI. Tell me.

She pinches him. He cries out, whips his arm away.

Tell me.

'

YOUNG ZHANG LIN. My bed was broken. I was walking to buy a new bed. I had the money in my pocket. I'm walking down the street and I see this woman in the window of a store, a store that sells appliances. And she's electric. She's so beautiful, I have to stop for a moment and watch her, as she opens the door of this brand-new refrigerator and looks inside. And I cannot stop watching this. And I thought, whatever I have to do, whatever it takes, I've got to, I've got to have… that refrigerator.

LIULI *shrieks, hits him in delighted outrage.* YOUNG ZHANG LIN *laughs, fends her off.*

That refrigerator would change my life, so I go in and I hand over the money in my pocket. And the store owner helps me carry it home. And I plug in my refrigerator and it starts to hum. And I already feel like a different person.

I fall asleep and when I wake up it's hot in my apartment so I think, I know, I'll put my face into the cold refrigerator. So I open the door and this girl jumps out. The girl from the store, she's hidden inside my beautiful new machine. A stowaway. She's been there the whole time.

Like a rat on a ship. Like a spider in a crate of melons.

She's shivering. Her eyelashes are frosted up. She says 'I'm so cold.' I touch her skin and she is, she's freezing. I think, she's going to die if I don't do something, so I say, let's go to bed. It's warmer there. She nods and her teeth clatter together like spoons in a bowl. So I take her hand. Her cold little hand.

And then I remembered, I don't have a bed. I spent my money on a refrigerator. I completely forgot, I was supposed to buy a bed.

So we made love on the floor instead.

He looks at her. A kiss. In 2012, a knock on the door. ZHANG LIN *switches off the microphone. 1989 disappears.* ZHANG WEI *enters, wearing a face mask, a cardboard box under his arm.*

ZHANG WEI (*Mandarin*). You alright?

ZHANG LIN (*Mandarin*). Yeah. You?

ZHANG WEI. I bought you some new dishes. They're seconds. From work. The glaze is flawed, but you can eat off them fine.

ZHANG LIN. I don't need new dishes.

ZHANG WEI. Yours are all chipped. It harbours bacteria, it's unhygienic.

ZHANG LIN. You shouldn't go out, not when the smog's like this.

ZHANG WEI. You can just say 'thank you', you know that?

ZHANG LIN. It's from the factories, you know?

ZHANG WEI. Sure. The factories and the trucks. They're talking about suspending production. Stressing me out, we're behind schedule as it is. Have you spoken to Joe yet?

ZHANG LIN. Yeah. Yeah. Yeah. Yeah.

ZHANG WEI *puts down the box, turns to leave.*

Zhang Wei? Zhang Wei?

ZHANG WEI. What?

ZHANG LIN. Thank you for the dishes.

ZHANG WEI. You're welcome.

ZHANG LIN. Will you get me a beer?

ZHANG WEI *goes.* ZHANG LIN *looks at the refrigerator. Hesitates. Opens the door.* LIULI *is inside. She hands him a beer. He takes it, closes the door. Yanks the plug from the socket.*

Scene Four

JOE*'s dingy apartment.* TESS, *taking it in, as* JOE *produces a number of large folders, lays them on the floor.*

JOE. And you found it okay?

TESS. Your streets are too long.

JOE. Well, you'll have to take that up with the Dutch. You want a beer?

TESS. I can't stay.

JOE. No, sure, I just wanted to – I felt kind of awful, about how I spoke to you the other night, and – anyway so I sorted through my China archive. They might not be of any interest to you, they're mostly still-life or landscape but... for the credit card, I mean?

TESS. Oh. Thank you. That's – wow, thanks.

TESS *opens a folder.* JOE *realises his mistake. A panic.*

JOE. No, sorry, that's not. That's the wrong, you don't want to look at those –

But TESS *has taken a printout and is examining it.*

Tess, please. Don't. I didn't mean to –

He goes to take it from her, she moves it out of his reach, still looking at it. JOE *hesitates.*

Sudan. '94, I think.

TESS *goes to the next print.*

That's Colombia.

Pause. He points to a detail on the print.

He was a trade unionist. Worked at a Coca-Cola bottling plant in Carepa.

Pause. The next print. JOE *points to a detail on it.*

That's the paramilitaries arriving.

Pause. The next print. TESS *covers her mouth.* JOE *indicates something.*

The light wasn't good. I followed them into the bushes but I couldn't risk a flash.

TESS *puts down the print. A pause. Then she takes a breath. And picks up another.*

That's a cemetery in Gaza. Palestinian woman, that's her boys in the background.

TESS. You must have been standing, quite close...

JOE. Pretty close yeah.

,

TESS. You can see every wrinkle / in her –

JOE. You see the flare coming off that iron bar in her hand, I love that, total fluke.

TESS. Looks like she's about to –

JOE. Yeah. Caught me right across the eye. See?

He shows TESS *his scar. She feels it.*

The restaurant. I'm sorry about, you know –

TESS. Throwing a wobbly?

JOE. Yeah. I guess.

TESS. It's alright. I had a toffee apple.

She retracts her hand.

Can I see the Tank Man?

JOE *finds a print of the Tank Man photograph in a folder. Gives it to her. She examines it.*

Have you found him yet?

JOE *shakes his head. She looks at the print.*

I always used to wonder about his shopping bags.

JOE. Why is everyone so hung up on that, what he bought from the *store* that morning?

TESS. Because I think that's amazing. A man goes out to buy a paper, or a new shirt or something, and by the end of the day, he's part of history.

JOE. Yeah but forget the shopping. That's a picture of heroism. It changed things.

TESS. Yeah but don't most of your photographs do that?

JOE *takes out his tobacco, rolls a cigarette.*

JOE. I wish.

JOE *fumbles his tobacco.* TESS *takes the papers from him, she rolls the cigarette, deftly.*

TESS. So why d'you bother then?

JOE *shrugs.*

The Vietnam War wasn't lost on the battlefields of Vietnam, it was lost in the living rooms of America, right?

JOE. Right. Right and that *was* because of photographs. No one could forget what was happening when the blood was right there in Technicolor for the very first time. But living rooms now, they're full of war. Full of famine, full of genocide. Atrocity's just another pattern in the chintz.

,

TESS. I bet you're really fun at parties, aren't you?

JOE. Look, there are schoolkids armed with iPhones who do my job way better than me now. And maybe photographs are like people. The more there are of them, the less any individual one means.

But, you know, I don't know how to do anything else. Kodak ergo sum. I read that somewhere, I didn't come up with that or anything, you want a beer?

TESS. No, I. I have to go in a minute.

JOE. Come on. I'm trying to apologise here.

TESS. By talking about Vietnam?

JOE. Come on, have a beer with me. Or tea, I have tea, you guys like that, right?

'

TESS. I prefer beer.

JOE grins, gets two beers, opens them.

So why don't you want kids?

JOE. World's a shitty place. Seems kind of unfair to bring a child into that. And, you know, I just get really violent when I'm drunk, so. Cheers.

He hands her a beer. Clinks her bottle with his. They drink. He opens a correct folder of prints for her. She looks through them, picks one up.

TESS. Oh, wow. This is it, that's just, can I have this?

JOE. That? I just took that one to test a new lens. Don't you think it's kind of / bland?

TESS. Bland, yes, it's perfect. I love it. It's so… white-bread.

JOE. Then have it. You probably want a high-res TIFF, right?

TESS nods. JOE opens his laptop, keeps working, finding and sending the file, TESS hands him the rollie, he lights it, smokes. She looks at his tobacco packet. She takes out her straights.

TESS. *American Spirit.* Will you throw me out if I smoke an immoral Marlboro?

JOE. Sure, go on. You can say your Hail Marys after.

TESS *laughs. Lights a cigarette. Pause.*

TESS. I was really glad you called. I don't really know anyone in New York. Except this drug dealer I bought some speed off when I first got here.

JOE. I used to take so much speed in the nineties. I stayed up for four days once, in Kosovo.

TESS. She keeps calling me up crying all the time, wants to talk about her boyfriend. She came round last night with a *Sex and the City* box-set. She made me plait her hair. She keeps making me say 'oregano', then laughing. If I still lived in London, she's exactly the kind of woman I would avoid at all costs. She's my only friend in New York.

JOE *keeps his eyes on the screen.*

JOE. Nah, you got at least two.

Outside, it starts to rain. TESS *looks out of the window, drinks her beer. Smokes.*

TESS. They can control the weather, you know.

JOE. What?

TESS. In Beijing. They fire rockets, into the sky, to disperse the clouds.

If they don't want it to rain, then it doesn't. Terrifying.

She looks around; at JOE, *and at his gloomy apartment.*

I'm going to buy you a lamp.

Scene Five

JOE *consults* MICHELLE, *an Asian-American NYPD cop for information.* MICHELLE *is in the middle of an arrest with her partner,* OFFICER HYTE, *outside a house in Harlem. Blue flashing lights from off.* MICHELLE *is wearing disposable gloves and tagging an enormous bag of white powder.*

MICHELLE. This is a one-off, okay? Why you so interested in Chinese newspapers?

JOE. C'mon, Shelly, I'm a voracious reader, you know that.

MICHELLE. Okay. So we have three Feng Meihuis on record in Manhattan. One, she died last year, the second's in Penn State, attacked a real-estate agent with a fire iron. The last one lives in Chinatown, on Mott Street. Clean record except for a speeding ticket up in Maine in 2002, one daughter. It's a fish stall –

JOE. Address?

MICHELLE (*chiding*). *Please.* I wrote it down for you. If I get a report in of some sweet Chinese businesswoman being harassed by some prick with a camera I will find you and throw away the key.

JOE. Remind me why we broke up?

OFFICER HYTE *leads out a* DEALER *clad in garish Bermuda shorts.*

MICHELLE. Because you were cheating on me with the Lebanon.

DEALER. ...I know my rights!

MICHELLE. Great, well, Officer Hyte's gonna remind you of them anyway.

* OFFICER HYTE. You have the right to remain silent, anything you say may later be used against you in court, you have the right to consult with an attorney and have attorney present with you during questioning, if you cannot afford an attorney, you have the right to an attorney appointed at public expense.

* JOE (*grins*). How're the kids?

MICHELLE. Hannah's got head lice and Liam hit a Little Leaguer in the face with a sports sock full of pennies.

JOE. Ouch. What'd you do?

MICHELLE. Put him in a cell for a half hour with a really mean hooker.

JOE. Nice job.

MICHELLE. Protect and serve.

MICHELLE *and* OFFICER HYTE *lead the* DEALER *away.*

Scene Six

The back of a Chinatown fish stall. MEL *checks his phone as* JOE *takes shots on his camera. His natural instinct.* JENNIFER LEE *enters, dragging her mother,* FENG MEIHUI. *Both in aprons, pink with fish-blood.* MEIHUI *sees* JOE, *alarmed.*

MEIHUI. No photo. No photo.

JOE. Sorry. Feng Meihui?

He shakes her hand.

MEIHUI. This, my daughter. Jennifer.

JOE. Hi. Joe Schofield. This is Mel Stanwyck, he's a writer.

MEL. Thanks for speaking with us.

MEIHUI (*nods*). You got the money?

MEL. Yeah.

MEIHUI. You give it?

JOE *looks at* MEL. MEL *nods.* JOE *hands the money to* MEIHUI.

I do this for her. She going to college in the fall. We need money.

MEL. Absolutely, ma'am. So, we wanted to speak with you about a couple of advertisements you placed in the *Beijing Evening News* earlier this year. The first one. Mothers of 64. 64 means June 4th? Tiananmen Square, right? I'm sorry to ask but did you lose someone?

MEIHUI *looks at* JENNIFER. *Nods her permission.*

JENNIFER. My brother. We were twins.

MEIHUI. They were very small, babies. We were in the apartment.
Bullet, comes through the window. Into the kitchen. Into the crib.

JOE. I'm so sorry.

MEIHUI (*to* JENNIFER). I need a Fresca. Get me a Fresca.

JENNIFER goes out. MEIHUI *takes out a picture, shows* JOE
and MEL.

This is him. On the left. When I have twins, I think, 'I am
so lucky' right? I beat the one-child policy. Yeah. They get you
in the end.

MEL. The second advertisement. About the Unknown Hero –

MEIHUI. I don't know nothing about that.

MEL. You placed it though, right?

MEIHUI. I do it for someone else. He don't have a credit card.

MEL. Could you tell us his name?

MEIHUI *shakes her head.* JENNIFER *comes back with the
Fresca.* MEIHUI *takes it, cracks it open, slurps. Scratches her
leg.* JOE *takes out more money, gives it to her. Pause.*

MEIHUI. He call himself Jimmy Wang. You don't hassle him,
right?

MEL. Is it possible his Chinese name might be Pengfei? Wang
Pengfei?

MEIHUI. Possible. I don't know.

JOE. The advertisement. You placed it for Jimmy as a favour. Like,
guanxi?

MEIHUI (*laughs*). Not guanxi. Just money. People pay me, I do
them a favour. They don't pay me –

MEL. You don't, right, so how do you know him?

MEIHUI *shrugs.* MEL *nods,* JOE *gives her more money. They
wait.* MEIHUI, *uneasy.*

I promise you, ma'am, this won't go any further –

MEIHUI. I help him come. Into the country.

MEL. Thank you, and when was this?

MEIHUI (*thinks*). Fall. Maybe October 1989.

JOE. 1989. You're sure?

MEIHUI. Yeah because he was one of the first we help, after we come here. He stay in safe house near New York State border. We wait till river freeze. Drive them over.

MEL. Okay. And where is he now?

MEIHUI (*shrugs*). I put them always at Brooklyn Bridge. He worked in restaurant. Then some flower store for a time but… now I don't know. I don't see him for months.

MEL. Which flower store?

MEIHUI. I don't know! My friend Fan, she work in funeral home, over in Flushing. He used to bring them white uh, *ju hua*?

She speaks to JENNIFER *in Mandarin: 'What's the word?'*

JENNIFER. Chrysanthemums.

JOE *shows her the picture of the Tank Man*.

JOE. Do you know who this man is?

MEHUI. Yeah, I know. He's famous. He's a famous man.

JENNIFER *takes the picture. Scrutinises it.*

JOE. Did you bring him to New York?

MEIHUI *says nothing*. MEL *nods at* JOE. JOE *gives her more money. She puts it in her pocket.*

Did you bring him to New York?

MEIHUI. No.

JOE (*pissed off*). How do we know you're telling the truth?

MEIHUI. Why should I lie? You think I talk with people like you for fun?

JOE. Maybe you could ask your boss / if he –

MEIHUI. Boss?

JOE. Like, I don't know, boss like – *Godfather*? You know that movie?

MEIHUI. No Godfather. Just me. American dream. Family business. My sister in Fuzhou make documents, her husband is Passport Inspector, very good, I deliver client to the safe house, collect the money. Family business. I help China. Money goes back there. You know how much poor there are there still? Not us –

MEIHUI*'s pride erodes her bad temper, she looks at* JENNIFER, *loving.*

She gonna be next Hillary Clinton!

JOE. You like Hillary huh?

MEIHUI. Last election, I give a thousand dollars to Hillary Clinton.

JOE. You did? How come?

MEIHUI. She helps illegals get papers. To be associated with such great a figure. Is an honour. Women hold up half the sky, right?

You go now?

JOE. Yeah. Thank you.

MEIHUI *goes out.* MEL *follows her out to the front of the store.*

MEL. You coming?

JOE *nods, as* MEIHUI *comes back holding something in her gloved hands.*

MEIHUI. Here. You want a fish?

JOE. Uh, sure. What is it?

MEIHUI. Pollock. Like cod. Very good.

MEIHUI *speaks to* JENNIFER *in Mandarin, telling her to wrap the fish.*

JOE. Well, thanks.

MEIHUI *goes.* JENNIFER *does as she's told. Gives* JOE *the wrapped fish.*

JENNIFER. If you find him, tell him 'Li Jiang's sister says, "have a nice day".'

Scene Seven

JOE *and* MEL. *The Glorious City Flower Shop, Queens. Buckets of flowers, a cash register. Amid various Interflora posters, a yellowing campaign poster from 2008 for Hillary Clinton.*

MEL. I need a drink. Ninety flower stores in three days. Sinuses are fucking on fire.

JOE. I told you, take a pill or something. This is the last one on the / list, just –

MEL *sneezes*. PENGSI *enters*.

MEL. Hi, my name is Mel Stanwyck, this is Joe Schofield, lovely store you have here, I don't know if you can help us out, we're looking for someone called Jimmy Wang? Or Wang Pengfei? We're not cops.

PENGSI. Sorry, not here.

MEL. No one of that name working here?

PENGSI. No. I can't help you.

MEL. There are apartments upstairs, right? I saw the AC units.

PENGSI. No, he doesn't live there.

MEL. Okay, well, thanks for your time.

MEL *makes to leave,* JOE *holds his position.*

JOE. So where *does* he live then?

PENGSI. What?

MEL. What are you doing?

JOE. He didn't answer the question, he just said he doesn't live *upstairs* so – (*To* PENGSI.) so where *does* he live?

PENGSI. I don't… sorry, I don't understand?

MEL. Joe, he doesn't know / anything –

JOE. Wait a second – do you know this man? We're not cops.

MEL. Will you leave the guy in peace? Let's go. I need a piss.

JOE. Just give me a second, alright! Sorry, I promise you, I'm not a cop, just, take a look at the picture.

PENGSI *scrutinises the picture. Shakes his head, hands the photo back.* PENGSI'S WIFE *enters.*

He doesn't live there, that's what you said, not you don't know him, 'he doesn't live there', so, so –

MEL. Joe, that's enough.

JOE. So I'm just wondering what you meant by that?

PENGSI. I didn't mean nothing. My English is… not good. I'm sorry.

PENGSI *and his* WIFE *speak in Mandarin as* MEL *addresses* JOE.

* PENGSI'S WIFE. Who are they?

PENGSI. Just cops, go upstairs.

* MEL (*sneezes*). This is not how you do this, you can't walk into a guy's store and Columbo him just cos English isn't his first language!

PENGSI *turns back to* JOE.

PENGSI. Can I help you with anything else?

MEL *looks at* JOE.

MEL. I'm catching a cab.

MEL *exits.* JOE *hesitates.*

PENGSI'S WIFE (*English*). You want to buy something?

,

JOE. Yeah. Sorry, yeah I, can I get some flowers?

PENGSI'S WIFE *exits.*

PENGSI. Sure. Uh. What do you want?

JOE. Uh – roses? Roses are nice, right?

As PENGSI *starts to gather and wrap a bunch of yellow roses,* JOE *takes out his phone, surreptitiously takes a shot of* PENGSI. *His thumbs move as he quickly types an email. He sends it. Lights up on* ZHANG LIN, *slumped at his table as his iPhone beeps. He picks it up, reads the email. Quickly deletes it, consumed with rage. He calls* JOE. *Split scene between* JOE *and* ZHANG LIN.

Hey, Zhang Lin!

ZHANG LIN. What is wrong with you?

JOE. What the –

ZHANG LIN. Do you think you are James Bond? You don't put such fucking words in an email to me, okay?

JOE. What? What words?

ZHANG LIN. You think an email like that from an American journalist does not get seen by the censors? 'Tank man', in the subject line, Joe, in the subject line, are you stupid or something?

,

JOE (*appalled*). Shit. Shit, what a fucking moron, I didn't think, I'm so sorry, I was, I got carried away – what I can do, can we fix this or –

ZHANG LIN. Fuck you.

JOE. You sound a little – it must be three in the morning there, what are you –

ZHANG LIN. I'm not sleeping very… good, well. I'm not sleeping well. My neighbour, Ming Xiaoli, she's dying.

JOE. What's the matter with her?

ZHANG LIN. She has Beijing Lung, I think. She coughs through the wall all night, I can't sleep with it. Why haven't you called Benny?

JOE. Who?

ZHANG LIN. My nephew, you promised my brother you would –

JOE. Sure, I'll call him tomorrow, but what about the email, can I do anything there?

,

ZHANG LIN. Just call Benny.

ZHANG LIN *hangs up.* JOE *looks at his phone. Lights down on* ZHANG LIN. PENGSI *hands* JOE *the flowers.*

PENGSI. Fifteen dollars.

JOE. Uh. Thanks. That's – shit, I'm sorry, I'm a little light on cash.

PENGSI. It's no problem. We take American Express. Or Visa.

Lights down on JOE *and* PENGSI, *we rejoin* ZHANG LIN *in his apartment.*

Scene Eight

ZHANG LIN *sits, turns on the TV, play a movie. Perhaps the first few lines or opening bars of the score to* Casablanca. *Then* ZHANG LIN *mutes the TV, opens his laptop, his face is lit by the screen. The microphone is plugged in, he hits the controls.*

ZHANG LIN. When I look back, it seems obvious, and I feel stupid. But I want to be honest. And I was stupid. If I wasn't, I would've put her in a taxi. I would have carried her home on my back. I would've told the English journalist to go away. In my head, I've done all of these things.

We see YOUNG ZHANG LIN *and* LIULI *in 1989.*

YOUNG ZHANG LIN. You need to eat something.

LIULI. It's too acidic.

YOUNG ZHANG LIN. No, okay, but – Liuli.

LIULI. It's my body.

YOUNG ZHANG LIN. So I don't have a say?

LIULI. You have a say. You just can't make me.

YOUNG ZHANG LIN. You're going to have a baby, you have to eat –

LIULI. Why?

YOUNG ZHANG LIN. Because, because I'm your husband and I'm ordering you to.

LIULI *grabs the bag of peaches, takes one and eats it, hungrily. Juice running down her face. She wipes her hand across her chin.* YOUNG ZHANG LIN *laughs.*

You pig. You piglet. Come here.

LIULI *shakes her head. Defiant.*

Come here.

She relents, jumps into his arms, wrapping her legs around him. They kiss.

LIULI. We're going to have a baby.

YOUNG ZHANG LIN. Don't draw attention. We don't have a licence.

KATE, *a British reporter in a flak jacket, enters, followed by a* CAMERAMAN.

KATE. Excuse me? Do you speak English?

YOUNG ZHANG LIN. I do. My wife doesn't.

LIULI. What does she want? Is she a journalist?

KATE. I wonder if I might talk to you?

LIULI. Let me speak to her –

YOUNG ZHANG LIN. Shh, she won't understand you.

LIULI *looks at* KATE, *laughs. Somewhere, speakers blast Beethoven's 'Ode to Joy'. Tinny and distorted.* KATE *gestures to her* CAMERAMAN *to record* LIULI. *During this, coughing starts, off.*

LIULI. We're going to have a baby. It's going to be born in the future. It's going to be a great artist. It's going to be a doctor. It's going to own a shop. It's going to have a doorbell with an electric chime. It's going to have a car with a refrigerator in it and a rubber dinghy and three pairs of Levi's. It's going to have five brothers and sisters who look just like it and all my children, will be fat and happy and clever and kind. You wait. Just you wait.

,

KATE. Can we check that / for sound?

ZHANG LIN. 'Can we check that for sound?' she said. I can find no record of this footage ever being televised.

MING XIAOLI *enters. She carries a large pot plant. Beat.*

MING XIAOLI. I brought you a plant. You have to water it once a week.

ZHANG LIN. Thank you.

MING XIAOLI. I want a striptease.

ZHANG LIN. I'm too tired.

MING XIAOLI (*tuts*). At my funeral.

ZHANG LIN. We don't need to talk about this now.

MING XIAOLI. They had one at my brother's, in Jiangsu, it was good fun. Cheered everyone up. And it helps to attract a crowd. I want a lot of / people –

ZHANG LIN. Ming Da Ma, don't –

MING XIAOLI. A lot of people having a good time, that's what I want. You'll have to call my daughter. I had a dream last night, she lectured me about smoking. She hit me with a coat hanger. This was in my own bedroom, only when I looked out of the window, we were by the sea and the sea was full of pigs.

ZHANG LIN. It was only a bad dream.

MING XIAOLI (*defensive*). I don't smoke.

MING XIAOLI *starts to cry.*

It's not fair. Telling me off, I never smoked in my whole life. She must've mixed me up with my sister. I'm a good girl. I was on a poster, you know. A Party poster, it was called 'Through Cooperation the Electric Light was Fixed'. I was twelve, I had to stand like this:

She stands, holds up her arm like the Statue of Liberty.

Holding out the light bulb. I stood like this for hours.

The effort it takes to keep her arm up is clear, but she continues, wheezing.

For months, everywhere I went, people had this picture of me on their walls.

ZHANG LIN. You'd think something like that would go to your head.

MING XIAOLI. Yes, it's amazing I stayed so modest.

ZHANG LIN *gently lowers her arm. She leans against him, regaining her breath.*

I hear you talking to your wife.

ZHANG LIN *doesn't respond. He picks up* MING XIAOLI*'s hands, massages them again.*

I don't mind. I remember you moving in. Seventeen years old. Children. I used to lie awake and listen to you making love. It made me happy. My husband was no great shakes in that department.

MING XIAOLI *breaks off, wracked with coughing.* ZHANG LIN *lets go of her hands. She covers her mouth with her sleeve. When she brings it down, there is a little blood on it.*

Gimme a beer.

ZHANG LIN. It's warm.

MING XIAOLI. So is the ground. Let's get drunk.

ACT THREE

Scene One

JOE*'s apartment. The yellow roses stuck in a jug. A new lamp.*
TESS *is bringing in stacks of files.* JOE *holds up the fish* FENG
MEIHUI *gave him and a bag of Doritos.*

JOE (*Dick Van Dyke*). 'Fish and chips.'

TESS (*laughs*). Idiot.

JOE. You just fry it with a little butter and lemon. Good for the
brain cells.

TESS. I don't cook. (*The flowers.*) Nice. Whose grave you nick
'em off?

JOE. No, they're for you.

TESS. Oh. Thanks, Joe. Listen, if you need to get off, I can / just –

JOE. No, we have time, Mel's late, okay, these are the keys, the
heat's on a timer, I left you a fresh towel on the bed, in case you
want to, you know, like –

TESS. Wash?

JOE. Yeah.

TESS. It's all mod-cons here, isn't it?

JOE. I don't know what that means, by the way, I've got a pull-out
so you're welcome to stay on after I get back if you need to –

TESS. I should be okay. Apparently they just need a day to fill the
apartment with chemicals, and then another day to sweep up the
corpses.

JOE. Okay. Only you brought a lot of stuff, I didn't know if / you
were –

TESS. I know, it's just, it's work. They brought my presentation
forward, I'm totally fucked.

She takes a bottle of whiskey from her bag.

JOE. Uh-uh. (Very nice.) So quit.

JOE fetches glasses. She pours them both a drink.

TESS (*laughs*). Yeah, okay! And do what?

JOE. What? I don't know, go join the Red Cross or something, if you need the / super, his cell is –

TESS. Join the Red Cross?

JOE. I wasn't serious, I was just –

TESS. So why did you say it?

JOE. I was joking, it was a / joke –

TESS. No, I'm just interested in why would you / say something like –

JOE. I don't know, (Jesus) cos you bitch about your job basically constantly and you might get off on doing something that has, whatever, more of a... an effect?

TESS. I have an effect.

JOE. I wasn't, come on, you know what I mean.

TESS. No, Joe, what do you mean? Maybe I could set up a soup kitchen? Rescue some prostitutes? Go and work in a, in a children's home? Wear a nylon tabard, drug dealers trying to get in through the windows, rats and chicken dippers?

JOE. What the fuck's a tabard? I'm not suggesting you go dig wells in Africa, I / just –

TESS. Good. Cos I don't give a shit about Africa.

JOE. That's nice, Tess, very nice, d'you ever actually listen to the words that come out your mouth?

TESS. I don't know, do you ever step outside your pious, holier-than-thou, sanctimonious pedestal?

JOE. You can't step outside a pedestal. Just, forget I opened my mouth.

The buzzer goes. JOE answers it, opens the door.

TESS. Joe? I do give a shit about Africa.

JOE. I know.

MEL *enters, in a flak jacket. He carries a backpack.*

JOE. What are you wearing?

MEL. Statement of intent. Long Island on debate night. Place is going to be lousy with cooze, you got a new lamp.

JOE. Yeah. You like it?

MEL....no, is that whiskey?

MEL *picks up the whiskey, pours himself a mug.*

TESS. Hello, Mel.

MEL *throws her a cursory glance.*

MEL. Oh, hey, Tess, how you doing?

TESS. Great thanks. You?

MEL. Uh-uh. (*To* JOE.) We gotta go.

TESS *turns.* MEL *gestures to* JOE*: 'Are you two… ?',* JOE *shakes his head, mouths: 'No, shut up.'* MEL *puts his hands together, silently thanks the heavens.* JOE *double-checks his bag, goes out. An awkward pause between* TESS *and* MEL.

TESS. So. Second debate, right? Any predictions?

MEL. Romney's going to be ramping on China, no prizes for guessing that.

TESS. Sure, 'What if the big boy comes and steals our sweets?' Maybe they don't want your sweets.

MEL. Well, that's a radical interpretation of the facts. You know how much they've expanded their military? How much of Africa they've got in their shopping carts? Plus, you know, they seem pretty intent on putting every factory in Ohio out of business, so –

TESS. Yeah you lot've got a real bee in your bonnet about that, haven't you?

MEL. About thousands of American jobs going overseas? Yeah people get a little worked up! I don't know if you can imagine what losing your entire manufacturing industry to / another nation would –

TESS. Can I imagine? Oh, love, stable door, horse. We don't
    manufacture shit. Everything in Britain's been made in Taiwan
    since the sixties. Every child born since Thatcher has it stamped
    on its bottom. You want to see?

    JOE *enters, with his toothbrush, packs it.*

MEL (*to* JOE). What is she even doing here?

JOE. Her apartment's / full of roaches!

TESS. You think you're a *liberal* because you're voting for the
    black guy? Obama can't even get a basic Medicare bill through
    intact, there's a good chance another Democrat term right now
    is the worst thing could happen to them, you let the Republicans
    break their neck on the fiscal cliff then, in 2016, if I had a vote,
    I'd vote for Hillary Clinton. And if I didn't have a vote I'd give
    her all the money in my pocket.

JOE (*sotto*). Oh / my God. Oh, shit.

    He is suddenly feverish with excitement. JOE *unzips his bag,*
    takes his own out, starts it up, types.

MEL. If you don't like this country, I can get you a cab to JFK
    right now.

TESS (*to* JOE). What's up with you?

JOE. How do you change things if you don't have a vote? Money.
    No one poor ever got near the White House. Look – under
    federal law, all party contributions over $200 must be itemised,
    with the donor's occupation and employer.

MEL. So?

JOE. Remember what I said, in Denver? About checking the
    electoral roll, you laughed but maybe – look, you can search
    online.

    JOE *clicks on a link, Opensecrets.org.*

MEL (*points*). There –

JOE (*types*). No, I think we need to go back to '08. You pick your
    candidate –

MEL. Clinton? Think you're looking for a Hillary fan?

JOE. Just a hunch. Come on. Come on…

JOE *scans the website. Clicks the next one. Scans. The next. Scans.*

MEL. There.

JOE. *Yes.* Jimmy Wang. Three hundred dollars.

MEL. Jimmy Wang, there must be a few of them, we don't know that's him.

JOE. But if it is, he was alive and solvent on the 14th of October, 2008. And if he's registered here that means there's a record of his address.

MEL. Yeah but we can't access that.

JOE. You know who could though, right?

    ,

MEL. She wouldn't. I mean, she wouldn't, that's got to be illegal, right?

JOE. She'll be down there in Long Island, right?

MEL. She's a Senator, Joe, she's a public servant, it's not cool.

JOE. But –

MEL. Not cool, Joe! Come on, I'm parked in a tow zone.

   MEL *grabs his bag, exits.* JOE *closes his laptop, puts it in his bag.*

TESS. Bye, Mel! Have a safe trip!

MEL (*bad English accent*). Tally-ho!

   JOE *picks up his bag. Hesitates. Gives* TESS *a hug. She is slightly surprised by this.*

JOE. Eat the fish. It's good.

   JOE *goes.* TESS *looks at the fish. Unwraps it. Picks up her phone. Dials.*

TESS. Hi, will you deliver to Hudson Heights? Okay, this is what I want:

Scene Two

FRANK *at a chess table in Washington Square Gardens, with a coffee.* JOE *enters.*

FRANK. You're late.

JOE. We said ten thirty. It's ten thirty.

FRANK. Well, I was early. You should've known I'd be early. You see what they did to this place? Fucking Giuliani. I slept in this square for a month when I was twenty-two. Over there. Amazing, isn't it, what a young body will tolerate. Tina made me go camping last summer, one night in a tent, I've been in PT four months.

JOE. Wait – you were homeless?

FRANK. God, no. Vietnam. There were about five hundred of us here. The stink of people, that's what I remember. I wore the same pair of jeans for a month straight.

JOE. You *protested*?

FRANK. That is not the big surprise. The big surprise is, I used to wear jeans.

MEL *enters, bleary-eyed, hungover, muffled up against the cold.*

JOE. What's going on, Frank?

FRANK. Mel! You look like shit! How was Long Island?

MEL. Don't drink the iced tea.

JOE. Frank?

FRANK. I need you to drop the story.

,

JOE. Which story?

FRANK. The China story.

JOE. The Tank Man?

MEL. What?

JOE. Frank, come on, you can't – we haven't even found him yet.

FRANK. So you won't mind.

JOE. I do mind. I absolutely mind –

  JOE *stands up*.

FRANK. I talked with Lou about it, she's not happy, / sit down.

JOE. Fuck Lou.

MEL. Woman's a bureaucrat.

JOE. She doesn't know the first thing about how a newspaper works –

FRANK. No. But she happens to be extremely talented at running the company that owns us. And Verico is seeking to acquire one cable network and two newspapers in the Asian territories. Which means it's seeking investment capital, and it's seeking it from about the only place in the world there is any right now.

  ,

JOE. China.

MEL. Ah, Jesus. Okay. Jesus.

FRANK. Am I saying I like it? No, but – and I'm sorry if this complicates your video-game view of the world – but Verico are not the bad guys. They're trying to keep thousands of employees from the breadline.

MEL. And China has them by the pocketbook.

FRANK. No, Mel, they have the whole country by the pocketbook. This is a means to an end.

JOE. It's collusion.

FRANK. I don't think it's possible to sum up what this is in just one word. Sit down.

JOE. You could fight this if you wanted.

FRANK. No, I couldn't, not in the way you want, sit down, Joe.

JOE. Why not?

FRANK. Because you get a lot of medical bills when your kid has leukaemia, it's kind of a side effect. Siddown.

  ,

MEL. Sit down, Joe.

JOE *sits*.

JOE. Okay, listen to me – you run a *newspaper*. You cover the *news*.

FRANK. Yeah well when you owe a guy one-point-three trillion dollars it's prudent not to make a big deal out the fact he knocks his wife around a little.

JOE. Anyway, you think the PSB read your newspaper?

FRANK. A month ago, Xi Jinping cancelled his meeting with Hillary Clinton because she criticised China's support for Assad. The *Times* has been blacked out for their investigation into the Chinese Prime Minister –

JOE. So? The Party's corrupt, everyone knows that, even a state-run media is covering *that* story, you really want to run a newspaper with less transparency than *The People's Daily*? You're supposed to be a guardian of a free fucking press –

FRANK. Do you think this is *vanity* publishing, what I get up at five a.m. every day to do? This newspaper is some sort of *catalogue* of my favourite things, do I look like fucking Oprah? Don't you dare sit there and suffer at me, hell I suffer too! You think I enjoy using the word 'multi-platform'? That I think it's *desirable* to employ the best writers in the country, then stick a comments section under their articles, so whatever no-neck grain-fucker from Arkansas can chip in his five uninformed, mispelled, hateful cents because God *forbid* an opinion should go unvoiced? Assholes Anonymous validating each other in packs under my banner, that's not a democratic press, it's a nationwide circle-jerk for imbeciles.

JOE. Yeah, well the internet isn't going anywhere, so –

FRANK. I'm still hoping it's a fad. I have a meeting. Consider yourself spiked.

JOE *advances on* FRANK.

Go on. You can hit me. If it makes you feel better.

JOE *knocks the coffee out of* FRANK*'s hand. It's a dismal gesture and he knows it.* FRANK *takes out a handkerchief, wipes the splashes from his shoes, pulls his coat round him.*

Fucking liberals. Too much spilt coffee, not enough split lips.

FRANK *leaves.* JOE *hollers after him.*

JOE. You voted for Bill Clinton!

FRANK (*disappearing*). Prove it.

    ,

JOE. You know what, fuck him. Right?

MEL. Sure.

JOE. Anyway, we get that story? No way he isn't gonna print it.

MEL. Did we just hear the same conversation?

JOE. Fine, so we take to a different newspaper.

MEL. And breach our contracts. Believe me, I wish I was a happy little helium balloon like you, but I have alimony payments like you wouldn't believe.

JOE. You think you'll have trouble getting *hired* after a story like that?

MEL. We don't have an address, we don't even know if this guy is still alive. I think this is an appropriate moment to admit defeat, don't you?

JOE. We should resign, that's what we should do.

MEL. Joey, this new Nancy Drew thing you have going on, it's adorable, but –

JOE. This is censorship, what's happening here, what you're / endorsing –

MEL. You've lost the patient, Joey! Stop the heart massage!

JOE. I haven't lost anything, you seem to have lost your fucking balls somewhere, but I haven't lost / anything –

MEL. You ever consider buying a new shirt, you know, one that's not made of hair? I can't believe I let you drag me all over five fucking boroughs with this shit. 'America must be shown!' Shown what? That some guy who took a great picture twenty-three years ago finally completed his difficult second album? You think you helped *make* that man? Bull*shit*, point and click, that's all *you* did, now you're trying to recycle an old photograph and call it a crusade, it's not a crusade, Joe, it's desperate masturbation, and I get my fill of that at home.

JOE. You're walking away from this so you can do what? Go back to your apartment to read your take-out menus, and your precious fucking first editions? Sniffing dust jackets, hoping you inhale some fucking talent, cos I tell you what, Mel, you might drink like Henry Miller, you might catch the clap like Henry Miller, but whatever your deluded fucking ego tells you, you sure as hell never wrote like him, cos unlike you, he understood the grey areas, / he –

MEL. You're a grey fucking area!

,

This isn't Watergate. This isn't Vietnam. You get your picture of Jimmy Wang, fifty, of Queens, and the fleeting attention it receives will only prove to you how inadequate you are.

JOE. Mel.

,

Jesus.

,

MEL. I know. I know.

Look at that. I did it, didn't I?

Scene Three

ZHANG LIN*'s apartment.* LIULI *climbs into the refrigerator and closes the door as* ZHANG LIN *enters with* DENG, *a prospective buyer. An efficient young businesswoman with an iPhone to her ear. She examines the refrigerator as* ZHANG LIN *watches. When she opens the door, the refrigerator is empty and clean. But* ZHANG LIN *cannot look at it.*

DENG (*Mandarin, on phone*). Yes. Yes. I'll ask him. (*To* ZHANG LIN.) Is it still under warranty?

ZHANG LIN (*Mandarin*). No.

DENG (*Mandarin, on phone*). I'll call you back.

She hangs up.

Is there something wrong with it? I won't buy faulty goods.

ZHANG LIN. No, it works perfectly.

DENG. So why are you selling it?

'

ZHANG LIN. My wife doesn't like it.

The sound of MING XIAOLI *coughing through the wall.*

DENG. She probably wants something more modern. Your walls are as thin as ours.

ZHANG LIN. My neighbour.

DENG *looks round the back of the refrigerator.*

DENG. What's wrong with her?

ZHANG LIN. Have you looked out the window today? Look at that. I've been reading about it, the smog, it makes the blood sticky. Something about particles in the lungs.

DENG. I know, it's atmospheric.

ZHANG LIN. I don't think so.

DENG. You want to dust back here.

ZHANG LIN. I check the US Embassy website, they've got a monitor on their roof. Says it's at 540 today. The Party numbers never go above 200.

DENG. You think it's propaganda, is that it?

ZHANG LIN. No. I wasn't implying –

DENG. No but is that what you're trying to say, it's propaganda? It's not. These stories you've read, this stuff about the Embassy, that's propaganda, that's Americans trying to undermine us, our growth.

ZHANG LIN. I don't know. Maybe.

DENG. No, trust me, this is my business, I deal with this kind of behaviour every day, only we call it corporate sabotage.

The coughing erupts again, through the wall.

No, sounds nasty though. I'm sorry for her.

ZHANG LIN. She's fifty-nine.

DENG. Right, so the China she was born in was still medieval, thanks to the Party, she's going to die in a space age. She's a time traveller. She has motion sickness, is all. There's no icebox?

ZHANG LIN. No. It's quite old.

DENG. I was really looking for something with an icebox, it's for my mother. I'll give you one hundred and fifty yuan.

ZHANG LIN. I was hoping for a little more.

DENG. When did you buy this?

ZHANG LIN. 1987. It was new then.

DENG. It's not new now, is it? One hundred and fifty yuan.

Scene Four

FRANK *in his office, phone in one hand, a dripping, oily jiffy bag in the other. Volcanic. Lights up on* JOE, *also on the phone, as he takes* FRANK's *call.*

FRANK. Did you send me a fish?

JOE. Yes, Frank. Yes I did.

FRANK. You sent me a fucking – what the fuck is this?

JOE. A pollock, Frank. It's similar to cod.

FRANK. It's similar to me introducing your balls to my hunting knife. Doreen didn't get to it for two days, stunk my whole office up. I mean, Jesus! A pollock! You still pissed at me about pulling the Tank Man?

JOE. Yup.

FRANK. You wanna come in and talk about this?

JOE. Nope.

FRANK. Of course you don't, you know I'm still not gonna run it, right? I will *not* bow to terrorism, I hope you have this out of your system, because I want you and Mel in Boca Raton for the final debate and – Jesus H – DOREEN! There's fish juice all over my desk, you remember who gave me this desk, Joe?

JOE. Henry / Kissinger.

DOREEN *enters in rubber gloves. She takes the bag, exits with it at arm's length.*

FRANK. HENRY FUCKING KISSINGER. If you mail me a fish again, I swear to God I will kill you and make it look like an accident.

Scene Five

ZHANG LIN*'s apartment.* ZHANG LIN *dressed in white.* ZHANG WEI *in his normal clothes. Wailing, off.* ZHANG LIN *is stuffing* MING XIAOLI*'s plant, now dead, into a bin bag.*

ZHANG LIN (*Mandarin*). Can you hear that?

ZHANG WEI (*Mandarin*). I can hear it, calm down.

ZHANG LIN. She can wail all she likes now. Her mother's dying, she can't get on a plane?

ZHANG WEI. It's a long way from San Francisco. She made it for the funeral.

ZHANG LIN. Sure, after Ming Xiaoli had been *dead* for two days.

ZHANG LIN *goes to the window, gestures out.*

They say it's safe, look at it! I mean, what a miserable, what a really miserable way to – to be born on a farm, by the Yellow Sea –

ZHANG WEI. Poor.

ZHANG LIN. Yes poor, so what, poor, at least she could fucking breathe!

ZHANG WEI. Calm down. What happened to your fridge?

ZHANG LIN. Liuli wouldn't have allowed it, she would have been in there, every day!

ZHANG WEI. Zhang Lin, keep your voice down, where's your / fridge–

ZHANG LIN. I sold it. It made too much noise, all her old friends from the Party, checking their Rolexes, how long till lunch. You know how they bought them? With the shit from her lungs –

ZHANG WEI. You think the Party isn't looking into this? There are regulations, there / are rules –

ZHANG LIN. Oh, regulations, regulations, fantastic! No, that's wonderful, I'll make sure they put that on her memorial, 'Ming Xiaoli, dead of regulations'.

,

ZHANG WEI. When me and Yuanyuan were having trouble, she signed us up for this marriage counsellor, he made us write down all the things that were making us angry.

ZHANG LIN. Did it help?

ZHANG WEI. Yes. That's why we got divorced.

,

ZHANG LIN. Okay. I'll do that then.

ZHANG WEI. Okay. Good.

,

ZHANG LIN. I could send it to Joe.

ZHANG WEI. No, that's not / what I –

ZHANG LIN. I won't get it printed here, but the American press would be interested, right?

ZHANG WEI. Let's go next door, come on, pay / your respects.

ZHANG LIN. Joe would, anyway, Ming Xiaoli, she was on a poster, you know, poster girl for the Party, now she's dead because of, what? Because all they give a shit about is *growth*? That's a joke –

ZHANG WEI. You're upset, you mustn't / rush into anything.

ZHANG LIN *grabs his laptop, opens it, starts it up.*

ZHANG LIN. Through cooperation the electric light was fixed!

ZHANG WEI. My boss is in there. I have to show my face. Come and eat something, at least.

LIULI *emerges from the bin bag.* ZHANG LIN *sees her.* ZHANG WEI *does not. She proffers* ZHANG LIN *a peach.*

ZHANG LIN. I'll eat when I'm done.

ZHANG WEI. No, don't do anything!

Zhang Lin? Are you listening to me?

ZHANG LIN *doesn't answer.* ZHANG WEI *goes out.* ZHANG LIN *looks at* LIULI. *Many* LIULIS *enter. Red dresses flood the stage.* ZHANG LIN *is surrounded by them.* ZHANG LIN *begins to type. We keep sight of him, typing quickly, as, thousands of miles away:*

Scene Six

JOE, *without his camera, outside the Metropolitan Opera House. He's waiting. Cordoned off from a red carpet. A frenzy of camera flashes.* MARIA DUBIECKI *enters, with* DAVID. MARIA *is wearing an exquisite ball gown.* DAVID *is in black tie.* JOE *waves to* MARIA.

JOE. Hi, Maria! Maria, over here!

MARIA. Joe! Good to see you, you remember Dave, right?

DAVID. David. David Barker.

JOE. Hey. So that's a hell of a gown. Beethoven doesn't stand a chance tonight.

MARIA. These galas, I don't even know who half of these people *are*, I was going to pretend I had pink eye but Dave here basically got down on his knees and *begged* me, he wants to meet the Dixie Chicks – so listen, what happened, Frank demote you to the gossip column?

JOE. Nah, I was in the area, just wanted to say good luck. For next week.

MARIA. Luck? Honey, it'll be over by Ohio. Romney's about to get crushed by binderfuls of women. Good to see you, Joe.

MARIA *makes to go.* JOE *hesitates. Then:*

JOE. Wait a sec, while I have you, I'm trying to trace someone. His name is Jimmy Wang. He donated three hundred dollars to Senator Clinton's campaign / back in '08 –

MARIA. *Three hundred dollars?* Joe, I hope this doesn't sound self-important but: you know I'm kind of a big deal, don't you?

JOE. Just, come on, Maria, just help me out, will you?

MARIA. It's protected information, you know that.

JOE. I know. I just thought –

MARIA. Yeah, I know, you thought wrong, don't worry about it –

JOE. Look. I didn't want to do this but. But, okay, I have this colleague. And he has these files.

A beat. MARIA *covers her panic beautifully, turns to* DAVID *with a dazzling smile.*

MARIA. Dave, would you check my wrap? Thank you so much.

DAVID *hesitates.*

DAVID. I think it's going to rain. Your hair will go flat.

MARIA (*smiling*). Dave, honey, will you just check the wrap, okay?

DAVID *goes.* MARIA *turns to* JOE, *hisses.*

What you talking about, Joe, what *colleague*?

JOE. You wouldn't know him. But he's a big fan of yours, we both are, and what we're concerned about, Maria, is… well, people remember pictures like that. The smell of them hangs around.

Shouts of 'Maria!', from off, she turns, smiles, waves as she speaks.

MARIA. I don't know what you're talking about –

JOE. I'm talking about you wearing nothing but a Nixon T-shirt snorting cocaine off a cheerleader's wrist.

,

MARIA. Hey, we all have *pasts*, right!

JOE. Obama still keeping that Secretary of Education seat warm for you, by the way?

A tiny beat. MARIA *moves much closer to* JOE. *She keeps a fixed smile on her face.*

MARIA. There's a hurricane coming. I hope she picks you up and drops you in the fucking Hudson.

JOE. Come on, don't be like that.

MARIA. I thought you were a nice man, Joe.

,

JOE. I am. Jimmy Wang. W-A-N-G. You can reach me here whenever you're ready.

JOE *hands her a card. She takes it. Slips it into her clutch. Shouts from off of 'Maria! Maria!' Camera flashes firing as she smiles dumbly into the lenses, and* JOE *slinks off into the night.*

Scene Seven

ZHANG LIN, *still typing.* ZHANG WEI *standing behind him. Music playing through the laptop. It is 'Ode to Joy' from Beethoven's Ninth.*

ZHANG WEI (*Mandarin*). What are you doing, Zhang Lin? What are you doing?

ZHANG LIN (*Mandarin*). Stop bothering me.

ZHANG WEI. What are you writing? What does it say?

ZHANG LIN. How much do the pollution inspectors fine you?

ZHANG WEI. I don't know, not much, about six thousand – don't do this. Please don't do this – (*Points.*) why are you writing about him, you know who that is?

ZHANG LIN. He's a Party Official, he's looking into the smog.

ZHANG WEI. Okay but don't use his name, he owns my factory! Let's just, stop and, think about this, have a beer, do you want a beer?

ZHANG LIN. No. What year was Ming Xiaoli born?

ZHANG WEI. How the hell should I know! Please, Zhang Lin, don't.

LIULI. 1953.

ZHANG WEI. What's this word? Zhang Lin, what's this word you keep using, that one, there? And there, you better not be mentioning me, what does that mean?

ZHANG LIN. It's nothing to do with you.

ZHANG LIN finishes. Leans back. 'Ode to Joy' fills the air around him. Very loud. He looks at LIULI.

It just means 'blood'.

ZHANG LIN hits send.

Black.

Interval.

ACT FOUR

Scene One

Lights up on PETER ROURKE *at his desk in Silicon Valley. The CEO of Mytel computer systems, a US company with an office in Beijing. He's typing, headphones on. Perhaps we hear the music he's listening to. His secretary,* DAWN, *enters. He looks up, pulls the headphones out.*

DAWN. Peter? I've been buzzing you. Judy's on line two / and –

PETER. Lawyer Judy or wife Judy?

DAWN. Lawyer Judy.

PETER. Got it.

> *He picks up the phone. Lights up on* JUDY, *in pyjamas and dressing gown.* DAWN *exits.*

Hey, Judy Tuesday! How you all doing out there in Manhattan, you battening down the hatches?

JUDY. I'm not in the office, I've been working from home Upstate this past month.

PETER. You take it easy on the East Coast, don't you?

JUDY. I had a heart attack, Peter.

PETER. Fuck. Judy, I'm so –

JUDY. I'm fine, Pete, I need to run something by you before I authorise it. The Beijing office has a request for some detail on a Chinese citizen.

> *Lights up on* ZHANG LIN. *His apartment is being searched by* SECURITY MEN.

PETER. Uh. Okay. He been a naughty boy?

JUDY. He posted an article online. Something about Party corruption over the smog in Beijing. It went through an anonymiser site but the Party picked it up.

PETER. He was using one of our systems?

JUDY. I didn't just call to hear your voice.

PETER. Okay, so what do they want? IP address I guess?

JUDY. And the location of the corresponding PC used to send it.

PETER. Dumb question: do we have any assurance as to what this data will be used for?

JUDY. You want the extended disco version again or –

PETER. Humour me.

JUDY (*sighs*). As a US company operating on Chinese soil you are required to comply with Chinese law. There's no assurance.

Peter? This is really just a courtesy –

PETER. Okay. Okay. Fine.

JUDY. I can give the clearance?

PETER. Yep. Sure.

ZHANG LIN*'s laptop is seized.* ZHANG LIN *is handcuffed, and dragged out.*

JUDY. Okay. See you Saturday.

PETER. What's that?

JUDY. Company paintballing? I'm flying in Friday, I'm at the Fremont if you want me.

PETER. Okay well, see you then. Safe trip.

PETER *hangs up, lights down on* JUDY. PETER *stares at his desk, shaken. Then calls off:*

Dawn! Get in here!

DAWN *comes in.*

Judy had a heart attack.

DAWN (*puts a hand to her mouth*). Oh my God.

PETER. I know, right?

PETER *puts his headphones back in and starts typing again.*

Scene Two

ZHANG LIN *and a* PSB GUARD *in a Beijing interview room, sitting at a table. The* GUARD *wears Nike trainers. He is writing. A long pause as he does so. Without looking up:*

GUARD. Do you want to get tuberculosis?

ZHANG LIN. What am I being accused of?

> *The* GUARD *hands him a written statement.*

GUARD. This is our first meeting. If there is a second, it won't be in a nice room like this. It will be, lying on bunks with old men. Coughing and sneezing.

ZHANG LIN. I didn't do anything.

GUARD. I thought you were a teacher.

ZHANG LIN. I am. I've taught the children of many / of your superiors –

GUARD. I thought teachers were smart. Sign just here.

> ,

ZHANG LIN. I didn't put my name on it. The article, I didn't put my name / on the –

GUARD. You know how easy it is to get that information? One phone call to New York.

ZHANG LIN. It was only online for six hours before it was firewalled.

GUARD. Chinese law states it is illegal to incite unrest.

> ,

ZHANG LIN. I'm sorry. I wasn't thinking straight. My neighbour is dead.

GUARD. The Party extends its sympathies. Sign, please. And the date.

> ,

> Or have I made a mistake? You did send this article to a foreign journalist, correct?

ZHANG LIN. He didn't publish it. He wasn't able to – he said the story was too small, and the Americans can't even solve their own problems, they –

GUARD. There's no problem here. This part I've underlined, what does that say?

The GUARD *shows* ZHANG LIN *a copy of his article.*

ZHANG LIN. It says the smog was at 801 –

GUARD. The fog.

ZHANG LIN. I'm sorry?

GUARD. You mean the fog.

ZHANG LIN. Yes, the fog was at 801.

GUARD. But that's wrong, isn't it?

ZHANG LIN. Yes.

GUARD. Yes, it's wrong. Because the scale doesn't go beyond 500.

ZHANG LIN. Yes. What happened was, I was looking at an American website, and it said the smog was at that level, but –

GUARD. The fog.

ZHANG LIN. The fog was at that level but –

GUARD. But this information was incorrect?

ZHANG LIN. Yes, the fog was below 500.

GUARD. It was well below that. The readings for the time show levels of around 190.

ZHANG LIN. Yes, I'm sorry, it was a mistake, a stupid. I would like to apologise –

,

I would like to apologise for the mistake. Please. Please. I won't –

GUARD. The same foreign journalist has been emailing you seditious material.

ZHANG LIN. That was, a mistake too.

GUARD. Lots of mistakes, eh? You think China would be a better place, without jobs, without industry?

ZHANG LIN. No.

GUARD. You prefer the economy to fail?

ZHANG LIN. No. No, I was only pointing out that the sm– the fog is, the fog is, it's a problem.

GUARD. It's not a problem. It's weather.

Beat. The GUARD *looks down at the article. Reads from it.*

This is a nice part: 'Somewhere in Beijing tonight, a woman dies a third-world death in a new-world China built on her sweat, and her blood, and her sacrifice. And across the city, an official scratches his belly in his sleep, and dreams of regulations...'

,

You see, I don't understand your complaint. Because you say, right here, you say the Party has made regulations, so –

ZHANG LIN. No. I said dreams. Dreams of regulations. There's a difference –

GUARD. God, I hate English teachers. The Party takes pollution very seriously. There are regulations. There are inspections. Nobody is exempt. Sign.

ZHANG LIN. I could write a retraction of the article. Would that help? Because I could do that –

GUARD. It's too late for retractions. Stand up.

ZHANG LIN *stands. The* GUARD *takes out a pen, hands it to* ZHANG LIN.

Sign it.

ZHANG LIN *hesitates.*

It's only a statement. I'm trying to help you.

ZHANG LIN. Help me how?

GUARD. Help you to be happy.

,

LIULI *enters. The* GUARD *does not see her.*

ZHANG LIN. I read a study recently. A scientific study, it claimed that the happiest people are the ones who are best at lying to themselves. For example, an athlete who believes, truly believes, there's no one faster than him, is happy. Even if he comes last every time, he's still happy.

GUARD. Is there a point to this?

ZHANG LIN. Yes. I think you are a happy man.

The GUARD *surveys* ZHANG LIN. *Then with great deliberation, he puts out his cigarette, takes the statement from the table, folds it, puts it in his pocket. Takes the pen from* ZHANG LIN, *replaces the cap.*

GUARD. Take off your shoes.

Scene Three

JOE*'s apartment. The night of the 2012 US Presidential election. The roses, now dead.* JOE, *watching the coverage as it's streamed through his laptop.* TESS, *off. They've been drinking.*

JOE. Tess! Get in here! They just called Ohio.

A toilet flushes, off. TESS *enters.*

TESS. It's over?

JOE. Not yet, it's just Fox. Wait for a proper news channel to call it.

JOE*'s cell rings.* JOE *grabs it, looks at it, puts it down again, disappointed.*

Frank. He's having some big election party.

TESS. You didn't want to go?

JOE. Wine and cheese with a hundred people who voted for the other guy? That sound like a fun night to you? You going to show me your thing or what?

TESS. How dare you.

JOE (*laughs*). Your thing, your presentation, that's the whole / reason you came over.

TESS. Yeah, I know! Wait a second, okay. Okay.

She pulls on a pair of high heels. Takes her position. Holds an imaginary clicker. Takes a breath.

Okay so – I've got a whole PowerPoint thing, this is just – that's my clicker. So. Thank you all for coming here today. Hello, Cleveland!

'

She waits for him to laugh. He doesn't.

JOE. Sorry – you're doing this in Cleveland? / Only –

TESS. No, it's – *Spinal Tap*, I thought, start with / a –

JOE. Lose it.

TESS. Okay. Okay so… where was I… (*Sotto*.) 'Thank you for coming here today…'

Pause.

Shit. I had the whole thing memorised. Don't – it isn't *funny*! I actually have to do this in, in, in – (*Looks at her wrist*.) where's my watch gone – in, in the morning, stop laughing! I have to start drinking water.

JOE*'s buzzer sounds, he rushes to the intercom.*

JOE. Hello?

Perhaps we hear a muffled voice, perhaps JOE *says 'come up'. *JOE *opens the door. His heartbeat increasing.* TESS *kicks off the heels.*

Okay. Okay. Give me some of that.

JOE *takes the water from* TESS. DAVID *enters. He sees* TESS, *looks at* JOE.

Hi, David. This is my friend, Tess.

DAVID. Pleased to meet you, Tess. I'm David, David Barker.

TESS. Hello.

'

TESS *looks at* JOE. JOE *closes the laptop.*

I might just step out for a cigarette.

DAVID. Thank you so much. Appreciate it.

TESS *steps out, takes a bottle of water.* DAVID *remains very still, looking at* JOE.

JOE. You want a – you want a drink or something?

DAVID. No. There's a party at the Sheraton. I have a cab waiting, I can't absent myself for too long. Senator Dubiecki doesn't know I'm here, if she ever speaks to you again, I'd be grateful if you didn't mention my visit.

,

JOE. Sorry, I don't –

DAVID. Look, I'm only someone's assistant so I'm sure you don't give a damn for what I have to say, but I've just been asked to meet you outside your apartment tomorrow, charged with a task I very much resent, and I've drunk half a bottle of champagne, so I'm going to say it anyway. Maria's not a perfect woman but she was born to a pair of immigrants in the back of a Ford Sedan and now she's a Senator, and she represents the interests of nearly twenty million people. And she represents them very well, for the most part. I don't know fully what your interests are here, but I'm guessing they are not shared by twenty million people. I'm guessing they're purely individual concerns. I know what you do, I know who you are –

JOE. You don't know / anything about me –

DAVID. I know your *type*. And there is nothing in your dwarf grasp you could hope to achieve in a lifetime that comes close to what that woman achieves in a single working week. So I hope that's something you can tango with during your more introspective moments, if indeed you have them, because I sure as hell couldn't.

,

JOE. Are you finished? Because –

DAVID. Four p.m., downstairs. If you're late I won't wait.

DAVID *leaves*.

TESS (*off*). Can I come in?

JOE. Yeah.

TESS *enters*. JOE *fills a coffee mug with champagne, downs it*. TESS *grins*.

TESS (*German accent*). Augustus, sweetheart, save some room for later!

JOE. What?

They both look up as distant, drunken voices become audible, singing 'The Star-Spangled Banner'. The sound of fireworks. JOE *opens his laptop. They sit, watching. Presently:*

(*Quiet.*) He got it. Four more years.

TESS. What about Florida?

JOE. Doesn't matter. He doesn't need it.

,

TESS. I wonder what it'll mean.

JOE. It means I never have to take another shot of Romney reflected in a pair of Ray-Bans.

,

I don't feel anything. Do you feel anything?

TESS (*yawns*). Bit pissed.

,

Do you owe money to the mob?

JOE. What?

TESS. That man, / what did he –

JOE. I think people need to know that there is heroism in the world, don't you?

TESS. Oh yeah. Definitely.

JOE. That's in the interest of people, right?

TESS. Absolutely.

JOE. No, but a lot of people. Like, more than twenty million? To see a picture of, just a normal man. Who stood up, and for that not to be a desolate thing, not a martyr, who can give a shit about martyrs these days, but a normal man who survived, carried on, made a life –

TESS. It's the sun and the wind.

JOE. Right, thank you. What?

TESS. The man. With the coat, how d'you make a man take his / coat off?

JOE. Right. Thank you, and that's not, I mean how is that masturbation?

TESS. It's completely not.

JOE. Because the other way doesn't work. You can't shock anyone into anything, not any more –

TESS *lights a cigarette.*

Not when kids line up at the movies to watch some guy who gets his kicks throwing teenagers into pits of needles, or sewing them mouth-to-asshole –

TESS. I saw that one.

JOE. Right, or whatever, so what's horror? Just, just something we watch, just a, thrill, a titillation –

TESS. Clip art. Fucking clip art.

JOE. Exactly. Exactly, the effect is gone. The shock is... too familiar so, so so I'm just looking for a, a different angle. A different kind of picture. Not of darkness, but light. I think that could be a, a *good* thing. I'm not trying to hurt anybody –

TESS. You're not going to hurt anybody. Look at you, you're a shrimp, you couldn't hurt anybody.

JOE. That's what I'm saying, I don't want to.

TESS. Then don't.

JOE *kisses* TESS. *She pulls away. Then kisses him. They start to make love.*

Scene Four

The Beijing interview room. ZHANG LIN *tied to a chair. No shoes, no shirt. Lash wounds on his feet and torso. Mouth stuffed with rags. Two* GUARDS. *Electrodes attached to his toes. Shocks are now administered. The chair shakes with the jolting of* ZHANG LIN*'s body.*

Scene Five

JOE's *apartment. JOE and* TESS *in a crumpled heap on the floor, under a blanket. A few hours later. JOE watches TESS sleeping. Gently shakes her. She stirs, sees him.*

JOE. Hey.

TESS. Hey.

JOE. Just you said you had an early start.

TESS. I did? No, that's –

JOE. I can call you a cab, if you like?

,

TESS. No. I can walk.

JOE. Just my wife'll be home soon.

> JOE *smiles.* TESS *laughs. Too loudly.*

> Wasn't that funny.

TESS. No, no I was just thinking. I bet they normally go for that line, don't they?

,

JOE. Come on, I wasn't – I'm not.

> TESS *starts to dress. JOE watches her, uncertain and self-conscious. TESS looks around. JOE reaches for something on the sofa, hands her bra to her. She takes it, quickly.*

TESS. It's okay, Joe! I know the drill, you have a morning, I have a morning, I'll just, shoes, bag, out the door, I won't even ask to borrow a toothbrush, because that's always mortifying, isn't it? Someone looking at their watch while you floss –

> TESS *pulls on her trainers. Grabs her bag.*

JOE. Tess, wait a second –

TESS. No, it's fine, just give me a minute, I'll be out of your hair.

> TESS *checks she has everything and heads for the door.*

JOE. Can I buy you dinner?

TESS. Yeah, great! Call me.

JOE. Can you. Just.

Stop – I'm trying to. I mean it, I'd like to see you tonight. In fact, since I've known you I, well I've wanted to see you most nights, which is, that's a little… new for me, so. So I have this dinner, with Zhang Lin's nephew, Benny, why don't you come? It's this steak place, Peter Luger's, in Williamsburg. Seven thirty, we'll have dinner with Benny, put him in a cab then –

TESS. I hate Williamsburg.

JOE. Of course you do. It's an awful place. Vintage clothing stores and, and, and… brunch, but it's just a couple hours, tops, then we'll get right back on the L train / and –

TESS. I got mugged on the L train.

JOE. Then we will take a cab, come on. Let me buy you a steak.

TESS. I'm a vegetarian.

JOE (*grins*). The hell you are.

He kisses her.

Scene Six

ZHANG LIN*'s apartment.* ZHANG LIN *sits or lies, covered with a blanket, very ill. In great pain. He retches into a bowl.* ZHANG WEI *is bathing his feet.*

ZHANG WEI (*Mandarin*). Where does it hurt?

ZHANG LIN (*Mandarin*). It hurts everywhere.

I'm so sorry. Zhang Wei, I'm so sorry I'm so –

ZHANG WEI. They let you go.

ZHANG LIN. I don't want to make trouble for you –

ZHANG WEI. Don't worry about me, I'm fine. If they'd put you on a surveillance list you'd know about it by now.

ZHANG LIN *makes a sound in pain.*

Shh. It's alright. You're safe. You said your piece. And she would've been proud of you, you know that? I'm proud of you too but you don't have to prove anything to anyone. Things can go back to normal now, it'll be easier than you think.

,

We need more iodine. I won't be long. I'll put the TV on. Okay?

ZHANG WEI puts the TV on. He leaves. ZHANG LIN turns off the TV. Grasps for his laptop. Picks up the microphone.

Lights up on LIULI and YOUNG ZHANG LIN in Tiananmen Square. The 3rd of June. A polystyrene Statue of Liberty being erected in the background. Music. A sense of an excitable, jubilant crowd. 'Ode to Joy' playing on a distant speaker system.

LIULI. What's the time?

YOUNG ZHANG LIN. Nearly ten thirty. You want to leave?

LIULI shakes her head.

LIULI. We've taken the square. The city belongs to us.

YOUNG ZHANG LIN lights a cigarette. Surveys the square. Conversational.

YOUNG ZHANG LIN. They're bringing the Army in now.

LIULI. So? The People's Army.

YOUNG ZHANG LIN. No, I know.

,

LIULI. You remember all those boys from school? Sun Ho and Wang Pengfei and Li Fu-Han, showing off their uniforms. Stupid boys with shiny buttons.

YOUNG ZHANG LIN. And little Qiu Hong Wen who couldn't grow a moustache.

They laugh. Observe. Pause.

YOUNG ZHANG LIN. They're pushing forward.

LIULI. There's too many of us.

,

YOUNG ZHANG LIN. You look tired. Maybe we should think about –

LIULI. We haven't got what we came for, not yet.

,

YOUNG ZHANG LIN. Are you cold?

LIULI. No.

  ,

YOUNG ZHANG LIN. You look cold.

LIULI. I'm not.

  ,

YOUNG ZHANG LIN. Maybe. Just to be on the safe side.

LIULI. They're just here for show!

YOUNG ZHANG LIN. But there's a small chance they might –

LIULI. Rubber bullets you said.

YOUNG ZHANG LIN. You're pregnant.

LIULI. And?

YOUNG ZHANG LIN. And a pregnant woman shouldn't risk getting hit with bullets.

LIULI. Rubber bullets.

YOUNG ZHANG LIN. Any bullets.

He puts out his cigarette.

Let's go.

LIULI. Shh – do you hear that?

YOUNG ZHANG LIN. It's the tanks moving. The buses are burning, they're trying to get round.

LIULI *stares off. An approaching sound of a crowd, panicking.* YOUNG ZHANG LIN *looks. Alarm. He tries to remain calm, steer her away.* LIULI *twists from him. Mesmerised.*

LIULI. Why are they running?

YOUNG ZHANG LIN. I don't know.

LIULI. Why are they running?

YOUNG ZHANG LIN. I don't know. Let's go.

LIULI. I want to go home.

YOUNG ZHANG LIN. That's good –

LIULI. Why is everyone running?

Snap blackout. Gunfire. Feet on concrete, screams, the shouts of
the Army, a crowd panicking. Then sound and vision cut out. It's
quiet and dark. Lights up on ZHANG LIN, *weeping, wretched.*
ZHANG WEI *enters. Rushes to his brother.* ZHANG LIN
grasps at him.

ZHANG WEI. It's alright. It's alright. I'm here. It's all over now.

ZHANG LIN. No. I don't think so. My feet. Zhang Wei, / my feet
sting.

ZHANG WEI. Shh. Go to sleep.

ZHANG LIN. I don't want to go to sleep! I don't want to go to
sleep!

Scene Seven

TESS *is mid-speech, before her PowerPoint presentation, a clicker*
in her hand.

TESS....so we're late to the party, the road to the Chinese market
is already well-trodden, and you know what? It's littered with
the corpses of companies who blithely assumed that Chinese
consumers would bite off their hands for anything America
wanted to hawk to them. Disney, Mattel, Groupon, eBay, Nestlé,
these are not chicken-feed mom-and-pop operations. They're
multinational businesses, who've put vast resources into
researching the Chinese market. And they've all failed. Because
they believed China was looking over the fence wanting to *be*
America and nothing could be further from the truth.

What about the good-news stories? Starbucks, McDonald's,
KFC? There's no magic ingredient in their coffee, their burgers,
their buckets of chicken, their success lies in the fact they made
themselves Chinese enough in a country that values the
supremacy of its culture above all else. You can have congee for
breakfast at The Savoy. You walk into Givenchy or Hermès in
Paris, the staff speak Mandarin, because those companies
understand that China is not the drunk girl at the frat party. She's
the business major with an A-plus average, and really great hair.
She's in charge of this brave new economic world, you bend to
her or you die trying.

And how are those Chinese tourists paying for their room service, their ostrich-skin handbags? Not with our cards, or the cards of our rivals, even, but with the, singular, state-sponsored card, UnionPay. How do we change this? We can't, not unless we understand the Chinese consumer. Which is where I come in.

What I'm about to show you is a portfolio of seven customer segments. We'll get into the variations in a minute, but they're united by one thing. They love to shop. We have to abandon the myth that China is a nation of savers with no interest in credit cards. Because it is a myth, the only way the Chinese are different to us is they make sure they have the money before they spend it, but they do spend it. We only have to look at this picture to know that:

TESS *clicks, the Tank Man photograph appears.*

What is this an image of? Protest, of course, but more than that, this is a picture of the moment that China exchanged democracy for an economic miracle. For the opportunity to work, live, spend, progress. Aspire – and credit cards live and die on aspiration or desperation – so this is a photograph of the moment that our mission went from being unthinkable, to being tantalisingly *possible*. And then, of course, all we had to do was wait another twenty-three years for them to let us in! By the way, can I point out:

TESS *clicks. Two red circles appear around his shopping bags. She turns back to us.*

The Tank Man… has been shopping! One of the most iconic images to come out of China, and at its heart a man who's just been to the store, to buy, what? Rice, a newspaper, socks, dried…
'
…dried duck stomach.

TESS *is becoming less sure of herself; her voice wavers. She clicks. The first archetype appears.*

So, let's look at the segments. The first one I'm calling 'The Rural Dreamer'. They're often in their thirties, sorry, late teens to mid-twenties. They have, they have a high brand awareness, but minimal free time, and much of their money is sent home, a high brand awareness, they –

TESS *clicks on to the next one by mistake. Her hands are shaking.*

Oh, whoops, sorry, I just – Jaydene? How do I – is there a back button or something?

She looks out, lost. Trying to remain breezy.

Sorry, just I double-clicked, I'm still on the Rural Dreamer, I'm not sure how to –

Jaydene? Any joy?

Pause.

Well, that's okay, okay... okay... okay so, so let's talk about, 'The Luddite Shopper' instead, seeing as we're – okay, the Luddite Shopper. The Luddite Shopper is. It's (Jesus), it's the Rural Dreamer with a different picture on it.

Pause.

The Luddite – sorry, actually, these categories are. These categories are, well, for a start, these categories are, they're just versions of Western categories. Which is, it's what you asked for but. But I need five years to build a really accurate segmentation and, well, you have me on a six-month contract. And I'm used to that, that's business cycles, right, but China's moving faster than we can collect the data, I mean, this is a nation that's gone from famine to Slim-Fast in one generation. I know some of you've been out there, I mean, did you see the *smog*? My last trip, it rained one day, the puddles were black, the sky was yellow, they're growing so fast you can see it in the air! And, you know, in the fact there are like thousands of babies who can't breathe properly, but anyway, they've had, what? Forty years' worth of economic evolution in the last ten years and that's, you know, amazing but actually, that's not, it's not a safe speed to be moving at.

Because and also, I mean, I'm sorry if this is – but have we really thought about what happens when you turn one-point-three billion economic pragmatists into people who think about money like *us*? I mean, we're still breaking our nails on a recession now, right? But, what is it going to be *like* if one-point-three *billion* Chinese renege on their mortgages and credit-card payments?

And you know, this isn't me trying to tell you that the dog ate my homework, this work, it's fine, it's rushed but it's fine, it'll get you over the finishing line before American Express, but then what? Because you're about to get into bed with someone you don't really understand which is, it just seems a bit... lunatic, because, you know, this is the future. It's the next hundred years. And we don't understand. And I think that might a problem. Right?

The image behind her skips back to the Tank Man photograph.
TESS *glances at it.*

Thanks, Jaydene, that's – yep. I've got it now.

Scene Eight

Outside JOE's *apartment.* JOE *has been waiting here for a very long time. He has an A4 envelope on his lap and is smoking.* DAVID *enters, wheeling his bike which has a baby seat on the back and saddlebags. His cycle helmet unclipped, he wears a suit with a fluorescent jacket, bicycle clips. One trouser knee is ripped open, a bloody bandage around it.*

JOE. You said four p.m.! I've been sitting out here three hours, you couldn't call?

DAVID. I'm so sorry to hear that.

    DAVID *kicks down the stand on his bicycle.*

JOE. It's fine, I just. I have to be in Brooklyn in twenty minutes –

DAVID. You have something for me to collect?

JOE. Right, sure, I have it right here.

DAVID. This is the only copy?

JOE. Yeah. The negatives are in there too.

    JOE *gives him the envelope, unsealed.* DAVID *glances inside.*

DAVID. Do you have a pen?

    JOE *quickly takes out his pen and a notepad.*

One twelve 169th Street, Queens.

JOE. Work or home?

DAVID. He lives above the shop.

DAVID kicks up the stand on his bike.

JOE. Listen, David, about what you said, last night. I. I've been thinking about it a lot and, well, I wanted to say. It's not my fault you've got no fucking imagination.

Beat. DAVID goes. JOE examines the address. This precious information. Checks his watch. Takes out his phone, makes a call, scanning the street. He is feverish with excitement.

Shit. (*He's connected.*) Hi, Tess, I'm going to be like, ten minutes late, I just, I have an errand to run but I hope your thing went well and. And I can't wait to see you. It's Joe, by the way. And I can't wait to see you, I said that, didn't I, okay, bye –

He hangs up, flings out his arm –

Taxi!

Scene Nine

Outside the Glorious City Flower Shop. PENGSI is closing up for the day. JOE enters, excited and flushed.

JOE. Jimmy Wang.

PENGSI. Closed. Sorry. Tomorrow / at eight a.m., we open –

JOE. Your name is Jimmy Wang, right?

PENGSI. No.

JOE. No, it's okay. It just – I need you to tell me the truth. Feng Meihui placed that ad for you. And she brought you here, didn't she? In '89, why did you take out that ad?

PENGSI. No, not me. Wrong man.

He shows PENGSI the Tank Man picture.

JOE. The man in this photo? It's you, isn't it?

PENGSI. You go now.

JOE. Please. I think you can help me. Jimmy Wang, is your real name Wang Pengfei?

PENGSI. YOU GO PLEASE.

PENGSI'S WIFE *enters and speaks rapidly in Mandarin to her husband. He speaks back.*

JOE. What was that? I heard you, I speak Mandarin, you said brother, your brother.

PENGSI. No.

JOE. I speak Mandarin – you did you said your brother and then –

PENGSI *shouts in Mandarin at his* WIFE, *she runs out.*

I'm just asking for a little cooperation here, I'm not –

PENGSI *tries to push him out.*

Is he your brother? This man, in the picture, he's your brother –

PENGSI *starts to manhandle him,* JOE *is stronger. He shoves* PENGSI *against the wall. Jolts him a few times.* PENGSI *yells for help.*

Shut up! Shhh just – be quiet okay?

PENGSI. Get off!

JOE. Just be quiet –

PENGSI. Fuck you. Get out my store.

JOE. Please –

PENGSI *spits in his face,* JOE *reacts lightning quick, punches him in the face,* PENGSI *crumples,* JOE *hauls him up, shoves him to the wall.*

I didn't mean to – that was a mistake, you shouldn't've, just tell me –

PENGSI *swings for* JOE, *misses,* JOE *slams him onto the floor, holds him there.*

Just tell me. Just tell me. I don't want to hurt you / just –

PENGSI. Please. My brother was…

JOE. Your brother was what?

JOE *shakes him again.*

Your brother was what?

PENGSI. Yes.

JOE. Yes what? The Tank Man?

PENGSI. Yes. Tank Man.

Pause. JOE *releases* PENGSI. *Stumbles away. Holds his fist.*

JOE. Is he... is he okay? Is Wang Pengfei alive?

PENGSI *shakes his head,* JOE *shows him the Tank Man photo again.*

Are you sure? Look. This man, you're sure he's not –

PENGSI. I don't know about this man.

JOE. But you just said, he's your brother.

PENGSI. No, not my brother this man.

JOE. But you just / said –

PENGSI. Not my brother, this man.

JOE. You're not making sense!

PENGSI. The man... the tank...

JOE (*points*). This man.

PENGSI. No. (*Moves* JOE*'s finger.*) This man. Here. The soldier. In the tank, he was my brother. Unknown hero, my brother.

PENGSI*'s wife runs in. Smashes* JOE *in the face with a wrench.* JOE*'s nose explodes in blood. He stumbles.* PENGSI'S WIFE *yells in Mandarin.* PENGSI *hollers back. She storms out.*

She'll call the police! You go now.

JOE *moves onto his knees, clutching his nose.*

JOE. You're illegal, she's not going to bring the cops here – ah, shit. Where is he now? Your brother?

,

PENGSI. He was executed.

JOE. But... he was a solider, why would they –

PENGSI. He never killed. He would not drive tank forward when someone was there.

JOE. Someone? You mean the man with the shopping bags?

PENGSI. Yes. He could not go round, so he would not go. The Party were angry. Everyone looks at the man. With the shopping bag. But here, you can see, very small, a man coming out. Then he disappear again. Inside the tank. And that man was my brother. And he was very brave.

Sirens, faint at first. Getting louder. PENGSI'S WIFE *comes out, panicked and fearful. She says in Mandarin: 'Can you hear that! Can you hear that! It's her, next door, she called them!'*

JOE. She called them? They'll take you in! Why did she / do that –

PENGSI. Not her. Must be next door, a lady. Nosy on this block. We try to live quiet.

,

JOE. I – I'm sorry. I'm so sorry, I don't – here. Here, take this.

He takes out money, thrusts it at PENGSI. JOE *wipes blood from his nose. The sirens get louder. Blue and red lights flash.*

Scene Ten

TESS, *dressed up, and* BENNY *sit in awkward silence in Peter Luger's steakhouse at a table for three. A* WAITER *enters, puts two steaks down in front of them and clears the cutlery from the third place.*

Scene Eleven

A Queens police station. JOE *comes out from the cells into the foyer. His nose is busted. He has a dressing splayed over it.* OFFICER HYTE *is escorting him.*

OFFICER HYTE. We have all we need from you. Bail's been posted so don't you go taking a winter cruise or anything now.

JOE (*looking about*). Where is she? Who posted my bail?

OFFICER HYTE. How should I know? I am not your concierge! (Fucking night shift), you'll get your court date in a couple weeks. Should only be a fine if you're lucky.

JOE. Is he – was he legal?

OFFICER HYTE. Don't believe so. Won't affect your case, that's brought by the State of New York.

JOE. No but, will he be deported?

OFFICER HYTE. Depends. How good a lawyer you think he can afford?

OFFICER HYTE *goes as* FRANK *enters. He and* JOE *look at each other.*

FRANK. Nice nose-job. It hurt?

JOE. Little bit.

FRANK. Good.

,

JOE. You posted my bail?

FRANK. I did.

JOE. Well, / thanks, Frank. I really –

FRANK. You want to tell me why Senator Dubiecki's office called me and cancelled Jim and Heather's access to the press conference today?

JOE. Why would I know that?

FRANK. Because after Maria's office called, I called Maria. And Maria put me on *hold*, Joe. D'you know when I was last put on hold? I can't remember the time, I cannot actually remember, but Maria did it, she had me listening to Handel's fucking *Water Music* for a full eight minutes, and when I finally got through she was awful frosty with me, which, I couldn't understand it cos me and Maria, we have form, so I say to her 'What's this I'm hearing about the conference, why are my guys in the fucking ejector seats?', except I didn't curse, I was very calm, very breezy, but she wasn't, she was not breezy, fucking arctic *wind* coming down the line, and d'you know what she said to me? / Joe?

JOE. No.

FRANK. She said 'Ask your fuck-weasel photographer.' One of the most eloquent, elegant, orators of her generation, she uses the word 'fuck-weasel' and hangs up on me. Which is not, it doesn't happen to me a lot, so it resonated, so I'm thinking whatever it is, she's probably right. You are a fuck-weasel. So you're fired.

,

JOE. Oh by the way I called your cell yesterday. It was so weird, Mary Chang picked up.

,

Mary Chang the stripper? Should be careful, I could've been Tina, / or the girls –

FRANK. I gave her a *job*, you little prick. I'm sponsoring her green card application, you didn't even give me her résumé when she / asked you –

JOE. Because I knew you wouldn't –

FRANK. *But I did*.

,

JOE. Well, I'm –

FRANK. What did you do to Maria, Joey? What the hell did you do?

JOE. I didn't do anything! I needed her help, she was resisting, I just… greased the… whatever. Look, okay, Frank / this is –

FRANK. It's the day after a fucking election, they kicked my embeds out! Do you understand what that means? Do you even get how many fires I'm fighting here? Joe, I hope your greasy whatever was worth it, because by the way, this is not me blowing off steam, this is it, you and I are finished, I free you from the terrible compromise of being employed by me, I hope you go fucking blind.

FRANK *goes as* OFFICER HYTE *returns with* JOE's *wallet, keys, phone, etc. Hands them to* JOE, *as* TESS *enters.*

OFFICER HYTE. You left your stuff.

JOE. Thanks.

OFFICER HYTE *goes.* JOE *moves towards* TESS.

I'm so sorry.

Tess? I didn't mean to –

TESS. They brought them in while I was at the desk. They put them in a cell.

,

I just came to see if you were alright. And you are, so I'm, I'll go now.

JOE. I was coming, Tess, I meant to be there, things / just got –

TESS. Yes, I know. I listened to that voicemail you left, you sounded so, you were so excited. And I was excited too. I got fired today, but I didn't even care, not much, I came home, tried on dresses, stomach in knots, skipping down Broadway like some fucking cunt from a musical, and it took me all the time, how slow is this, all the time till I was sitting opposite Benny, in Williamsburg, holding a steak knife and understanding you weren't late, you just weren't coming, to realise: we were excited about completely different things.

JOE. That's not true. That's not true –

TESS. A photograph? Two people, destroyed, for that? What a bloody waste, I hope you find him, I do, but I am not… insignificant just because I never stepped in front of a fucking tank.

JOE. I know that.

TESS. Well, good. Anyway, I think. I think I'm in love with you. I think I have been for

well, quite a long time now. And it's nothing to do with… what you do, your work, my work isn't who I am, it's because, I think it's mostly just that I was scared, on a plane. And you held my hand. And you were very kind.

JOE *sits, hides his face.* TESS *stands over him. Pulls his hands from his face. He looks up at her. She runs her fingers over the scar by his eye.*

They made her take off her wedding ring. Jimmy Wang's wife. It was so awful, Joe. She screamed and screamed and screamed.

TESS *goes.* JOE *takes out his phone. Split scene with* ZHANG LIN, *in his apartment, as he answers the call.*

ZHANG LIN. Joe? Are you okay? Zhang Wei heard from Benny. He said you didn't show up to your dinner. He was very disappointed.

JOE. Yeah well, I'm disappointed too, that name you gave me, I found his brother.

ZHANG LIN. Really? How is he?

JOE. He's not the fucking Tank Man and he's not the fucking Tank Man's brother is how he is, Wang Pengfei was a solider, some soldier, some teenager who'd probably just spent two days gunning down civilians –

ZHANG LIN. He was a hero.

JOE. He's not a fucking hero, he was on the side of the Party, how / is that a –

ZHANG LIN. Sides? What does sides have to do with anything, he was a, he was a good man, even the Party saw that, you know how they used your picture? As a portrait of their humanity, look, we went around him! Did you know you were in the propaganda business? But it wasn't them, it was Wang Pengfei. And I don't know what happened to him.

JOE. His brother said he was shot.

,

ZHANG LIN. I'm sorry I wasted your time. I thought it was a good story. Sometimes a uniform makes it much harder to be a hero. And I thought you were interested in what happened that day.

JOE. I was interested in the Tank Man.

ZHANG LIN. Yes. I misunderstood.

,

JOE. I'm sorry about Benny. I'll call him. How are you?

ZHANG LIN. A new family moved into Ming Xiaoli's apartment. They have triplets.

JOE. Yeah, by the way, sorry about that I just, one old lady and some smog, I couldn't –

ZHANG LIN. She was only fifty-nine.

JOE. Okay, well. I, I'm kind of between things just now. You should come and visit.

ZHANG LIN. I wouldn't get a visa. And I don't have a work permit.

JOE. Well, I could help you out with that.

ZHANG LIN. Really?

JOE. Sure. I told you that, or, you know, we could just get married.

ZHANG LIN. I'll think about it.

ACT FIVE

Scene One

ZHANG LIN, *with a megaphone, addressing a crowd.*

ZHANG LIN. We call for a Party that refuses to get rich on our blood. We call for a Party that puts its people over its profits. We call for a Party that does not turn a blind eye as young men walk wheezing upstairs. We call for these things, at the top of our voices, while there is still breath in our lungs to do so.

Scene Two

April 2013. ZHANG LIN *and* ZHANG WEI. *Looking up at a security camera that has been mounted on the wall outside of* ZHANG LIN's *apartment.* ZHANG WEI *is furious.*

ZHANG WEI (*Mandarin*). Do you see that?

ZHANG LIN (*Mandarin*). Yes, I've seen it. I'm sorry.

ZHANG WEI. What's wrong with you? My secretary saw you in the park!

ZHANG LIN. There were lots of other people there too.

ZHANG WEI. Did they all come home to find security cameras outside their homes?

ZHANG LIN. I'm sorry, Zhang Wei.

ZHANG WEI. I left the office, no one would even look me in the eye, felt like I was contagious or something.

ZHANG LIN. The Party won't hurt you.

ZHANG WEI. I wish they would, a beating, I could deal with a beating, that would be better than this, better than being unemployable for the rest of my fucking life. I won't get another job now, you know that, don't you? I'll have to leave the city.

ZHANG LIN. You could visit Benny. You'll get a visa no problem that way. Just tell them you're visiting Benny. Then it's the truth. Just make sure you pretend you're coming back.

ZHANG WEI. I can't live with people like that, you know the stuff they say about us? What about you? What are you going to do?

ZHANG LIN. I have Joe.

ZHANG WEI. Oh sure, the ghost who won't return your phone calls. Americans don't understand guanxi.

ZHANG LIN. That one does. I taught him. He asked me to marry him, did I tell you?

ZHANG WEI. He must be desperate. I hope you got this off your chest, I hope it was worth it, to do that.

,

ZHANG LIN. We used to want the same things.

ZHANG WEI. Yes. I know we did. And then after, you took to your bed, like a little boy. And I went to work, like a man.

,

Call him again.

ZHANG LIN. I'll call him when I get in.

,

ZHANG WEI. Americans, I hate Americans. Their teeth are too white.

ZHANG WEI *goes.* ZHANG LIN *looks up into the security camera. He walks closer to it. Peering up into the lens. Framing his own close-up. Then he quietly takes out his camera phone, and takes a picture of the security camera.*

Scene Three

May 2013. Somewhere near a kettling, New York. TESS enters.
She appears to be crying, eyes streaming, but her manner, though
irritated, is not upset. She is six months pregnant but she wears
a tailored dress and jacket, and stiletto heels. She blinks furiously,
in pain.

TESS. jesuschristjesusfuckingchrist

> *She makes out the shape of* JOE *but cannot see him with any*
> *clarity.*

Excuse me? Excuse me? Could you give me a hand?

> JOE, *absorbed in his camera, now a digital one, rather than the*
> *film camera we have seen him using, does not hear her. She wipes*
> *her hand across her streaming eyes. Does a sharp whistle,* JOE
> *turns, sees her. Contemplates walking away. Does not.*

JOE. Hey. Tess. Hey.

TESS. Who is that?

JOE. It's me, it's Joe –

TESS. Joe? As in… Joe?

JOE. Joe Schofield.

TESS. Oh my God –

> *He moves towards her, registers her pregnancy; her streaming*
> *eyes.*

JOE. What happened? Are you okay?

TESS. Oh, it's, no it's just pepper spray, I'm / fine –

JOE. Shit, you want some water –

> *She dumps her bags, pulls a carton of milk from the shopping*
> *bag, tries to open it.*

TESS. No, you have to put milk on it – here, help me out. Hang
on –

> *She gives him the carton.* JOE *rips it open,* TESS *takes off her*
> *jacket, rummages in her handbag, pulls out a rain poncho,*
> *shakes it out, pulls the poncho on over her head to protect her*
> *dress.*

JOE. Has this happened before?

TESS. Yeah, little bit. Okay. You can, you can pour it now.

TESS leans back. JOE *hesitantly pours the milk into her eyes, trying to steer clear of the bump.*

JOE. Does it sting?

TESS. It's pepper spray, Joe.

She laughs. JOE *takes her picture.*

Did you just take my picture?

JOE. Sorry. Force of habit. I thought you went back to England.

TESS. I got a stay of execution. Landed a new contract, Tesco, it's this British company, they set up over here, cocked the whole thing up, tried to sell packets of four rolls of loo paper when Americans want to buy forty at a time, that kind of basic, you know, total incompetence.

JOE. So what are you doing here?

TESS. This is just, it's a side project, it's extra-curricular. *Pro bono.* I'm helping them out, just a bit of basic profiling, improving their outreach.

JOE. You're working for a… multi-national corporation and an anti-capitalist protest?

TESS. Right.

JOE. Right. I mean, that's kind of schizophrenic –

TESS (*laughs*). Isn't it though! They can't work me out, it's hilarious.

,

JOE. Anyway. Congratulations.

TESS. For what?

JOE. The – the baby.

TESS. Oh, right, yep. Thanks.

JOE. What. I mean, what's that like?

TESS. It's okay. I had constant morning sickness for like, five months but my hair looks like a fucking Pantene advert so. You know, swings and roundabouts.

JOE. Do you think – I mean, is that safe? Being here?

TESS. Oh, the doctor says it's really got its feet under the table now. So how are you, you look well, are you well?

   TESS *takes out a packet of gum, concentrates on retrieving a piece.*

JOE. Uh, yeah. Fine. Just, you know, I'm, I'm seeing someone, Heidi.

TESS. Uh-uh, that's great, you want some gum?

JOE. No thanks. She's a model. Not like, catwalk or anything. Hand model.

TESS. Oh, right. Sorry, what?

JOE. It's like a regular photographic model but only for jewellery, or nail polish.

TESS. Okay. That's. Has she got nice hands then?

JOE. Yeah, no they're… nice. Nice hands.

TESS. You live together?

JOE. Yeah. It's cheaper this way.

TESS. The four words every girl wants to hear! 'My darling… it's cheaper this way.'
   ,
   No, but that's great! I'm really, good for you, so listen, you have an exhibition coming up, right? Howard Greenberg, very nice, I saw the poster.

JOE. Yeah. They approached me a couple years ago but I wasn't. I wasn't sure I wanted to, but now, / I'm –

TESS. Now you're broke.

JOE. (*laughs*). Now I'm broke, right. No, I mean, I am but I also think that if it gets people to look at them then… the opening's next week, I'd love it if you, I mean if you could make it I would. I would love that. I can send you an invitation.

TESS. Yeah. Thanks. I'll see.

JOE. Because actually it's, I know the poster probably made it look all ritzy and all –

TESS. Sponsored by American Express.

JOE. Yeah, that's the gallery, that's not me, I mean I didn't –

TESS. Yeah but you're *in* the gallery, right? They didn't, like put a gun to your head, 'Show us your portfolio!'

JOE. No. No they didn't do that.

TESS. Do you get one of those big shiny coffee-table books?

JOE. I do. Give you one if you come.

TESS. Well. Yeah, send the invitation.

JOE. You can bring your... the father, I'd love to meet him.

A very long pause.

Oh. Oh. Right.

TESS. I did try to call you, I called... quite a few times, when / I –

JOE. Yeah, I know, I just. I went a little, after we. I went travelling. Round the country, for a. Long time, sorry, I'm just... I'm just...

,

TESS. I didn't want to leave some voicemail. And I knew your... position, you were very clear about that. And well I sort of thought I couldn't. Have them. I have a, well they call it a 'hostile environment', so, yeah. Congratulations. On your... tenacious... semen.

Sorry, what a fucking stupid thing to, listen you don't have to – I do have someone, in my life, his name is Mike, so you don't have to –

JOE. Can I...?

He gestures. She nods. He puts his hand on her belly. Holds it there.

TESS. If you're waiting for it to kick, don't bother. It's incredibly lazy.

JOE's phone rings. JOE takes his hand away. Checks the phone. Puts it away again.

You want to take that?

JOE. No. No, it's just Zhang Lin, / listen.

TESS. I don't mind. It's long-distance, you / should –

JOE. I said, don't worry about it, I'll call him back, listen, I would have said this anyway:

TESS. No, don't, / you don't have to –

JOE. I miss you. I can't stop – I think about you all the, so I mean, I know the timing is a little, and this guy, Mike, he sounds like a great – and I know I wasn't, that we met at a time when I was – but it's our lives isn't it, it's our lives so if there's any, even if you, you know, just for a coffee or something, even if there's the smallest, you know, a trace / of –

TESS. Joe –

JOE. I know.

TESS. Because –

JOE. I love you.

TESS. No.

JOE. No I know, I just had to. I just, I had to.

> JOE *kisses* TESS. *She lets him. Pulls away.* TESS *looks off.*

TESS. I have to go. I have a meeting. I smell of milk. My mum says I should get used to that.

> ,

Did you ever find him?

> ,

JOE. He's dead, Tess.

> ,

> JOE *puts his camera to his eye, takes her picture again. Pause.*

You look so beautiful. You look exactly like I imagined you would.

Scene Four

A gallery, Midtown Manhattan. Images of protest on the walls.
JOE's shot of the Tank Man. Next to a close-up of TESS, grinning,
milk running down her face. Applause greets JOE as he steps up to
the microphone, clutching his notes.

JOE. I've spent a lot of time lately, apologising. For things I've done.
   Not done. Things I've asked of other people. For myself, in
   general, I guess. Which is, well, it's not an unfamiliar feeling. So
   it's a pleasure for me to stand here in front of you, and be able to
   say, well, just this: that these are some pictures I've taken.

   He glances behind him, gestures to the Tank Man photograph.
   A tiny beat, then he looks back.

   And of all the things I've done, I make no apology for them.

   JOE hesitates. Then folds his notes, nods, leaves the stage.
   Uncertain applause. MEL approaches, wearing an eye patch.
   The men look at each other. Pleased to see each other, but
   damned if they're going to say it. MEL gestures to the Tank Man.

MEL. I know the guy who took that. He's kind of an asshole.

JOE. Hello, Mel.

MEL. And he can't write a speech for shit.

JOE. Yeah well, you aren't going to make any kind of
   photographer. What happened?

MEL. Impertinent piece of Syrian shrapnel up and bit me.

JOE. Shit.

MEL (*pirate*). Oo-arr. You shoulda stuck around. Party got
   interesting after you left.

JOE. Is it – did you lose the eye?

MEL. Got a socket like chopped liver. Wanna see? Scares the crap
   out of the kids.

JOE. No, I don't want to – what was that like?

MEL. Hurt like hell afterwards. Didn't know what hit me during.
   Moment before it happened I felt very alive. So anyway, I just
   came to see you in your splendour.

JOE. Well, thanks. It's pretty splendid, right?

BENNY comes rushing up. Ignores MEL, *shakes* JOE*'s hand enthusiastically. Dressed in American sports-casual, and a pair of box-fresh Nike trainers.*

BENNY. Hey, man, I'm Benny. My uncle's a friend of yours, Zhang Lin? We were sposed to go to Peter Luger's!

JOE. Hey, yeah, yeah. Good to meet you.

MEL *is sloping off.*

You going? You don't want to stay for a drink or something?

MEL. Nah.

JOE. Okay but, you didn't – I mean, what did you think of the, of the exhibition?

,

MEL. I think. I think it's a hell of a store window, kid.

MEL *goes.* JOE *turns back to* BENNY.

JOE. I appreciate you coming down, I meant to call you but, I'm sorry about that night.

BENNY. Oh, man, don't even worry about it. Your girlfriend, ah, Tess? Very nice lady. She ate a thirty-two-ounce steak, no problem!

He puts up his hand for JOE *to high-five.*

JOE. Yeah, we broke up.

BENNY *takes his hand down. Gestures to the Tank Man picture.*

BENNY. Yeah so great picture, dude. Immense. So how much?

JOE. The gallery price them. I think that one's about eight thousand dollars.

BENNY. Okay, and is there any room for movement on that?

JOE. Sure. I could charge you nine thousand dollars.

,

BENNY. Look, dude, I never bought art before, I / don't know –

JOE. I'm sorry. That was. So you're studying at Harvard, right?

BENNY. I graduated last summer. I miss college, man, college was *awesome*! I work for this oil company now, they're like *the devil* but they helped me get a green card so I kind of have to stick it out for a while – hey! Ba!

ZHANG WEI has entered, looking a little lost, BENNY *waves to him.* ZHANG WEI *shakes* JOE*'s hand, formal.*

You've met my dad, right?

JOE. *Yeah, uh nín hao ma?* [How are you?]

ZHANG WEI. *Hái hao.* [So so.] *Ní hao ma?*

JOE. *Hen hao.* [Very well.]

ZHANG WEI hands JOE *an iPod.* ZHANG WEI *speaks to* BENNY *in Mandarin. Gestures to* BENNY *to explain.*

BENNY. So Zhang Lin asked him to give you this. He wants you to listen to it. He says to tell you: 'I hope this story is big enough.'

ZHANG WEI speaks very quickly and fiercely in Mandarin. JOE *tries to follow, looks to* BENNY.

JOE. My Mandarin is really – I'm sorry, what is he saying?

BENNY. He just, he says it's awesome to be here and, he's jetlagged, don't worry about it.

JOE. I'd like to know.

BENNY. Aw, man, this is super awkward.

He speaks to ZHANG WEI *in Mandarin, 'I asked you not to do this, Dad.' Turns to* JOE.

He says he is wondering what is wrong with you. He says his brother made guanxi with you. You took his hospitality and his gifts and his friendship and profited from them. When it was your turn you, like, failed him. He wanted your help and you didn't even return his phone calls. He is angry and disappointed. He said you're neither East nor West, which is, it's like a pretty bad insult. Shit, sorry, man.

ZHANG WEI speaks in Mandarin again.

He would also like me to say, what a wonderful exhibition. You are clearly a very talented man.

ZHANG WEI *nods his goodbye, and goes.*

Sorry, man. He's, like, I mean I like *love* him, but he can be kind of an asshole.

JOE. No, that's okay.

BENNY (*the Tank Man*). You know I think my dad knew him.

JOE. Yeah, well, your uncle said he did too.

BENNY. When I was growing up, I was the only kid at school who knew about 64. My dad had this tiny copy of this picture, and he used to get it out, sit on the floor by my bed with a candle and he'd go –

BENNY *laughs. Hands* JOE *a cigarette. Starts to roll one for himself.*

He'd point at the Tank Man and go: 'That little Dog-face! That little Dog-face nearly got me killed!'

JOE *looks up sharply.* BENNY *shakes his head, continues to roll his cigarette.*

At the time I just was like –

JOE. Dog-face?

BENNY. Yeah, it's a milk name, like a Chinese custom. Listen, so eight grand, that's totally cool, I mean it's an investment, right? It's like, enjoy your greenbacks while you can, dude. All gonna be yuan soon. We're coming for you, bitches!

JOE. What?

BENNY. It's a joke, man. Little… economics, like, joke –

JOE. Excuse me. I have to make a phone call.

JOE *quickly moves away, impatient, takes out his phone. Dials, waits. Lights up on* ZHANG LIN, *in his Beijing apartment, as he answers his mobile. He is sitting, eating his breakfast.*

Zhang Lin. It's Joe.

ZHANG LIN. I've been having some problems with my phone line.

JOE. Uh-uh, listen – I just saw Zhang Wei. And I met your nephew. Benny.

ZHANG LIN. Did Zhang Wei give you something?

JOE. Yeah. I haven't listened to it yet but. Does it say. What I think it's going to –

A PUBLIC SECURITY GUARD *passes behind* ZHANG LIN, *searching his apartment.* ZHANG LIN *watches him.*

ZHANG LIN. Yes, there's been some interference on the line. It's been causing me some trouble so our conversation may have to be quite… short. Do you understand me?

Joe?

ZHANG LIN *takes a bite of food.*

JOE. Yeah, Zhang Lin, I'm so. I'm / so –

ZHANG LIN. Your photograph made me look important.

I was frightened of it.

People looking at your picture, and seeing something.

And you try but you can't see what they see. Only what happened before, what happened after.

He was never me. Only a man who looked a bit like me.

And I wanted so much to look like him.

,

JOE. There's so much stuff I want to ask you.

ZHANG LIN. Yes. Another time, maybe? I have company.

,

JOE. What time is it there?

ZHANG LIN. Seven thirty. You're spoiling my breakfast.

JOE. Yeah? What you having?

ZHANG LIN. For breakfast?

JOE. Yeah.

ZHANG LIN. Crullers.

JOE. With congee?

ZHANG LIN. No, I hate congee. With soy milk.

The SECURITY GUARD *stands over* ZHANG LIN. *Holds his hand out.* ZHANG LIN *looks up at him.*

JOE. Sweet or salty?

ZHANG LIN dips his cruller in the milk. Takes a bite, still looking up at the GUARD.

ZHANG LIN. Sweet.

The GUARD *takes* ZHANG LIN*'s phone from him. The line goes dead.* ZHANG LIN *wipes his mouth, picks up the possessions he has been allowed to take with him, in two carrier bags.*

JOE. Zhang Lin? Zhang Lin, hello?

Lights down on ZHANG LIN, *as he leaves his apartment, followed by the* GUARD, *a shopping bag in each hand. Hands shaking,* JOE *puts the earphones to the iPod in. Plays the track.*

ZHANG LIN (*voice-over*). The 1st of May. 1989.

JOE *works the controls, impatient. The track fast-forwards.* JOE *stops, plays the recording. Sudden black. Chaos. Tiananmen Square, 1989. June 5th.* ZHANG LIN *enters. Bare-chested, blood-spattered, he holds his arms around himself. A* NURSE *runs on.*

NURSE. They've stopped firing, you should go home!

ZHANG LIN. Excuse me – that was – the woman, you just – that's my wife. (*Louder.*) That's my wife. Please. That's my wife.

NURSE. Where's your shirt?

ZHANG LIN (*thinks*). I ripped it up. For bandages.

NURSE. Wait there.

She runs off. ZHANG LIN *shivers, he wipes his hand across his face, blood comes off, he stares at it. The* NURSE *runs on again, clutching an armful of things.*

Here, you can't go home like that.

She pulls a white shirt from the pile, gives it to him. He tries to thrust it back at her.

ZHANG LIN. Whose is it? I don't want it.

NURSE. You want her things? It's just, her dress, bag. Shoes. Jewellery, you'll want that.

She thrusts the items into ZHANG LIN*'s arms, takes two carrier bags from her pocket, then kneels on the floor and puts* LIULI*'s things into the grocery bags.*

ZHANG LIN. What about. What about the body.

The NURSE *shakes her head, kind.* ZHANG LIN *understands.*

NURSE. Will you be okay?

ZHANG LIN. I think. I think I'll take a walk.

The NURSE *runs off. Moving slowly, automatically,* ZHANG LIN *pulls the white shirt on. Numbly picks up the bags. Turns to us. Looking out, holding a grocery bag in each hand, full of the last scraps of* LIULI. *We are looking, for the first time, at a front view of the Tank Man.*

A lighting change. ZHANG LIN *walks, into the gallery. He has reached the avenue.* ZHANG LIN *turns. His back, more familiar view. The tanks approach.* ZHANG LIN *walks into the tank's path.* ZHANG LIN*'s movements are synchronised with the projected, real film of the Tank Man.* JOE, *and we, watch it with the knowledge of who this man is for the first time. Of how he came to be there and what is in his bags.*

ZHANG LIN *turns to* JOE.

The two men look at one another.

Lights down.